Rich
Wolfe

# All It Takes
# Is All Ya Got

# Craig Counsell

## by Rich Wolfe

*Page Two. In 1941, the news director at a small radio station in Kalamazoo, Michigan hired Harry Caray who had been employed at a station in Joliet, Illinois. The news director's name was Paul Harvey. Yes, that PAUL HARVEY! "And now, you have the rest of the story...... ➡

# DEDICATION

**To**

**The late Jim Fitzgerald of Janesville—the classiest
NBA team owner ever...**

And

Jane Kannell-O'Neill of Barrington, Illinois,
Darby Kelly of Colorado Springs,
Bill Meeker in Santa Barbara and
Nick Muller in Denver...friends all!

# CHAT ROOMS

Dedication. . . . . . . . . . . . . . . . . . . . . . . . . . . 3
Preface . . . . . . . . . . . . . . . . . . . . . . . . . . . . 7

**CHAPER ONE: WE ARE FAMILY**     **13**
Father Knows Best . . . . . . . . . . . . . . . . . . . . 14
City Counsell . . . . . . . . . . . . . . . . . . . . . . . 50
No, Mother Knows Best . . . . . . . . . . . . . . . . . 56

**CHAPTER TWO: THE CHICKEN RAN AT MIDNIGHT**     **73**
Maybe there's a Separate God for Children . . . . . . . . . . . . 74
Craig Counsell was Just a Regular Guy Who Some Days Wore a Cape . . 97

**CHAPTER THREE: WHEN WE WERE YOUNG AND
OUR WORLD WAS NEW**     **105**
Having Craig Counsell for a Friend Is Like Playing Hooky from Life . . . 106
The Twin Cities: Half as Good as the Quad Cities . . . . . . . . . 120
A Driver with Concentration . . . . . . . . . . . . . . . . . . 131
Doctor, Doctor Tell Me the News How Craig Counsell Paid His Dues. 136
Put Me In Coach. . . . . . . . . . . . . . . . . . . . . . . 145

**CHAPTER FOUR: SHAKE DOWN THE THUNDER**     **153**
Murphy's Law . . . . . . . . . . . . . . . . . . . . . . . 154
Of Mikes and Men . . . . . . . . . . . . . . . . . . . . . 161
A Roomie With a View . . . . . . . . . . . . . . . . . . . 172
Iowa? It's On All the Maps Now . . . . . . . . . . . . . . . 176
Notre Dame Needs a Halfback, a Fullback and Rockne Back . . . . 183

**CHAPTER FIVE: FLORIDA MARLINS**     **185**
It Was Magic, I Tells Ya . . . . . . . . . . . . . . . . . . 186
A Writer and a Friend . . . . . . . . . . . . . . . . . . . 192

## CHAPTER SIX: A HOT TIME IN OLD ARIZONA      203

Clones are People, Too. . . . . . . . . . . . . . . . . . . . . . .204
We Saw it on the Radio . . . . . . . . . . . . . . . . . . . . . .209
Luis, Luis, Oh, No, Me Gotta Go . . . . . . . . . . . . . . . .214
It's Easier Managing from the Press Box . . . . . . . . . . . .217
The Heat Was on Counsell When He Replaced an All-Star.
But it Was a Dry Heat.. . . . . . . . . . . . . . . . . . . . . . .223

## CHAPTER SEVEN: HOME, SWEET HOME MILWAUKEE      227

It's Good to Be the Boss . . . . . . . . . . . . . . . . . . . . . .228
Hear Me Now, Listen to Me Later  . . . . . . . . . . . . . . . .230
Take this Job and Love It  . . . . . . . . . . . . . . . . . . . . .234
Inside Trader  . . . . . . . . . . . . . . . . . . . . . . . . . . . .245
The Fourth Estate Doesn't Take the Fifth  . . . . . . . . . . .247
When Milwaukee Calls Ya Gotta Accept the Charges . . . . . . .253
The Son Also Rises  . . . . . . . . . . . . . . . . . . . . . . . . .258
A Real Pro in Every Way . . . . . . . . . . . . . . . . . . . . . .265

# PREFACE

My first introduction to what would become the Milwaukee Brewers began before almost anyone else. It was a beautiful March spring training game in 1966 at Al Lang Field in St. Petersburg, Florida, the spring training facility of both the St. Louis baseball Cardinals and the relatively new New York Mets. As a big Cardinal fan, even though I was a pretty young guy, I was able to get into the ball park before almost anyone else other than the players. I'm sitting in the first row behind home plate when suddenly another man about my age came and sat right next to me. I started talking to him, found out he was from Milwaukee, worked for his father in a Ford car dealership. When he told me he was not a Cardinals fan, I asked him why he happened to be at this particular game. He said, "Well, as you probably know, the Milwaukee Braves are playing for the first time this year in Atlanta, and Milwaukee is left without a team. My goal is to bring major league baseball back to Milwaukee." I slowly turned to look at him, thinking, "What kind of pipe dreamer is this guy?" That's how I met Bud Selig and my hat's off to him. He brought major league baseball back to Milwaukee four years later, when he bought the Seattle Pilots and moved them to Milwaukee. He previously came very close to a deal on buying the Chicago White Sox and moving them to Milwaukee.

This is my 54th book. While I've enjoyed all of them but one, I make no bones of telling people that my very favorite is the one I did on Tom Brady at the request of his father the day before Brady's first Super Bowl in February of 2002. We're sitting at a lunch in New Orleans when Tom Brady, Sr. (in the family, the dad is Tom Brady, and the quarterback is Tommy Brady), and Tom Brady said, "Rich, I see that two years ago when Kurt Warner was MVP of the Super Bowl, you did a book on him. If Tommy's MVP tomorrow, will you do a book on him?" I said sure, knowing that the Patriots were 15 point underdogs, still the second largest underdog in Super Bowl history. I was more likely to be struck by lightning while honeymoning with Christy Brinkley than for Tom Brady to be MVP of that Super Bowl. After all, Tom Brady had only played two series of downs in the NFL before that season. Brady started his first game ever in Game 3 of that season when Drew Bledsoe, the highest paid player in the history of the NFL at the time, went down due to an injury. It was a very difficult book to do as Brady was only 24 years old, was a clean liver, rarely drank, never got in any fights, only dated one woman at a time, and was about as clean-cut as you could hope for. But Tom Brady has the best manners and is the hardest working of any athlete that I've ever met. It was an absolute joy to do the book.

Believe it or not, the similarities between Tom Brady and Craig Counsell are striking. Neither one of them cares if they ever get their name in the paper. Each of them is very family-oriented, each of them has an undying love for their sport, each of them is a very cerebral player, each is also thoroughly prepared for all circumstances during a game. I happen to like players like that. Add that to the fact that Craig's father and I were classmates and teammates in college back when the earth was still cooling. I've been privileged to know the Counsell family for almost sixty years, and it has been an absolute pleasure. I hope you enjoy reading this book as much as I did putting it together.

One of the biggest problems in doing a book about a person who has lived his or her life properly is constant repetition. Since this is a book of tributes from over 50 of Craig Counsell's friends, obviously, there is going to be some repetition. Repetition is always a problem. For example, in my **MIKE DITKA\***

*When Joe Girardi played for the Cubs, he caught a ceremonial first pitch from **MIKE DITKA**. Girardi had a football curled behind his back. After catching Ditka's pitch, Girardi fired the football at Ditka which Iron Mike caught easily.

book, seven people described a run Ditka made in Pittsburgh the week of JFK's assassination as the greatest run they had ever seen. Yet, only one of those made the book. The editor didn't understand that when the reader was through with the book, few would remember the importance or singularity of that catch and run; whereas, if most of the seven stories had remained intact, everyone would realize that one play summarized Ditka's persona and his career.

So, too, the repetition with Craig Counsell, except many times greater. It was overwhelming. Almost eighty pages were deleted from this book because there were constant, similar or duplicate testimonials. Even so, many remained.

In doing over four dozen books, I've never encountered as much repetition. It's a tribute to Counsell, but a real challenge to the editors. On the other hand, there has never been a book that I worked on out of 54 books that was such a pleasure to hear stories about the subject.

Craig Counsell is terrific.

When you find out more about Counsell and how he achieved his success while keeping his values, you have to ask the question, "Why can't everybody live like Craig Counsell?" There is nothing that he does that is very difficult. He is very kind. He is hard working. He has all these values that everyone could possess if they desired.

I write books only on people who seem admirable from a distance. The fear, once you start a project, is the subject will turn out to be a jerk. As you will soon find out, you would want your son, your brother, your husband or your friends to possess these qualities of humbleness, thoughtfulness, joy for living, a passion for his job and the love of life that Craig Counsell has.

Growing up on a farm in **IOWA\***, I avidly read all the Horatio Alger-style books of John R. Tunis, the Frank Merriwell collection and Clair Bee's Chip Hilton series, all which preach the values of hard work, perseverance, obedience and sportsmanship where sooner or later, one way or another, some forlorn, underweight underdog would succeed beyond his wildest dreams in the arena of life. Frank Merriwell, thy name is Craig Counsell. Craig Counsell was better than Frank Merriwell. He was real life...more natural than Roy Hobbs...a Rudy with talent. Counsell was manna from heaven to MLB and every other beleaguered professional sports league.

From the age of ten, I've been a serious collector of books, mainly sports books. During that time—for the sake of argument, let's call it thirty years—my favorite book style is the "eavesdropping" type where the subject talks in his own words...In his own words, without the 'then he said,' or 'the air was so thick you could cut it with a butter knife' waste of verbiage that makes it hard to get to the meat of the matter. Books like Lawrence Ritter's *The Glory of Their Times* or Donald Honig's *Baseball When the Grass was Real*. Thus I adopted that style when I started compiling the oral histories of the **VIN SCULLYS\*** and Ron Santos of the world.

There is a big difference in doing a book on Mike Ditka or Harry Caray and doing one on Craig Counsell. Ditka and Caray were much older than Counsell, thus, they had many more years to

\*For decades, the Chicago Cubs have had a guest sing "Take Me Out to the Ball Game" during the seventh inning stretch. Cubs organist Gary Pressly says that **VIN SCULLY** had the best singing voice of the over 3,000 warblers.

\*Between his junior and senior years at Van Meter (**IOWA**) High School, Bob Feller struck out 15 St. Louis Browns in a regular season game. Two years earlier, Feller's catcher in American Legion ball was Nile Kinnick, the 1939 Heisman Trophy winner at Iowa.

create their stories and build on their legends. Furthermore, unlike Counsell, they both liked to enjoy liquid fortification against the unknown, which leads to even more and wilder tales...and multiple divorces.

I don't even pretend to be an author. This book with its unusual format is designed solely for fans. I really don't care what the publishers, editors or critics think, but am vitally concerned that Counsell fans have an enjoyable read and get their money's worth. Sometimes, the person being interviewed will drift off the subject, but if the feeling is that the reader would enjoy their digression, it stays in the book.

In an effort to include more material, the editor decided to merge some of the paragraphs and omit some of the punctuation which will allow for the reader to receive an additional 20,000 words—the equivalent of fifty pages. More bang for your buck...more fodder for English teachers...fewer dead trees.

It's also interesting—as you'll find in this book—how some people will view the same happening in completely different terms....There was a thought of omitting the attempts at humorous headlines—some of the headlines in this book prove that truly great comedy is not funny.

Craig Counsell is a man in a society where orthodox behavior has stifled creativity, adventure and fun...a society where posturing and positioning one's image in order to maximize income has replaced honesty and bluntness...Craig Counsell is a once-in-a-lifetime person...a principled man in a world of rapidly dwindling principles...a difference-maker on an indifferent planet...a man the way men used to be in an America that is not the way it used to be...a loyal man to colleagues, family, teammates and friends in an age when most people's loyalties are in the wallet...A good man!

Go now.

*Teammates Moises Alou and Craig Counsell, 97 World Series Champions*

Chapter One

# WE ARE FAMILY

## Wisconsin Proud

# FATHER KNOWS BEST

## JOHN COUNSELL

*John Counsell grew up a huge Milwaukee Braves fan in Oconomowoc, Wisconsin. A star athlete in high school, he walked-on for the Notre Dame baseball team. Named Captain his senior year, allergies played havoc with his career. A sweet swing coupled with a rifle arm led to a nice bonus with the Minnesota Twins where he spent his first three years playing for Wisconsin Rapids in the Midwest League. Counsell became assistant Baseball Coach at Notre Dame and later joined the Brewers in community relations and head of the Speakers Bureau. Eleven years later he formed Marketing Counsell before moving to Ft. Myers, Florida in 1994. He and son Craig are the only Father-Son Captains in history of Notre Dame.*

For my training as a baseball player, I got a leaded bat. I literally had a friend bore it out, dump lead in it. I swung that bat at home. I had a big sign on my bedroom wall, "Swing bat fifty times a night." I did...every night. I had read that some player had gotten a leaded bat and swung it at least 50 times a day. It strengthened his arms, as he developed a level swing. I was eleven when I started doing it in my upstairs bedroom in our house in Oconomowoc. The player I read about also used to swing it over a chair to keep his swing level. I got in trouble one time. I don't know what happened to the metal folding chair that I used to swing over, but all of a sudden it disappeared. I shared a bedroom with my sister and my parents. It was a huge bedroom. I went downstairs and got a dining room chair, a good dining room chair. I swung level, swung level, swung level, I got distracted, and I hit the chair. I totally destroyed it.

I got one of my mom's friends to fix it, but Mom caught it right away. I couldn't swing over a chair anymore.

I carried that habit through high school, and I took that to **NOTRE DAME**\* with me. Dave DeBruyne was my roommate freshman year in a dorm room in Stanford Hall. The rooms weren't very wide. I would stand in the middle of the room. I'd swing the bat over my roommate's bed. He would always say to me, "I don't get it. Why don't you swing over your bed? "You're not in it." I'd say, "I'm left-handed, and I don't want to swing towards our desks. I might hit a chair or something. I want to swing towards our closets, and you're in that other bed," and he bought it. Dave nicknamed me "Larry Baseball", and still calls me that 55 years later!

I never got Craig a leaded bat. To me, that was my fanaticism. His fanaticism was different. He just wanted to play on every team he could play on, be there first, and take BP (batting prac- tice) all the time and ground balls by the million. When Craig was 7 we came up with a game called "fifty". The game was: I hit Craig fifty ground balls, and we go in. This was after a full workout. I'd say, "Okay, let's end it with our usual, fifty ground balls, and we go home. You've got to catch fifty in a row." He'd catch forty-seven, sometimes forty-eight, even forty-nine, and he'd drop one on purpose. I said, "You did that on purpose." "No, I didn't, Dad." We'd have to do another fifty. As much as I liked the game, it was just like me having a playing partner. I was like, "He's the little kid who plays like a bigger kid, and I get to do this with him every night." My wife Jan would shake her head sometimes. She would say, "Are you overdoing it? I said, "He hasn't told me I am."

---

\*The Oakland A's copied their green and gold colors from **NOTRE DAME.** When LaPorte, Indiana native Charles O. Finley bought the Kansas City A's in the 60s, he changed the colors to honor his friend, former Irish coach Frank Leahy...The Green Bay Packers took the Notre Dame colors because Curly Lambeau played at Notre Dame.

*Dad showing Craig how to bunt at 10 months old.*

We always had crazy games. The craziest game we ever invented was when we lived in Madison. We had built a new house with a garage on the end of the house with a side entrance and a gable roof, the typical slanted roof. Craig was only seven. We invented this game for fly balls where I'm throwing a tennis ball up in the air to simulate fly balls. I tried throwing a hard ball up in the air, and a couple times, it hit him, not in the head, but it hit him in the shoulder, and Jan said, "You can't use a hard ball yet. He's too young, and you're throwing it too high." I'm throwing it way up there.

I went to a tennis ball. I'm throwing the tennis ball up, and it's killing my arm. To throw a ball straight up in the air, it's just hard. Accidentally, one ball flies out of my hand and goes up above the garage roof, hits the slanted garage roof, bounces out to us, he catches it. I said, "There it is, right there." He said, "What?" I said, "We're playing Garage Ball from now on."

Since then, I've introduced Garage Ball to a whole bunch of kids. Garage Ball is you throw the tennis ball up in the air. You bounce it off a slanted roof. Here's what happens. If you throw it high on the roof where the beams are close together and it's rock solid, it bounces way off. If you throw it up and it lands in the middle of the garage roof, it's fairly bouncy on the roof. It's not as rock solid, and it will come off a normal distance. If you throw it short, and it hits near the gutter, it barely trickles off and takes a short hop. We began playing that game. We've been playing it for about two months, and I started to notice something that I could not even begin to describe. Craig would recognize where the ball hit on the roof, and he would go to a spot, and the ball would go right to him. If I threw it high on the roof and it was going to go way off, he'd go back. If I threw it and he saw it was going to hit near the bottom of the roof, he'd run like crazy and sometimes have to dive and catch the ball. It would just trickle off.

I went into the house and said, "Honey, come out, I want you to see something." She said, "What?" I said, "Watch." I threw a couple up, and he did it. She'd say, "What?" I said, "You don't see what he's doing?" She said, "I don't have any idea what he's doing." I said, "He's judging the ball, where it's going to go. He's like an outfielder. It's like the crack of the bat, he knows where it's going to go."

That was one of the breakthrough times in my mind that he understood the game better than most, and it was all by accident because we invented Garage Ball.

His focus began to show probably as soon as he started Tee Ball when we lived in Madison. The moment we put him in Tee Ball, I said to my wife, "We've got a ballplayer," meaning, "He's going to really like this. He's going to just thrive on baseball" because the coach recognized that he was an above average athlete for his age and for his size. In Tee Ball, where do you think the coach put him? Not at shortstop, not second base. He put him at pitcher because the pitcher doesn't throw a pitch, but when the ball is hit off the tee, he stands on the mound, and he's a fielder. Craig would field every ball in the infield to a point where one game I had to walk out to the pitcher's mound as a parent. I said to the coach, "Time out a minute. Let me tell him something." I went out to the mound, and I said, "Hey, guess what? You're not the only fielder. You've got to let those balls to third base go." "But, Dad, he can't catch and he can't throw it over there." I said, "I don't care. His mom and dad want to see him throw it." He said, "He's going to throw it away." I said, "His mom and dad want to see that." I said, "The same thing at first, you can't catch the ball and go and step on first base. That's his ball." "But he can't catch, Dad."

Then he just stood on the mound and sulked, I remember. The balls would go almost right to him, and he'd let it go. He put up his hands like, "There you go, Dad. What do you want?" This is a six-year-old. That's when I knew that he had an idea of what was going on on the field, and it was fun. It was weird, but it was fun.

From there, we moved back to the Milwaukee area. He started his first Little League game ever in Grafton, Wisconsin in 1979, a small city north of Milwaukee. He made the All-Star team at age nine. He was the smallest kid out there. They definitely couldn't pitch to him. He **WALKED\*** almost every time. He stole second base almost every time he walked. He would score tons of runs. He didn't hit the ball that often the first year because they never threw him a strike. He was determined from the father-son-daughter games at County Stadium when he would play on Family Day...he was determined to score in those games.

One Sunday each year, usually in June, the Brewers would have Family Day, and we'd come out early for the Father-Son-Daughter Game. We'd have a picnic after the game on the field.

\*In 2002 B\*rry B\*nds received 68 intentional **WALKS**...Eight came when no one was on base.

The Father-Son-Daughter Game was huge for Craig...full Brewers uniform, usually there'd be 20,000 in the Stadium by then on a Sunday. They'd play at about 12:30 p.m. on a 1:15 start game. The players would come out with their kids. Those of us who worked in the front office also got uniforms for our kids. We could have our kids play along with the player's kids. Craig always chose #4, Molitor's number. A player would pitch underhand, and the kids would hit. If they were really little, they'd use the fat bat, and a Wiffle ball. But for kids like Craig that were a little older, five or six or seven, they would use a hard ball and pitch it underhand. Craig would take every pitch if it wasn't a strike and then he'd run to first. I'd say, "Wait a minute. You get to hit." "No, I walked," he'd say. He would go to first. Every other kid would stay up and hit until they hit the ball.

*Craig (age 8) and Jennifer (age 6) in 1978 with Brewers' outfielder Ben Ogilvie before annual Brewers Father-Son-Daughter Game. Since John Counsell was a Brewers' employee, the kids could play on the field in this annual promotional game. There were usually 20,000 fans in the stands pre-game.*

In the meantime, he's proceeding to second on a ground ball, or if a kid hit the ball and he was on third he'd score, and he'd slide every time. It didn't matter, no throw, no play on him... he'd slide into home. When I asked him about taking those walks, Craig said, "I've got to score, Dad. That's the name of the game. "He already knew that, and he'd ask me after the game, "Did we win?" I said, "Yes, you guys won." I didn't remind him that the Brewers players didn't hit. I'd always tell him, "You guys won." I would just walk away shaking my head. I was like, "He's already figured this thing out, ....that it's the guy that scores and wins the game, not that he personally wins the game, but his team wins the game, and you score by getting on base, and it doesn't matter how you get on. A walk to him was very big.

That whole concept carried over into **LITTLE LEAGUE**\* and then high school ball. He always led his team in walks. It would drive his coaches crazy. I remember the first thing Pat Murphy said to me after his freshman year at Notre Dame where he started in left field fifty-one games. Murphy said to me, "If he gets another 3-2 count, I'm going to kill him." He said, "He takes the count to 3-2 almost every at-bat. He's just not afraid to work the count." He still holds the all-time record for career walks at Notre Dame (166 in 236 games). That was all part of his "always high on-base percentage" characteristic. That carried over into his pro career.

Craig always played second or short, mostly second because of his size. He was just on base all the time, scored all the time. Obviously in Little League a base hit was a big deal because he seldom got a pitch to hit. If I didn't know better, I'd guess his on-base percentage throughout Little League was .600 easily, always on base, always dirtied the uniform, couldn't

*At the **LITTLE LEAGUE** World Series in Williamsport—for $16 total— a family of four can each get a ticket, program, hot dog and soda.

get enough of that. He'd be in the car waiting for me to drive him to a game. I didn't ever have to walk out and say, "Come on. Let's go." He was always waiting for me in the car. In that sense, it was a father's dream. He just couldn't get enough. I can't remember coaching him. I think like any father that had played baseball I said the usual things, Stay down on ground balls, throw overhand, don't squeeze the ball or the bat to death...all that little stuff. My biggest piece of advice, and it's still to this day, make sure you have fun today. He really always adopted that philosophy. It was so much fun for him to play baseball. That is what he lived for. I can say the same thing about baseball when I was growing up. He was more in love with the game than I was. That made me very happy.

Craig and his friends had so much fun playing Strike Out, a made-up game, way back in grade school. Jan used to say, "I don't know. I'm a little worried about Craig." I said, "Why?" She said, "He plays Strike Out in the morning, and then I make him come home and eat something, and then he goes back. He doesn't come home until 6:00 p.m. I can see him out the window. I can see what they're doing. He's going through at least four different kids a day. They don't want to do it that long. Plus he wins all the time. I don't know. Is he going to not like this after a while?" I said, "I have no idea. As long as he likes it now, let's let him go."

The best story I have about Craig as a youth and hitting balls at the school was that because I worked for the Brewers, I used to bring a bag of near new baseballs home every night and take BP with him whenever I could. The best times we had were Sundays.... after a Sunday day game. He'd be waiting on the porch. This is pre-cellphone time. Jan couldn't call me ahead of time, saying, "Hey, Craig's waiting here on the porch. He's been there an hour. He's got the bag of balls, two gloves, a bat. He's ready to go when you get home." When I'd pull up, I'd see him.... I'd say, "Oh my, he's ready to go." I'd go in, change, literally get a drink of water, and go right back out.

The first couple of years, we would walk only a hundred yards to the grade school. It had a little backstop in the far corner of the playground and you'd hit back at the school. The first couple years we hit there, Craig couldn't get near the school. He might hit a bouncer that hit the playground and roll to the school. The balls were just barely getting to the school, a brick school, two-story, with large windows on the first and second story.

A couple of times he hit one on the playground that would bounce into the school below the windows on the first floor, but they were Plexiglass, and they wouldn't break. I said, "We're good here." Then the second or third year, he hit the longest ball he ever hit in his life to that point, and he broke a window on the second floor, and I said, "That's it. We can't hit here anymore. That was a 225-250 foot shot. It was a pretty long ball. I never thought he could do it. He was tiny. He and I both packed the balls up and ran like hell. I don't know why. It was a Sunday. Nobody was going to catch us. It made a lot of noise. It just scared the heck out of us. We ran, and my wife recognized that we both had strange, scared looks, on our faces. She said, "What happened? Did you guys kill somebody?" We said, "No, we broke a window on the second floor, and we can't play there anymore." This was at Richards Elementary of course, where Craig played all of his Strike Out games with his friends for so many years. Craig was excited about that hit, but he was also scared to death. That was his school.

We moved four blocks away to the Jewish Community Center where Bud Selig and his wife Sue later donated a bunch of money and built a beautiful field there. So we went there. There's another funny story where I realized he was going to be a pretty good player. Some time during our second year hitting at the Jewish Community Field it happened. I had never used a screen...the protective screen for me throwing BP to him. When he was eleven he hit me in the leg with a line drive, and I thought I broke my leg. We went home immediately. It was swollen up....I iced it. I had a nice bump on my right leg. I still have that bump.

We built a protective screen. I had protection from then on. He was a left-hand hitter, and I remember the first time we built the screen, we built it backwards. I said, "What am I thinking? You're a lefty. I need protection on the other side. I'm a right-hand thrower, and you're a left-hand hitter." It got mixed up. We didn't build a very good screen. When we had to build that protective screen, around age 13-14, I said to myself, "Wow, he's really hitting the ball hard"—I still had pretty good reactions but I couldn't always catch it.

By the time he got to Notre Dame, **COACH**\* Murphy wanted Craig to try switch hitting. He had experimented with it for a couple of years in high school, but not in games. But sophomore year, he called me and said, "Hey, Dad. I talked to Murph, and I don't want to be a switch-hitter anymore." I said, "Uh oh. Which way do you want to hit?" He said, "I just want to hit lefty."

I smiled. I copied my dad as a hitter and hit lefty. I think Craig copied me essentially. However after 3 generations of lefty hitters and righty throwers Craig's two sons are both righty.

So at 15 I began to think, "Okay, he's got the ability to hit the ball really hard. We've seen him hit the ball fairly far at a young age." That's when he started to become a better hitter instead of just the walking concept. He still walked a lot. He was still not very big, but he could hit. That was at the end of Little League, age thirteen-fourteen and then in high school, Frank Klode, Craig's high school coach, recognized him as a real good player as soon as he got him, tiny, but he knew the game. He could play short and play it well, and he got on base all the time.

It bothered me that he was tiny in the sense that I would talk about it in the family, and my sisters would always say, "You were tiny. He'll grow. You were tiny, too." Jan and I looked at each other. Okay, fine. We'll accept it. We don't know when,

*The highest paid public employee in 40 states is either a football or a basketball **COACH**.

but it's going to happen. It didn't happen until junior year in college. It seemed like overnight, but I'm sure it was gradual over 12-15 months between ages 19-20 He eventually got to around 6', 175 lbs. So, coming from 5'10", 160 lbs. in his Sophomore and Junior college years that was quite a growth spurt.

In grade school, he did go out for football. The sixth grade at Richards Elementary had full tackle football. He was a running back. He got hurt in a game...got a slight concussion. Even back then, they diagnosed it as a slight concussion. There wasn't any concussion protocol. Jan and Jennifer were gone to Chicago shopping with friends. I was at the game. I ran out on the field. Craig was a little out of it.

He stumbled off the field, and we took him for a check-up at a hospital Emergency Room, and they diagnosed it as a very mild concussion. The instructions were written out on a piece of paper. "After he goes to sleep tonight, wake him up every two hours." That was to make sure he could wake up. Based upon the doctors mild concern I didn't think twice about it as a father. I had played grade school football. I had played high school football. I had gotten hit hard before and I had seen the hit he took....it was more a piling on hit than a direct hit.

Jan came home, and that piece of paper was on the counter. She read it, and I thought she was going to kill me. "What happened?" "How is he" "Are you waking him...?" We didn't know what concussions were then. It was just a diagnosis. That was all the instructions said. I had talked extensively with the doctor and wasn't worried. She said, "That's it. He's done with football. No more football," and he agreed to it. He thought it would jeopardize his baseball and Mom may have hinted at that. That's what his Mom had said to him. "If you get hurt, you might never be able to play baseball." That's all you had to say to him. "What? No baseball? Then I'm not playing football."

That's when he became a one-sport kid, even though he was probably—I would call him an exceptional basketball player—

but he didn't have a good experience on the freshman team at WFB H.S. He felt that the coach favored certain players, and Craig said, "I don't want to play if it's going to be like that. I'll play intramural, and it's just as much fun. I'll get to play with my friends," and he did.

Craig's good friend in grade school and high school, Jeff Margolis, said Craig was probably an exceptional basketball player, a really good shooter, quick. I played with him a lot in the alley behind our garage. We had a basketball hoop and backboard mounted on the garage. I was a fairly good player in high school. I wanted him to play high school basketball because it's so much fun. It's a great part of growing up. But he didn't want to. That's another reason why he became so dedicated to his own sport. He simply decided to concentrate on baseball and just play intramural basketball.

Jennifer was two years younger than Craig. He was born in '70. She was born in '72. They were typical brother and sister. They had their own rooms. They'd get in little scrapes, but basically they got along. They were in the same grade school, the same high school together and the same college together, think about that. They were around each other a lot. After college they lived together again for a couple of years in Craig's condo in Ft. Lauderdale while he was with the Marlins.

Jennifer was a gymnast in a high school that was tops in the state almost every year. Her junior year, they won the state in gymnastics. She was like the fifth or sixth or whatever. She was low man on the totem pole, but she had her role, was good at her particular exercises and got to share in the glory. I went to all her matches. I used to almost die when she would be on the balance beam and have to dismount. I knew it was coming. I knew it had to be a flip and I was scared to death. I wanted her to stick the landing, but I was always so afraid she was going to hit her head on the beam or fall. I was so nervous. To me, jumping off the balance beam when I knew it was going to be a flip was pretty dramatic. She handled it well.

For some unknown reason, when he was young, Craig was not totally in awe of the Brewers players, probably because I worked with the players closely and talked about them all the time. I became fairly good friends with Paul Molitor and Jan became close friends with Linda Molitor. Paul and I played racquetball a lot. We went out to eat with our wives, and he would be over at the house once in a while. We'd go over to his house. Many years at Thanksgiving they'd stay home in Milwaukee. We'd go to their house for a big holiday dinner.

I'd take Craig on speaking engagements with me. I'd go to the player's house, pick up the player, go on the engagement. Craig would sit at the head table with us a lot of times. He would ride in the car with the players, not say much.

*Craig, age 8, with father and Brewers pitcher Mike Caldwell at banquet. John often took Craig on speaking engagements/player appearances and Craig would sit at the head table.*

When Craig would go down into the clubhouse players would often say, "Hey, Craig, good to see you again." It was easy for him to be down there. Maybe it was that way the first day. I don't recall him saying anything. He was so quiet. That was one thing the players said to me, "Does he talk?," that kind of thing. He would essentially do anything they asked him. "Hey, kid, could you run and get me this...get me that?" In the clubhouse, players are constantly asking the clubbies to go get something for them. It's the way it is down there. It's the routine. The relationship Craig had with players in the Brewers' Clubhouse was such that I never heard feedback of anything negative or anything at all.

He would just be down there doing whatever was needed. Those were also the days that at his age, eight to eighteen, when kids could be on the field for batting practice shagging balls. MLB didn't come down strongly on that until, I don't remember exactly when and what changed it eventually. There was liability, I'm sure, but eventually only the bat boys could do that, and then nobody, no kids.

Craig was not in amongst the players a lot at eight and nine years old. He would go down and find things to do through the clubhouse guy. They might put him in a backroom, cleaning and shining shoes, the really tough stuff that the clubbies had to do.

Eventually at ten, eleven, twelve, and then thirteen through eighteen where he had skills and could help on the field, run down balls in the outfield, and pick up all the shag balls at certain times, and help clean up the clubhouse.

There is a picture of Craig when he was really young sitting with Rollie Fingers and Dion James, a young outfielder. That was a Little League Awards Day, and he got one. He won the right to have his picture taken and get the trophy. He was excited about it, but he knew both of those players already.

I asked Craig one time when we were driving home from a speaking engagement....We had just dropped **ROBIN YOUNT**\* off at his home...I said to him, "I've never asked you this." He

\***ROBIN YOUNT**'s brother, Larry, is credited for being a MLB player even though he never got into a game. He was called up by the Astros and was listed in the starting line-up. Larry Yount injured his arm warming up and never appeared in a game.

was twelve. I said, "I've never asked you this.... Who are your favorite players?" He said, "You're going to be mad at me." I said, "Why am I going to be mad? Is it Gorman and Vuke?" They were two guys who very popular, owned a bar together... they were kind of the bandits of the team....but real popular with the fans. He said, "No, Robin (Yount) and Paul (Molitor)". I said, "Why would I be mad at you for liking them?"...and he said "Because they're the most popular players, and they're the best players. That's why you think I like them." I said, "Why do you like them?" He said, "Because they're the same at home as they are at the stadium." I said to myself, "Here's a twelve-year-old who recognizes that, that's important, and that's why he likes them," and that's what he's like. He's exactly like them. After he said this, I thought, "I've got to drive faster.... I've got to get home and tell his Mom this.

Craig was like a little "favorite" in the clubhouse. I'm sure he never said much, but he always did the right thing. I think the other thing that probably was amazing to them is he knew who they were. Some of our front office people would come down, "Who in the hell was that? Who was that player I was dealing with there?"

*Craig Counsell's two favorite players: Paul Molitor and Robin Yount.*

I was always having to tell the VP of Marketing or other front office-types that was a new player. That was so and so. Craig knew them all. It was easy for him to understand who he was dealing with. And his favorite players, the good players liked him. The other players accepted him. "Who is that?" "That's Counsell's kid." "Oh, okay, fine."

For the speaking engagements, Craig could be out late with me if it was a weekend. If it was a week night, and if it would be local, and it might be some charity deal, and we're in and out. The player might be there for a half hour to forty-five minutes just to sign autographs, award a trophy for an "Employee of the Month or Year". We did a lot of that stuff....community relations. Selig was huge in that. He always wanted to know what the fans were saying about the Brewers. I felt safe taking Craig to speaking engagements/player appearances just so he could see what I did, not so much that he'd be with a player, but so he could see what Dad did for a living.

Doug Melvin, Brewers GM, felt that Craig belonged in the dugout in uniform, but he knew that if he could get him upstairs in the Front Office, he'd learn a lot. I had the same feeling. I thought, "If I take him with me, he'll at least figure out another part of the game" because Major League Baseball has to be sold and marketed. You've got to understand the fans.

When Craig was maybe fourteen Jan and I had invested in Mike Hegan's **GRAND SLAM**\* Indoor Batting Cages. Craig did two things at Grand Slam. He got to hit year round and he learned how a business was run.

> \*Don Mattingly hit 6 **GRAND SLAMS** in 1987, an all-time Major League record for one season. Mattingly never hit a grand slam before or after that season.

I became acquainted with Ken Bigler, Sr., a baseball guy, a high school coach in and around the Milwaukee area. He had sons Craig's age. Bigler knew Hegan because their sons were friends. I didn't know Hegan as well even though he was one of the Brewers TV announcers. He had been a player with the Brewers before I joined the Brewers staff. He went from playing up to the booth and was the TV color guy.

We all got together one day, and started talking about our sons having the opportunity to compete to play college ball. I never talked pro ball. I talked college ball, competing with the kids from Florida, Texas, and California—those were the exact words we used—and be able to hit year around. Those kids could hit outside year around. We lived in Wisconsin. I said, "What about these batting cages we're reading about?" I said, "What about the Grand Slam company that makes these pitching machines and has franchises?" I'd read about Grand Slam which was the franchise side of the business owned by Atec the company that sold batting cages and pitching machines. I'd researched it, and they had these franchises. "We ought to look into it." I said, "I'm in."

Hegan put up most of the money. I put up $5,000. Bigler put up at least that much and there were other investors. We opened indoor batting cages in a warehouse setting in Brookfield, Wisconsin, the first one in the Milwaukee area in the early eighties. We had five cages. We were very close to the Briggs and Stratton plant. We had two softball and three hardball cages and room in back to take infield. All of our kids, Craig, Bigler's kids, and Hegan's kid worked there. Here's Craig making three, four bucks an hour working at Grand Slam, hitting year-round. He was fifteen.

Here was the beauty. Craig's gift of math and numbers from memorizing baseball cards came out. He could run the cash register better than anybody. He was the only fifteen-year-old that could close the business at night and balance the books. Sometimes the manager, Ken Bigler, Sr., would say, "I can't get this to come out," and Craig would figure it out. We're not talking about millions of dollars of revenue. We're talking about hundreds of dollars of revenue per night, but he would balance it. You've got to balance the books to be able to close the register. He would close.

Unfortunately that meant he got home late at night. That bothered Jan and I. I often times went and got him. We lived in Whitefish Bay, and Brookfield was way across town. He'd take the bus sometimes. It was forty minutes away. He loved it. At the end of the day, when they'd close, before I came to get him, a lot of times there he would be in the cage hitting. Other times when the dads weren't around the boys would turn the batting machine they were using up to 85-90 mph.

Eventually it morphed into a father-son contest where the three fathers would divide up into teams. Mike Hegan would choose a team. I would choose a team. We would have these contests. There was a point system. We didn't know it, but Mike and I had found out later that the kids had learned how you could turn the speed up. We had the machines set at around 70-80 for high school players, maybe 75. Other kids, we'd crank it down as low as 60, 65. Our kids took it up to 90. Craig, Jeff Bigler, and Hegan's kid had learned how to put this key in and turn it up to 90. So when we'd have these father/son contests, they said, "Why don't we turn it up a little?" We were like, "You guys won't be able to hit it. We might be able to foul off a few, but you guys aren't going to be able to touch it." They turned it up and just the opposite. Our machines at Grand Slam had an iron arm that came around, and flung the ball at you. It came through an opening, and it wasn't like a pitcher winding up. You saw no windup. It was just, "Here comes the ball."

The kids had memorized the timing and they usually dominated these hitting sessions with the dads. Jeff Bigler was more mechanically inclined than any of them. I think he must have figured it out. Once he showed the other kids, they all learned how to turn up the speed...just like putting apps on a phone today.

When I saw that Craig was able to hit the ball when they turned it up to 90, I thought he had a chance to be a pretty good player. I think we made the right investment. That's all I could think. The bonus was he knows numbers. He knew how to close the cash register on this place. He also learned how to interact with customers. Craig was like a gym rat at Grand Slam. It was like the basketball court for many kids. Ironically, we put in basketball courts in the back of Grand Slam. It did create large crowds and some problems, but we made a little more money. It helped.

The concept of wanting our kids to be able to hit year around, to level the playing field to compete for college scholarships down the road...was the simple idea of Grand Slam. It had no other reason for me and look what happened. Quite frankly, for years, Jan said, "When are we going to get our $5,000 back?" I would look at her and say, "Are you kidding me? We got it back tenfold, a hundred fold."

The point is that the small investment paid dividends. I don't think anybody else that went through Grand Slam as a kid made the major leagues. A lot of kids did get college scholarships. It's just like Travel Ball today. A lot of kids got a chance to play, not necessarily all major colleges, but a lot of them played, and some of them got minor league contracts. All three of the sons, the original sons, Hegan, Bigler, Counsell, signed minor league contracts. Anyway, it did do what we wanted....it provided opportunity. I don't think the other two would have been pro players if it hadn't been for Grand Slam. I don't think they would have hit the amount of balls they hit. I don't think they would have turned the machine up to the high 80s and 90 and had no fear of a fastball. They wouldn't have made it to professional ball. Grand Slam has now been replaced by several competitors. Somebody bought it from us and later moved it. We did not get our $5,000 back. We did not get a cent from the buyout. We were minority stockholders. Preferred stockholders got their money, but we did not get ours, but I think we got our payback.

Grand Slam lasted at least another ten years after Craig went to college. When he'd come home from school, he'd go out there to hit, but he was not home often during summers.

In terms of Craig playing professional baseball, the concept in my mind was always, "Don't get ahead of yourself. Let's hope he can play at the next level. Get ready for the next level. Don't jump a level. Don't say, "Oh, I'm really good in Little League. So I'm going to college on a scholarship. No. You've got to play high school ball first. In high school I remember fathers of other players coming up to me when Craig was a junior and senior. He was all-conference and MVP of the team each of those two years. Whitefish Bay began winning baseball games, which they had never done to any great extent before. Several fathers said, "You've got it made. He's going to play pro ball." I said, "Pro ball? We're hoping he plays college ball." That was the goal. I didn't say, "I hope he plays at Notre Dame," but that was my hope. I figured he'd play somewhere in college. By the time he got to senior year, I was certain he could play at Notre Dame based on the level of players we had seen. I'd been watching Notre Dame games in the fall, when we'd go down for a football game.

It all started to come together. Craig grew a little bit and went to Notre Dame at 5′ 9″, 140-150 lbs. He was small. The first time I walked out on the field at Fall Practice his freshman year inside the fence, Coach Murphy was standing there. I walked up to Pat…. The only reason I felt I could walk out there—many of the fathers were there, but I had been the Assistant Baseball Coach there in the early 70's and I felt like "Okay, I'm a former assistant and player here…. I can walk out and talk to the coach…" Murphy without moving his lips says to me, "I don't remember him being this small." I laughed. I put my hand on his shoulder. I said, "Murph, Murph, I told you before. Just let him play. You'll see. Let him play." He just shook his head and said, "Okay, but I don't know how I can do that. He's so small."

He starts him in left field, and it was the best thing that ever happened to Craig for his arm. He had to make all those throws pregame where you throw to second, you throw to third, and you throw to home. It strengthened his arm. He learned a lot about positioning, just another perspective about the game that he hadn't had before. Here he is, a corner outfielder all of a sudden, starting fifty-one of the sixty games in Division I College Baseball at 18-years-old, and getting a 3-2 count about every second at-bat, driving Murphy crazy.

Craig had no offers out of high school. Notre Dame was the only offer, and I sort of created that by telling Pat Murphy, "Look, if you travel up to Milwaukee during the upcoming Yankees series, I will provide you tickets, but if you come two hours early"—there were some recruiting rules that we had to be careful of—"you might be able to observe Sal Bando, Sr. pitching batting practice to Sal Bando, Jr. and Craig Counsell, and it might be worth the trip." He said, "Shoot, the Yankee tickets are worth the trip."

He came up, and sure enough, here are two college prospects hitting...Sal Bando, Jr. was probably 6'1", 180 then, maybe 190. Craig was 5'9, 145. They were in a major league batting cage in **COUNTY STADIUM\***. The ball was making that great sound when you have an empty stadium, and Bando was throwing a good BP. He was throwing brand new baseballs, right down the middle. The sad part is, his son could barely get the ball out of

*Milwaukee **COUNTY STADIUM** was the first major league ballpark originally built with lights. The capacity was expanded from 35,911 to 43,000 over the first few years the Braves were in Milwaukee. Its dimensions from left to right field generally were 320-402-315.

the infield the whole BP that particular day. He never hit a ball deeper than shallow outfield. He kept popping them up. He was pressing, and Sal, Sr. was frustrated. Craig hit nothing but line drives. None out of the park, just line drives all over.

Sal Bando, Jr. was a nice player. Craig was on a team with him. They were on an American Legion team together along with Sal, Jr.'s brother, Sonny, and Larry Hisle, Jr., son of Larry Hisle, Sr., one of the Brewers top outfielders ever. These were great teammates for Craig to be around as all of them had been raised in the game.

Sal Bando, Jr. played in college. He started out at Oklahoma State, which then was a big college powerhouse. It didn't work for some reason and he ended up transferring I believe to Arizona State.

Whitefish Bay played regular high school baseball. It's just that they played summer baseball. They chose to play summer baseball, but they instituted a rule and got a ruling by the Wisconsin Interscholastic Association that any kid playing summer high school baseball could play on other teams, whereas spring baseball kids could not. There were two state tournaments. There was the state tournaments for high schools who chose to play spring baseball—the reason why Whitefish chose not to play spring baseball because the weather was always so unpredictable. They couldn't get enough games in. They did not have a very good field. It was at Cahill Park, adjacent to the high school. It was always muddy. It was always a mess, and they just couldn't get many games in.

They went to summer baseball. There was a limited group of schools. They were in the North Shore Conference. It wasn't all the regular ones, but it was certified for high school baseball. They scheduled twenty to twenty-five games and usually got in twenty. They didn't make up rainouts because there was no time to fit rainouts back into the schedule.

Craig also played on two other teams. He played on a Legion team with Larry Hisle, Jr., Sal and Sonny Bando, and some other kids out in Germantown. He was also playing on what's called a semi-pro team, they called it an Industrial League team. Most of the industrial companies in and around Milwaukee had baseball teams. The firemen had a baseball team. The policemen had a baseball team. The Falk Corporation had a team. Allen Bradley had a team. They were all financed by those respective organizations. It was a good league, a lot of ex-pros, mostly minor leaguers, an occasional ex-major leaguer. Craig played on all three of those for at least two of his summers before college.

He had three uniforms, and some of the uniforms had two tops. He went to a park to play one of the semi-pro games. I dropped him off, came home. By the time I got home, Jan said, "Craig called, and there's a problem." I said, "What? Did he get hurt?" She said no.

By the way, he had to borrow a dime or quarter—I don't remember what it was—to go to a pay phone and call us. There were no cellphones, and his message to me was, "Dad, I have the wrong top. You've got to get the other top." After I got there, he said, "Mom packed the wrong top. She packed the Legion top, and this is my semipro team!"

Maybe I took the phone call because I told him to borrow a top from another player, go in the field, and then when I get there with his jersey—he could switch. But being on three teams, he had so many uniforms, he couldn't keep track.

He did great on those teams. On that team, he was near the league lead in hitting at like sixteen, playing against a lot of twenty-year-olds, some thirty-year-olds. He had an exceptionally good season the first year he played in that league.

Craig always wanted to be the first one there to the game. It drove me crazy. He'd be waiting in the car. Sometimes he'd honk the horn, "Let's go, Dad."

It was a father's dream, inside me, to know that he liked it that much. Jan kept saying to me, "When's he going to not like it?" I said, "So far, we're good." I used to always say that to her, "So far, we're good. I haven't heard one thing that he didn't like."

Even if he had a bad day, hey, it's a good day. We get to play baseball. That's a line from the movie, *The Rookie*. For him, if he got to play baseball, that was a good day.

Craig was very consistent about everything he did. He very seldom wavered way off here or way off there. He was always consistent with his homework, consistent with just the way he acted. He was quietly smart. We didn't know how smart because he was so quiet, and he was dedicated to things. If he had something that had to get done, he wanted to get it done, if it was a school project, whatever it was.

The first summer after college freshman year, Craig stayed in South Bend to go to summer school to make sure he would keep enough credits ahead. A business degree (accounting) at Notre Dame, required that you take eighteen credits a semester. That's generally six three-credit courses. It was a very difficult major.

*Craig pictured with Wichita Broncos teammate just after winning National Baseball Congress National Championship, Summer 1989.*

The second summer he went to Red Oak, Iowa in the Jayhawk League, a league for college players. At the end of the season, teams that were in contention for the NBC, the National Baseball Congress Tournament, could pick up players from teams who didn't qualify. He got picked up by the Wichita team, the Wichita Broncos. They won the whole thing, the national championship. Craig was a key contributor. This was another very good experience adding to his resume of being a winner.

Between junior and senior year, he went to the Alaskan Summer League. This is where he called me and said, "Dad, what should I do? I've got these opportunities....I could go to the Cape Cod League, or I can go to the Alaskan Summer League." I said, "I don't know. I didn't play in either one. I played in the one in the middle. I played in Central Illinois Collegiate League. I said, "Cape Cod is a hitters' league, and the other one's a pitchers' league. If you want to learn how to hit, I'd go to the pitchers' league and see if you can hit good pitching." All of the West Coast colleges, Stanford and Southern Cal, Oregon, Cal-State Fullerton send their guys to Alaska.

He chose to go to Alaska where he struggled the first half of the season. He lived with a family that was originally from Milwaukee. That turned out to be a good thing for him. The second half, he did really well and figured it out. I think he hit .260. That was good.

I didn't see any of his summer games in **SOUTH BEND**\* or Alaska. My job with the Brewers...and later I founded Counsell Marketing Group, kept me busy. It was tough. We're (Brewers) playing weekends, and he's playing weekends and then I was trying to build a sports marketing business.

\*The man who wrote the Michigan fight song, "(Hail to) The Victors," lived in **SOUTH BEND**, Indiana on what was later the site of the College Football Hall of Fame.

Jan and I ventured out to Red Oak a couple of times to see him play. I remember going to Red Oak…it's way in the Southwest corner of Iowa, not terribly far from Omaha.

I remember going to Iowa without GPS, cell phones, or anything. We were trying to read the map. We had to literally stop at intersections and get out. The corn was so tall; it didn't allow you to see the signs.

He was playing on an all-dirt infield. He was the shortstop for this team. He had played all summer on a skin infield, as it was called…the first skin infield he'd played on since high school.

We did not go to Alaska to see him play. He struggled and wanted to come home. He did not think playing in this league was going to help him They were supposed to get jobs and have some money. The jobs fell through. I know we sent him some money. I simply said, "You've got to hang in there and learn how to hit". He did stay and eventually began to hit. He played for the Mat-Su Minors, a small city in Alaska

It was fun. He was living with that family originally from Milwaukee. It was much like Harrison Bader, current Cardinals center fielder, who lived with Craig and family for one summer when he was in college and playing for the Lakeshore Chinooks. The dad of the family in Alaska he lived with had an airplane, either as a hobby or part of his work. Craig did go up in it, and we never thought two things about it. He went up in the small airplane with him several times. Jan knew about it, but we didn't have any concept of what that meant then. We weren't scared.

He only flew one other time in an airplane with another guy. It was when he was with the Diamondbacks and had just won the World Series in '01. In '02 they were going to close Luke Air Force base near Phoenix. The Defense Department was going to close a lot of bases, and that was one of them. They were going to put 4,000 civilians out of work. The people at Luke AFB called the Diamondbacks and said, "We are going to launch a marketing campaign to go on the airwaves…television, radio and the newspapers to convince the general public to write to their Senators and Representatives, so that 4,000 jobs are not lost in the Phoenix area. They wanted to know if the Diamondbacks have a player that they could get to help them with their campaign?" The Diamondbacks said, "We'll ask around."

*Craig in flight suit (which he got to keep) after flight in F-15 in 2002. They flew upside down over the Grand Canyon.*

The Luke people wanted Randy Johnson. They wanted Curt Schilling. They wanted Luis Gonzalez. They got Craig. That was one of their choices, by the way. He was very popular in Arizona, and he still is. He called to ask us about it. "Dad, Mom I've got a chance to do this promotion, and the fee, there's no money. They don't have a budget." "So we asked, "What do you get?" He said, "I get to fly in an F-15." I said, "Oh, my god." I said, "You don't even like to go on Ferris wheels. How are you going to do it?" He said, "First of all, would you do it?" I said, "I would do it in a minute." He said, "I'm thinking about doing it." I said, "Do it. It's a once in a lifetime. You've got to do it.". Then he calls us later. He said, "Dad, guess what? I get to keep the flight suit if I don't throw up when they go Mach

2." I asked how fast is Mach 2?" He said, "1500 miles an hour." I said, "Good luck on that one. Fine. If you think you want the flight suit, then do it." He said, "Yeah, but I don't get the helmet. I guess those are like $5,000 to $6,000 apiece." He did it. Then he tells us about it later. He says, "Dad, we were flying over the Grand Canyon. The pilot says to me, 'Hey, we're going to fly over the Grand Canyon. So when we get there, I'll tell you, okay?' 'Okay, we're over the Grand Canyon. What do you think?'" Then he yelled at Craig, "Don't look down. Look up." He says, "How can I look up to see the Grand Canyon?" The pilot said, 'Because we're flying upside down!'"

It was neat. He's so glad he did that. He met all the flight guys, all the young kids that prepare the airplane. Some of these kids were eighteen-years-old. Craig said, "They have a thousand more responsibilities than I've ever had, preparing the pilot and getting the plane ready, and making sure the fuel tanks, the landing gear, just everything all checks out. It's incredible". Craig said, "He let me steer for a little while." Then Craig said, "You barely breathe on the stick, and the plane moves." He was just fascinated by that. I think in another lifetime, he would have wanted to be a pilot.

## Injuries—Rub Some Dirt On It

Craig had a lot of injuries in the minor leagues, two major injuries in the major leagues. His first injury in the minor leagues was his first year in Bend, Oregon. After fourteen games, he fouled a ball off his shin and cracked it. It was a hairline fracture. He was out for the rest of the season. Craig was the shortstop. Quinton McCracken was the second baseman. McCracken moved to short, became a more prominent player, and eventually made the big leagues. He was a Duke graduate, and they've been friends. They've played together a couple of different times throughout their careers.

In July '96, Craig was running to first base, got into a collision, broke his leg, and was out for the rest of the season. It happened in Tacoma, where my brother lived and worked as a lawyer. My brother called me and said, "Hey, I was at the game. I think Craig got hurt seriously." I said, "Get to the hospital. You can represent him. Don't let them do anything crazy to his leg." It was the fracture of the smaller bone in his leg, and eventually he had to go to the Olympic ski team orthopedic doctor to get it fixed with a very unusual procedure. Instead of putting a rod in his leg, which we think would have slowed him down, they did a different procedure. It did not slow him down at all. He completely recovered. That was pretty serious.

It was a key decision in his playing career. I went to four MLB GMs, and Craig dealt with his GM with the Rockies, Bob Gebhard, to ask their opinion on what to do. Obviously I went to Joe **GARAGIOLA***, Jr. of the Diamondbacks who I had coached at Notre Dame. I went to Sal Bando, then Brewers GM who I had played against in the minor leagues and dealt with him as a player with the Brewers. I went to Terry Ryan, the Twins GM, and I consulted with Red Sox GM Theo Epstein. In all cases, they said, "Let the team doctor give you the advice. They've seen a lot of injuries."

However it was Bando who said, "Boy, I don't know. We've had luck with sending people to the Olympic ski-team orthopedic doctors because they have seen so many leg injuries." Since Craig was playing for the Rockies, they agreed because the Olympic ski team doctor was in Vail, in the same state. That was an easy decision for a second opinion. It turned out to be the best thing Craig ever did. Craig was very worried about this injury. He was very concerned that his career was over. This was the second time that he had broken something in his leg/ foot area. One was from a foul ball, so he began to wear a guard. He wore that guard the rest of his career until he retired in 2011. The leg thing was scary. The most important thing was

*When **JOE GARAGIOLA**, Sr. played for the Cardinals, his wife Audrey was the organist. Both were St. Louis natives.

the Rockies accepted the Olympic ski team doctor's decision to put him in this special brace instead of inserting a rod into his leg. That was a major coup to get them to agree to that.

He had a broken nose the previous season in New Haven, Double A when a guy took him out on a double play, forearmed him and broke it. He went to Yale University Hospital, sat in the waiting room for hours, bleeding all over his uniform. They finally fixed it. He went right back and played the next day. Jan had gone out there. She didn't want him to play. He said, "No, I've got to play." Yale University Hospital Emergency Room almost screwed it up. They cauterized some veins in his nose and it was going to leave him with a noticeable scar. Fortunately, he ended up going to a plastic surgeon, and it was fixed. Yale just did it on their own. They didn't ask him. He just said, "Fix it, stop the bleeding". He didn't know any better. He was thinking, "I've got to get back in the lineup. I've got at-bats coming up."

In going to the big leagues, there were two major injuries. The second year with the **MARLINS**\* in '98, a left-handed pitcher, C.J. Nitkowski, hit Craig in the face and broke his jaw. We were not at that game. We were watching it on TV. I wouldn't let Jan watch the replay. She didn't see it the first time. The most dramatic thing about it was, he never went down. He tried to go to first base. The same concept, "I've got to get on base. I've got to score." Also, he was concerned about choking on all the blood if he went on the ground. There we called Jennifer. She lived with him in Miami. We told her to go to the hospital they were taking him to and represent him. "You're his sister. They can't deny you. You're family. Do not let them do anything dramatic until we get over there." That wasn't as hard to deal with as a broken jaw. It wasn't uncommon, though very serious.

*The Florida **MARLINS** have won the World Series twice but have never won their division—the NL East.

We got through the broken jaw in '98. It was the year after the World Series. The Marlins had unloaded everybody except Craig and Livan Hernandez. They were a shell of a team. In '99, he was also traded away, to the **DODGERS**\*.

In '02 another bad injury occurred with the Diamondbacks when he dove for a ball against Atlanta. Playing short, he dove for a ball up the middle, totally stretched out, and it took a bad hop up. As he had his body, arm and hand totally stretched out to get a ground ball he suddenly had to bend his elbow to snag the ball, and then he bounced. He got whiplash and essentially broke his neck. He broke a vertebrae in his neck. He played the rest of the game or at least another couple of innings. They took him out, and he couldn't turn his head at all the next day. He could barely walk. He didn't know what was wrong. The doctor said, "You've got a broken vertebrae in your neck." That's when he ended up again getting a third opinion. He went, first opinion, Diamondback doctors. The second opinion, the famous doctor in LA, Frank Jobe, at his Jobe Institute. From Jobe, he got a referral to the one of the Dallas Cowboys team doctors, Drew Dossett, an orthopedic guy, who had graduated from the Jobe Institute. He had been a linebacker at Southern Cal.

On his first visit to Dr. Dossett's office Craig runs into "Rocket" Ismail, former Notre Dame running back and kick returner and then a running back with the Cowboys. He was seeing Dr. Dossett for a similar injury...herniated disc in his neck. Craig meets with Dossett, and that's when he saw a sign on his office wall, "I put bull riders back up on bulls." When Craig saw that, he had the same reaction I did some years later. He said, "Well, that's stupid. Why would you do that?" Why would a bull rider get his back fixed and go back up on a bull? The answer is they do it because they love it. Craig said, "Maybe it makes sense."

\*Only 6,700 fans attended the **DODGERS**' finale at Ebbets Field in 1957. The park—built 44 years earlier—had a capacity of 32,000 with only 700 parking spaces. An apartment building now sits on that site.

Dossett says to Craig, "My job is to put you back on the field. I don't do fusion because people with back/neck fusion don't go back on the field (except Tiger Woods). "They can't", Dossett said, "I can fix your neck, and you can play again." He played nine more years.

Some years later, when I started having back problems, I said to Craig, "I don't know what to do about my back. I can't find anybody. I don't trust anybody." He said, "Dad, why don't we take the x-rays, bundle them up, send them to Dr. Dossett. I'll call him and ask him if he will give us an opinion. We're not asking him to fix you. We're just getting an opinion of what you should do." We did all that. I got on the phone with Dr. Dossett. He says, "If you want to come to Dallas, I can fix it." This was 2012.

I went to Dallas, and I had what's called a laminectomy. He said to me after the operation, "Essentially what I did was pretty simple. I shaved the bone down so that there are no bones rubbing together at the bottom of your back," It was lower discs. "But you have a definite back problem. You've got degenerative discs, which is a disease. It's incurable. We don't know how to fix it. It's hereditary probably in some cases." He said, "I will not see you again if you quit playing golf. I will see you again in five years if you play golf and don't do crazy things like one foot in a trap and one foot on the grass or swing from your heels to get the ball off the tee. Then I'll see you in a year. If you just play normal golf, I'll see you in five years." He said, "If you quit golf, I won't see you again."

I went home, and I played what I felt was mild golf. Four years later, I called him and said, "I've got problems. I'm going to send you my x-rays." He said okay. I sent him my x-rays. He said, "You need back fusion, and I don't do fusion. I put every-body back on the field. I can't put you back on the field. I can't put you back on the golf course, not with a fusion."

I felt like I was the smoker who didn't quit smoking. It was my fault. I said, "I understand. You don't do fusion." He said, "Yes, but I've got a friend that does." I said, "What do you mean?" He said, "It's a guy I went to the Jobe Institute with...Dr. John Small. He's right there in Tampa." We lived two hours south in Ft. Myers. That's how I fixed my back—Dr. John Small...the referral from Craig's doctor—Dr. Drew Dossett. That's all he does is fusions. I have a normal life, but I don't play golf.

I've had back problems for 20 years. My sleeping problem has been solved to a certain degree. I have a life. I'm going to be seventy-eight. I'm still flying everywhere. I don't throw BP anymore. I can still hit ground balls to my grandsons. I can play catch. I can't throw that good, but I have a life. The back does limit what you can do throwing a ball.

Up until maybe five years ago before my fusion surgery, I was throwing a lot of batting practice to my grandsons Brady and Jack, Craig's sons. I would shorten up and use a protective screen and throw from fifty feet, but I could throw strikes. I could throw hard. I could throw hard enough for them. I was always able to throw batting practice up until the fusion surgery. Then I had to stop. It was painful. Craig has a batting cage in his backyard, a full batting cage. He's always had that. His agent gave it to him years ago, but it's always been used by his kids and the neighborhood kids, which is really neat. Before a high school game, there'll be ten or twelve kids over there hitting.

During Craig's early career, many players were using PEDs (Performance Enhancing Drugs). He survived all of that. *The Onion,* the tongue-in-cheek magazine, during the steroid era, named Craig the National League home run leader with five. They said, "He's the only player that we know of that wasn't on steroids, so he's the home run leader in the National League".

# Turns Out Craig Counsell Was Actually Best Baseball Player Of Steroid Era

NEW YORK—After the records of players who used performance-enhancing drugs are carefully removed, statistics provided by the Elias Sports Bureau indicate that lifetime .255 hitter Craig Counsell was the best player of the past 15 years. "If you judge them on the basis of pure physical ability, you're left with Craig Counsell," said ESB representative Patrick Wondolowski, adding that Counsell's 35 career home runs narrowly beat out Quinton McCracken's 21 and pitcher Glendon Rusch's three. Upon hearing the news, broadcaster Bob Uecker lauded the Brewers utilityman as "one of the best I ever saw, if we're talking about those who I can say without a doubt never took steroids. He came this close to stealing a base off of Ivan Rodriguez, and I swear I heard him foul tip a Roger Clemens fastball. The kid could flat-out steroid-free play. One time he was playing third base and he caught a Rafael Palmeiro line drive—just caught it, right in his mitt." When asked about his Hall of Fame chances, Counsell dodged the question by asking if anyone had a few bucks so he could go buy a sandwich.

**Arizona Diamondbacks** basmith7 127 points · 4 years ago
Who needs steroids when you got that power hitting batter's stance.

> **Milwaukee Brewers** boatagainstthecurrent 71 points · 4 years ago
> Within the next month the entire Brewers lineup will be batting like this
> Continue this thread →

> **Toronto Blue Jays** tmlrule 37 points · 4 years ago
> He was so good, he needed a challenge. So he decided to make the strike zone as big as possible against him.
> Continue this thread →

> > **Milwaukee Brewers** 🏆 PocketWocket 15 points · 4 years ago
> > He did tone it down a ton later on. I think that season he hit .285 he was batting like a human.

> > **New York Mets** cheapdad 12 points · 4 years ago
> > That's not a real baseball action photo. It's a promotional shot for the film "Honey, I Shrunk the Utility Infielder".

> > **Los Angeles Dodgers** Quesly 5 points · 4 years ago
> > his stance always reminded me of someone trying to make themselves look big to scare off a bear

> > **McCovey Cove!** DrBeardyFace 2 points · 4 years ago
> > I hope he motions to the bullpen in a similar fashion for a pitching change.

> > **Cincinnati Reds** 🔴 JV19 2 points · 4 years ago
> > Ah, the ol' Cerveceros. The best Spanish MLB team name.
> >
> > And really, Counsell's stance is pretty similar to Ryan Braun from the other side.

> > **San Francisco Giants** scarface910 2 points · 4 years ago
> > "what're you trying to do, change a light bulb?"
> >
> > That was a heckle from a video game either the show or mlb 2k

**Milwaukee Brewers** necropaw 154 points · 4 years ago
> Upon hearing the news, broadcaster Bob Uecker lauded the Brewers utilityman as "one of the best I ever saw, if we're talking about those who I can say without a doubt never took steroids. He came this close to stealing a base off of Ivan Rodriguez, and I swear I heard him foul tip a Roger Clemens fastball.

The best part is i can actually hear Uke saying something like that in my mind, complete with Joe Block's muffled laughter

**New York Mets** caldera15 4 points · 4 years ago
I guess it makes some degree of sense when you can't rely on most statistics from that area due to inflated numbers from PED's. You have to look at the stats that don't get effected much, like GRITT. So I can see why Counsell came out on top - I mean the guy can play any positions, that has value that can't be measured in raw numbers.

> **Milwaukee Brewers** coolcool23 3 points · 4 years ago
> He was also way above in Hits Above Replacement Teammates and Batted Runs and Wins Normalized. By far and away the best in Fielding, Running and Errors per Innings at Night or Day.
> Continue this thread →

**Chicago Cubs** knm3 3 points · 4 years ago
Yea but that batting stance hurt to watch.

**Minnesota Twins** CantaloupeCamper 3 points · 4 years ago
The second Dead Ball Era passed us by and we didn't even know it.

**Arizona Diamondbacks** zuul99 2 points · 4 years ago
Dat batter stance.

**Boston Red Sox** ReginaldKD 1 point · 4 years ago
Ah, good ole Quinton McCracken.

When Craig retired, Brewers General Manager Doug Melvin asked Craig what he wanted. Craig said, "I want to be in a leadership position. I want to have an impact on the organization." As parents that's just something you love to hear.

*Craig, age 11, receiving a Little League award from Rollie Fingers and Dion James, 1981.*

# CITY COUNSELL

This John Counsell story was previously published in the author's book *For Milwaukee Braves Fans Only*.

When the Braves came to Milwaukee in 1953, my father owned a small insurance agency in Oconomowoc, 30 miles west of Milwaukee. He also did income tax consultation and prepared tax returns for people around tax time. Through a referral he began doing the individual tax return for the head of the ticket office for the Braves and in exchange for his services he received a fee and the ability to purchase Braves tickets. Because of this we were always able to get good seats at most Braves games including the '57 and '58 World Series and the '55 All-Star Game at Milwaukee County Stadium.

In 1955 I was 12 years old and very much into baseball. My favorite players were Hank Aaron and Mickey Mantle. My Dad got two prime seats for the '55 All-Star Game at County Stadium and took me on a summer school day! A couple of days before the game my dad came to me and said a guy had offered him $60 for our two tickets. They were $10 face value tickets in the lower grandstand. My dad said I could keep the $30 for my ticket if "I" decided we would take the money and not go to the game. $30 was a lot of money then for a 12-year-old, much less my father. Gas was around 20 cents a gallon. I'm certain now it was a test that my dad was putting me to regarding my "love" for the game and the privilege to see Willie, Mickey & the Duke (not to mention "Hammerin" Hank, "Stan the Man", Yogi, Ernie Banks, Ted Williams, Roy Campanella, "Big Ted Klu", Eddie Mathews and Harvey Kuenn). I had trouble sleeping that night thinking about the $30 because I wasn't sure if my dad needed the money or if he wanted me to make an important decision. I knew right away that I wanted to go...to me it was a baseball "candy store". I was going to see all these great players, in person, and be able to talk about it forever. The next morning I got up really early and went to my dad in bed and said "I want to go." He seemed really pleased, so I knew, later, I had passed the "test". Well, we went and it couldn't have been better. Mantle homered, all my favorites played and Stan the Man homered in the 10th to win it for the National League. I was "hot" stuff the next day at St. Jerome Grade School.

Again, one of the special benefits of my dad knowing this Braves ticket guy was occasionally we got the opportunity to buy really good seats. One particular game my brother, age 9, and I went to a Braves Sunday day game and got second row box seats between the Braves dugout and home plate. By that time my brother and I had been sending Hank Aaron birthday cards for about five years. We always signed them "John & Chuck from Oconomowoc, Your Biggest Fans." Of course we never asked for anything, or ever received any acknowledgement that he received the cards or even saw them. When Hank came up in the first inning that day and was in the on-deck circle right near our seats, we yelled to him we were the boys who were sending him the birthday cards from Oconomowoc...he turned and looked at us a couple of time and sort of smiled. He promptly homered in that at-bat and as he came near our seats on the way back to the dugout he looked over, pointed at us, and gave us a wink...everybody in our area was patting us on the back and congratulating us. We were convinced that was confirmation that he was getting our cards and the home run was for us. We were ten feet tall for weeks!

I went away to college at **NOTRE DAME**\*, on a baseball scholarship, and was able to sign a contract upon graduation with the

*The "**NOTRE DAME** Victory March" has won multiple polls as the greatest college fight song ever. It was written in 1908 by two alums, John and Mike Shea. John Shea, who wrote the words, lettered in baseball at Notre Dame before taking his volley cheer on high in 1965 in Holyoke, Massachusetts...In the late '60s, almost one-third of all junior high and high schools in the United States used some version of the "Notre Dame Victory March" as their school song.

Minnesota Twins for a sizable bonus. I struggled and never made it out of "A" ball in 5 years. However, I did get to play in one game in County Stadium (Wisconsin Rapids Twins vs. Fox City Foxes). In that game I fouled off a pitch that my future wife caught. We got married the last season of my minor league career and three years later, after accepting the Assistant Baseball Coaching job at Notre Dame, had a son. We named him Craig, after Graig Nettles, who I roomed with one season in "A" ball. As soon as Craig could hold a bat he was swinging it left-handed and, of course, throwing right-handed. After some years at Notre Dame, I accepted a job with the Brewers and in 1978 began a 10-year stint in the Front Office as Director of the Speakers Bureau and then Community Relations Director.

*John Counsell rounding third base in a Winter Instructional League game, Florida, 1964*

For those 10 years I had an office in Milwaukee County Stadium. I brought Craig to County Stadium often and he loved
it. He'd disappear for hours on end doing odd jobs in the clubhouse and around the Stadium. When he turned 16, he ran
the Speed Pitch concession behind the bleachers. His time at
County Stadium went for ten years (his ages 8-17) before he
left for Notre Dame, also on a baseball scholarship. We were
able to share a lot of moments at County Stadium. He took
batting practice with the players' kids many times on Sunday
mornings and shagged balls in early batting practice for the
players. He's the only kid I know who played in the Father-Son-
Daughter Games (played annually prior to a Sunday Brewers
game) that took four pitches (I'm pretty sure Mike Caldwell
was throwing, underhand, to the kids that day) and went to
first for a walk…and came around to score. He was 8 years old.
Those games were often played in front of 20,000 or more fans.

To have seen my son grow up in County Stadium, my favorite
ballpark, develop a lot of his baseball skills and knowledge of
the game, is obviously something a father can only hope for or
dream about. And now to have him completing an incredible
career as a professional is quite astounding. And in the words
of a famous Green Bay Packer coach "He's not done yet".

County Stadium is a place I frequented as a kid/fan, and later
as an employee/fan and I'll always cherish those many hours
watching Aaron, Covington and Mathews hit balls out of the
park, and then watching Counsell hit line drives, run the bases
and occasionally lift one over the right field fence in Sunday
morning BP. But I'll always remember the walk he took in that
Father-Son-Daughter game because unselfish play became his
trademark.

The Graig Nettles Story

Graig Nettles is from San Diag.
California. He played his first
season of Professional baseball
in Wisconsin Rapids with my Dac
He hit 28 home runs that year
And was the home run Champ for
the midwest League. The year wc
1966 In 1976 Graig was the
American League home run Cham
He hit 32 I was named After
Graig Nettles only my first
name is spelled with a C
Craig Counsell

*Assignment written by Craig Counsell as a sixth grader.*

I've heard the story that they named Craig after me but I just thought John probably thought my name was Craig. Turns out John wanted to spell it with the G but Jan argued they should change it to a C. I was in the Wisconsin Rapids in **1966**\* I remember John had already been playing for a couple years when I got there. So to me he was a veteran player I was just a rookie but I got along great with John. He was great player. One thing I remember about the Wisconsin Rapids is that it smells real bad. There was some kind of paper mill in town that just stunk like hell. Best part about their league was it was a 10-cent-beer league. Any bar you walk into it was 10 cents a beer. I followed Craig's career. I was doing scouting for the Yankees at one point. Once I scouted the Colorado Rockies and their AAA team in Colorado Springs. I saw Craig play and I liked him a lot.

——**GRAIG NETTLES\***, Farragut, Tennessee

\**Sports Illustrated* rated New York City in **1966** as the worst time and place to be a sports fan. The Yankees, Knicks and Rangers finished last, the Mets escaped last place for the first time and the Giants were 1–12–1. The best time and place to be a sports fan? Philadelphia, 1980.

\*In 1974, **GRAIG NETTLES** had a broken bat single and six Superballs bounced from inside the bat.

# NO, MOTHER KNOWS BEST

### JAN COUNSELL

*Jan (Rau)Counsell is the mother of Craig and Jennifer Counsell and wife of John for over fifty years. Raised on a dairy farm near Plymouth, Wisconsin, she graduated Wisconsin-Whitewater with a teaching degree. Her innovative classroom ideas helped hundreds of young Wisconsin students in her twenty year educational career.*

I was born and raised on a farm in Plymouth, Wisconsin, which is about an hour north of Miller Park. Of course, there was no Miller Park in those days. I had an older brother and an older sister. We had to work all the time. When you're on a farm, everybody works, and everybody goes into the house at the same time, and everybody comes out at the same time. The noon meal is called dinner, and the evening meal is called supper. There was a tremendous amount of work to do as we had a large farm. We had cows that had to be milked every morning and every evening. Our family—the Rau family—was close, very close, as we grew up. We all knew that we had a job to do, and we did it. We couldn't say no and go somewhere else. That was not acceptable at our place.

We were Congregational in denomination. We had a very special church we went to, where my mom was always involved in the ladies organizations. My dad would be the one who would always volunteer to fix something at the church because he was a good fixer-upper. As we got older, Craig and his sister Jennifer and my sister's boys sang a long German song in Church during Christmas services. Mom did a little of the choreographing. The congregation said, "The Raus! The Raus! Look what they're doing." The audience loved it and stood up and clapped heartily.

Oftentimes on an off day, Craig and I will work out in the garden together. I got the love of gardening from my mother. My mother took care of the garden and all the flowers around the house. Later even when I was teaching in Racine, Wisconsin and married, I would go up to the farm on weekends to help Mom in her later years with getting the plants all cut and getting rid of the weeds.

My mom taught me gardening, but my dad taught me how to be a mechanic. I had to help him. My sister had gone away to college. After high school, my brother worked on the farm for a couple of years before he decided he wanted to go to California to see what that was like. So I was home, and I was the helper except occasionally when my sister would come home for the summer.

My mother worked with the ladies in the church group. Down in the basement, they had meetings there. They made nice things for the old peoples' home. Mom was a hard worker. She never said, "No, I don't want to do that." My sister was probably the closest to being Betty Crocker.

Now, unfortunately, if you know anything at all about the farming business in the state of Wisconsin, farmers are in big trouble. The farmers are basically losing everything they've worked for their whole life. The big guys and the corporate farms are doing okay, but it's the little guy who's getting squeezed out.

Two years ago, my brother had twenty milk cows. After a while, it was costing him more to feed them than what he grossed for the milk. He sold all of the cows before it got really bad. One thing that really kills the dairy business in Wisconsin is milk that is being sold as almond milk or soy milk or other milks like that that aren't really milk at all, and it misleads the consumer.

After high school, I went to the University of Wisconsin at Whitewater. It was a business-oriented college where I studied teaching. I taught for twenty years, mainly business, typing, shorthand and business courses. When you're in those categories, there's always something new. I had to take typewriters, which were not electric in those days, and show the kids how to type, and then all of a sudden, we had to move up to electrics, and "Oh, now the school is going to buy us computers." So we had to get those set up. My dad had taught me how to put stuff together so I could do that with the machines that we were able to get new in the school from time to time.

I loved teaching. It was always something different. It was changing. The good thing that I did that was different from a lot of other business teachers in the area is I did a co-op program, what I called "getting girls ready to go to work in offices in downtown Milwaukee." I would go to some businesses in downtown Milwaukee and talk to the people in charge. I'd say, "I'm teaching some high school girls. They're in my class in the morning, but I'm looking to put them to work in the afternoon and for them to learn what it's like in an office at a regular business. Would you be interested in hiring some of them?" Many of the businesses said, "Of course we will."

I said to the kids, "The first thing you've got to do is you've got to learn how to type. Next you've got to learn how to file. If you put it away and they can't find it, you didn't put it in the right place. Then what's going to happen is that if you're really good, some of these companies will actually pay your tuition at some of the local colleges." The girls all looked at me and said, "I can't wait to go home and tell my mom that I can make some money."

It was a very good co-op program. After a few years, St. Joan's changed principals and they eliminated the program. They said, "we don't need the program anymore. The girls need to know how to read and write," which of course they were learning in other classes anyway. After twenty years, the whole program was scuttled. We had put this package together, and the kids loved it. When they'd get a job, they'd come in the next morning and said, "Mrs. Counsell, Mrs. Counsell, do you know what I did yesterday? I went down to the company's office, and I got a full-time job." They were just so excited.

I haven't see a lot of my students after they graduated. Every now and then I'll get together with some of the teachers. Where I taught most of the time was in a Catholic school called St. Joan Antida. It was a strict all-girls school. It was a good school near downtown Milwaukee. Ironically, I was back in the city a few years ago for a 5k race. Suddenly these three women came and said, "Oh, my god, it's Mrs. Counsell!" We just had a wonderful chat with them.

All the girls in school were hard workers. There was a group that had to be pushed a little bit, but they ended up doing well. Some days I'd say to them, "What are you going to do with your paycheck?" They'd say, "I'm going to spend it." I said, "No, you're not going to spend it. You're going to put it in the bank, and I'm going to teach you how to put it in the bank, and then how to take it out of the bank." "Well, my mom said I didn't have to go to the bank. She would take care of it." I said, "No, you take care of it. She's not going to be there when you're twenty-two years old, and you're dealing with money on your own."

I would give the students a pretend amount of money that they would get if they went to work. "Now if you don't want to live with Mom and Dad anymore, you'll probably want to live by yourself. Maybe you want to have a friend to room with. I want you to go into the Milwaukee Journal and find a place to rent with you and another girl." I tried to teach them real-life responsibilities.

St. Joan Antida was very diverse. We had many Spanish girls. We had Asian girls and African-American girls. There were about 16 girls usually in my classes. They would go to school in the morning, and then they would leave at 12:30, get to the offices downtown by 1:00 and work there until 5:00.

I also had some lawyer friends who I got to speak to the class. I told the lawyers, "You've got to give these girls a good lesson on what they can and can't do. They're going to have to make sure that they understand that you can't just drive a car over here or there with no insurance." That took quite a bit of twisting and turning to explain, but the girls in the long run really did appreciate that. That's one of the things when I met those three girls on the street, they said, "I have two bank accounts" or "I understand legal things really well." They got it. They really got it.

When I was at Whitewater, I did my student teaching in Oconomowoc, which is where I met John...his hometown. Whitewater was about an hour south of Oconomowoc. I stayed for a semester and was mentored by a man who was teaching in the business department at Oconomowoc H. S. He was a really nice guy who taught me a lot. The interesting thing was, this guy had a study hall that he was in charge of. He said, "Jan, could you oversee it sometimes? I have to go to the office and talk to the principal."

The first time it happens, he goes to the office, and all of a sudden, there's a lot of chit-chatting going on. I told the students, "Sit down. You all have enough homework. You need to get it done now." All of a sudden, I heard popping noises. I said to the student, "All right. Give it to me." The kid who I found out later was Chuck Counsell, John's brother, whom I didn't know at the time, said, "What do you mean? Give it to me?" I said, "You've just opened a can of soda, and I would like it please." Obviously I didn't drink it. I just poured it out.

That's how I met the Counsell family. What happened is John came to see his brother who was in this study hall. You're not supposed to talk when you're in study hall; you're supposed to study. But John's brother didn't take studying very hard even though he's a very successful lawyer in Tacoma, Washington these days.

When I was in Oconomowoc, I stayed at a friend's house. One night she said, "Hey, I'll show you some of the local bars." We went down to a local bar and walk in. Who's standing at the bar but John Counsell, my student Chuck's brother. John was with a couple of his buddies. We started talking. He said, "Did my brother ever shape up?" I said, "Yes, he did shape up."

We talked for a while and suddenly he said, "Hey, would you like to go to a movie?" Oconomowoc was not a very large town, but it did have a movie theatre. He said, "Let's go Tuesday night." We go to the theatre and saw a double feature. One of the films was called "Spy in Your Eye." Later I asked him, "Why did you want to go to a double feature?" and he said, "So I could spend more time with you."

I liked John. I was getting to know him better. Then suddenly he announces that he's going to be gone for eight weeks to something called spring training, and then he'll come back for a few days, and then from there, he goes off for four more months to play baseball somewhere. I said, "Oh, okay. You know, farmers have a lot of work to do in the summertime. My dad will appreciate the fact that I'm around."

He went to spring training, and he was assigned to the Midwest League team in Wisconsin Rapids. He had just gotten to Wisconsin Rapids when he was given a bonus check of $11,000, which was a tremendous amount of money in those days since the starting salary for a college graduate was about a $100 a week. What happened was he goes to a bank in Wisconsin Rapids to deposit the check and open an account. He asked the banker, who was very interested in John because he was going to be playing for the local team, if he could use his office phone. The banker said yes, and John called me. When he got the school, he asked for the teacher's lounge, and I happened to answer the phone. The voice on the other end said, "Hi, Jan, this is John." I said, "John who?" I knew a lot of guys named John. I found out later that John was very embarrassed because the banker overheard all of this and was laughing.

As John and I dated more, I introduced John to my family and the farm life. My dad was just looking at him, thinking, "What is this guy going to do? He's going to make money playing baseball?"

One peculiar thing on our farm was all of our tractors had a different way of starting. Some you would have to crank. Some you would have to push a button. There were various other ways of doing it. There was a tractor in the yard outside one Sunday afternoon when we're having our noon meal, and John was outside and decides he's going to put that tractor into the barn. The rest of us are inside eating, but we could see John out in the yard.

*The farm owned by Craig's grandparents (his mom's parents) in Sheboygan Falls where Craig spent many weekends with cousins.*

Suddenly he comes in and he says, "Hey, you know, I was out there working on that tractor, and I just couldn't find the right button to push to start it. Does it have a button? How does it start?" My dad is sitting at the table laughing. Everybody at the table knew how the tractor worked except for John. He had left it running in the barn.

Later when John was off playing baseball, but we were still dating, I started to sit down with my folks and watch baseball games on TV on Sunday when I would go to visit them on the farm. One day Dad said to me, "How come I never see John in any of the games on TV?" I said, "Well, he's trying to get there. He's working really hard."

After John and I were married, we had two children. Craig came first in 1970, and Jennifer came two years later. When Craig was little, as soon as he got finished with school, he would come home, go upstairs, put on a baseball shirt, and he would run out to any of three different fields. When he couldn't find enough guys available to play with, he would get one or two and just play a game called Strike Out. He did that on the wall of the school that he went to, Richards Elementary in Whitefish Bay, which was right across the street from our house.

*Craig with his grandparents, the Raus from Sheboygan Falls. The famous "Strike Out" wall is to the right on Richards Elementary School in Whitefish Bay, Craig's grade school. The second floor window, third one in was the one he broke with his first long fly ball at age 10.*

People at the school actually let him put up this box that outlined the strike zone. Two or three guys would go over, and they'd take a bunch of balls, and they would stay over there all day. Craig would play for two hours. In that two-hour period, somebody would say, "Yes, I'll play with you." Craig kept on going and kept on going. Finally I'd have to call him and say, "Craig, we're having dinner. Come on home." "Oh, no, I need to play some more. One more guy. One more round."

He was right across the street. I could just trot over and say, "Hey, dinnertime." That really helped him. He had guys around that he liked to play with, and they liked to play with him. They knew he was good at what he was doing. That was an interesting time in his life. With the playground being right across the street, he'd come home, get something to drink, something to eat, run back across to the schoolyard and say, "Okay, let's go."

Later when he was in high school, he played on three different teams. Every night he'd come home. He'd get something to eat. Someone would be driving him here or there to a ballgame somewhere. When he'd travel a little bit further away from Milwaukee with the team, he wouldn't get home till 10:00 or 10:30 at night. Earlier than that, I would look out the kitchen window, and there'd be four or five guys and girls sitting on our picnic table, waiting for Craig to come home. They didn't have anything else to do. They wanted to find out how Craig did that night.

It was interesting. One of the people waiting was Michelle McClone. After a while, we started to figure things out. Something's going on. Michelle was also very athletic. She ran track. She ended up getting her degree in elementary education from Drake University. She taught at a variety of schools as Craig was moving around the country playing baseball. They eventually married and settled in the Milwaukee area. By that time we had moved to Ft. Myers, Florida to work in a warmer climate. I ran a beach resort on the Gulf and John was involved in running golf tournaments for the PGA Tour.

*The invitations for "Couns" and "Mish" to their rehearsal dinner.*

In high school, Craig did not ask Michelle to the big home-coming dance. He asked another gal to it. Craig was rather shy. Once he was done with that, he said, "Oh, my gosh, I actually did it."

When John played college ball, there was no baseball draft like there is now. It started in 1965. John has signed with the Twins in 1964. We were hopeful that Craig would get drafted by a major league team in the annual June draft. You're eligible for the draft after your junior year in college, but no one had drafted him the year before.

I usually got home from work the same time that Craig and Jennifer got home. The first day of the draft, I came home, walked into the family room, saw Craig on the sofa and said, "Did somebody call? Did you get a chance?" He said he didn't hear anything. I said, "Well, you've got a couple more days."

The next day when I got home, he's lying on the couch again. I said, "Did you get a call today?" He said, "Yeah, I did," without making anything out of it. All of a sudden, he said, "Yes, I got a call. I got drafted by the Colorado Rockies." That was a happy day at the Counsell house. We were just hoping he would get drafted because he loved baseball so much.

**Robert H. Gebhard**
*Senior Vice President/General Manager*

™

November 18, 1994


Craig Counsell
5905 N. Berkley Blvd.
Whitefish Bay, WI 53217

Dear Craig:

Enclosed please find your Notice of the addition of your contract
to the Major League roster.

This move is an expression of our confidence in your ability and
we look forward to our third spring training with a great deal of
excitement.

Depending on the status of the labor situation, spring training
reporting information will be forwarded mid-January.

You should also be receiving your contract tender prior to the
December 20 deadline.

Craig, congratulations on this assignment. We look forward to a
wonderful inaugural year at Coors Field.

Sincerely,

Bob Gebhard
Senior Vice President/
  General Manager

Colorado Rockies Baseball Club · Suite 2100 · 1700 Broadway · Denver, Colorado 80290 · Phone (303) 292-0200 · Fax (303) 830-8977

*Letter from General Manager Bob Gebhard promoting Craig to the Rockies 40-man Major League Roster.*

Craig had several bad injuries playing in the minor leagues and a couple of bad ones in the major leagues. It was too bad that he had problems with injuries. I learned about one of the worst injuries on TV. When he was injured in Miami, we were watching the game. We were living in Ft. Myers, Florida, where we still live. It was like, "Oh, my gosh! He fell down." He tried to get to first base. He fell down. "Oh, my goodness! He's bleeding!" John and I were just sitting there, looking at each other, saying, "Oh, my god. That doesn't look good."

Our daughter Jennifer was living in **MIAMI**\* at the time and still does. We called her and she said, "I didn't go to the game tonight." She was watching it on TV. "Craig really got hit bad. I can't believe what he's going to look like in the morning." I said, "Okay. I'm going to come over. I'll be there at 6 in the morning."

The next morning I drove over to Miami, and when I walked into his hospital room, I almost fainted. His face was really mashed up. He could barely open his eyes. I just sat with him for a couple of days. We eventually took him home after the doctor said, "We can't do anything more." They wired his jaw together. They wanted to keep as many of his teeth as they could. Thank goodness that we still knew the name of our dentist from Wisconsin. We called and asked him to send us Craig's charts, the records he had kept on the shape of his mouth and other important material. He FedEx-ed it to us right away.

The doctors wired Craig's mouth shut. Now the challenge was, "How is he going to eat?" and "What is he going to eat?" Basically what I did was took food that you could put in a blender and make it in the style of a smoothie. That way he could eat something. Jennifer was there. She also made some stuff when I wasn't around.

Craig lost a lot of weight. He couldn't eat stuff that he normally ate, but he finally got through it and recovered. That was just one of the many things that he had to go through. That was one of those things that I really remember. "Oh, my god. What happened? He got hit in the head." I'm thinking, "Oh, my gosh! What's he going to look like? What's going to happen to him?"

\*Do you confuse Miami (Ohio) with MIAMI Florida? Miami of Ohio was a school before Florida was a state.

Today Craig lives in Whitefish Bay, Wisconsin, near where he grew up. With his kids and his children's friends, they do almost the same thing that he did with John. He plays with the kids at Cahill Ballpark for a couple of hours every week. When I see Craig with kids, he truly wants them to understand what baseball is all about and then what professional baseball is all about. It's about knowing how you can become a better player every time you go to the ballpark. If their dads can help them, fine. If their brothers can help them, fine. But he found out that there's not a lot of dads out there who really take the time to work with their kids.

Maybe that's different nowadays. Back then the kids were always coming out when John was out there. John was coaching them. Now that Craig has kids of his own, I enjoy it when we go up to Milwaukee for a week. On a Saturday morning, he'll call the boys and say, "Brady, Jack, call your buddies. Tell them to get to the ballpark down by the high school at 9:00. I'll play with them for two hours." They all come to the school. Everybody is out there. Craig will go to the field, and they will all be there, just waiting for him.

The parents came back to us whenever we'd see them and say, "Hey, we really do see how Craig got to where he did because he understands the kids. He understands the guys in the field." He's actually in between the two, I would say. He really did work his way up. He didn't get any favors from somebody. He just worked day after day. He was able to get what he needed. He got into the right position with the right people.

We are so proud of our daughter Jennifer who is two years younger than Craig. She also went to Notre Dame, and while there, she spent a semester in Australia in a program called Notre Dame-Australia. Jennifer has had an incredible business career, most of it based in Miami. She was many years with a company called Diageo, and when they downsized a year ago, she got a huge severance package. She had a wonderful, wonderful job with that company, and they were very good to her.

She started her business career in Atlanta working with Peat Marwick and Mitchell, a Big 8 accounting firm at the time. When she was with Peat Marwick in '96 or '97, they said, "We need someone to go to Australia on this project," and she was picked. She was delighted because she enjoyed Australia when she studied down there. That was the same year when Craig was traded to the Marlins and appeared in the World Series. We were talking with Jennifer in Australia, and we said, "We'd love to have you come to the World Series, but right now, we don't have enough money for your flight up here and your flight back down." "That's okay," she said. Later I was talking to Craig and and I said, "Jennifer's not going to be able to make it." Craig said, "Why not?" I said, "She doesn't have enough money, but said she'll figure out how to listen to it." Craig said, "No, she's not going to do that. I'll pay for it. Make the arrangements. I'll pay for it." That's what he did.

In Miami the night of the first game, John went out to the airport and picked her up. As they got to the stadium and were walking into the stadium, Craig was being announced, "And up now is Craig Counsell." Then, of course, the stadium went bonkers. There must have been twenty Wisconsin kids there— Craig's friends. Jennifer got all her friends to come. They had to pay for tickets, but they soaked up every bit of it. They'd never experienced anything like that, and neither had we.

Again, we're just so proud of Jennifer. She married a wonderful man, Michael Rock Hughes, who's been with the Miami Marlins for many years, and their kids are wonderful. Jen, as mentioned, has been very successful in business.

Jennifer's oldest daughter is thirteen. She sees me when I'm sewing. She said, "Grandma, will you teach me to sew?" I said, "Yes, I will." Last time when I was over in Miami, she and I cut out some patterns. The next time when she comes here, I'll have my machine with me, and then I'll just walk her through the steps of how to make a dress that has a place for your head to go through, your arms to go through, and sew it together. Then we make doll clothes.

Jennifer is always busy. She works so hard, and her girls work hard. They're going to their sports activities. Jennifer and Rock and the kids live in a cul-de-sac. There are maybe fifteen or twenty houses there, but they're near the end of the cul-de-sac. It's a miracle. There are kids all the same age that Jennifer's two girls are. They all come home from school. They have to come in and have a snack and something to drink. "Hey, Grandma, I'm going outside to play basketball." They're all out there. It's a great atmosphere. There's no fighting going on. They all want to do something physical because they've been sitting for six hours.

Craig's oldest child is Brady. He's a junior in high school, quiet, smart. He comes home, puts his books down, and he starts doing his homework right away. The other ones will say, "I don't want to do it now." I'm like, "Your Mom said you're supposed to do it." "Oh, all right." Brady is definitely the most disciplined of the group. When he has something to do, he gets it done, and then he goes out and does the baseball stuff. The other ones take a little bit longer to get engaged in what they're supposed to be doing. They've learned essentially that if they want to be successful, they're going to have to work at it.

Jennifer and Craig's wife, Michelle, get together. They really enjoy each other's company. They're both very much alike. They're both hard workers, and they want their kids to excel in what they're doing. Michelle's mom and I are very much alike. We compare notes on what bugs us about which kid, and other things. Whenever we get up to Wisconsin, Michelle's Mom and I go for coffee in a cafe down the street.

Michelle is a hard worker and has always been a hard worker. She has four children. She's creative with them. She knows who needs academic help, who doesn't. She makes sure that they are in their place. In other words, if she finds them doing something they're not supposed to do, she's not afraid to say, "Go up to your room. Give me your computer/phone, and we'll talk later." The kids' sports help them a great deal. Craig gives so much to the kids when they're around, not just to his kids, but all the kids in the area.

I've been very blessed in my life to be born in the great state of Wisconsin, to have parents like I had, to marry such a wonderful, wonderful man, to have the education I had in the state of Wisconsin, to have two wonderful kids and to have so many wonderful grandchildren. The Lord has been good to me, very good to me. I'm very grateful.

*Jan and John Counsell in the shadow of the Golden Dome, Notre Dame, 1972. Jennifer was six months old and Craig was two years old.*

*Counsell tagged out at home in Game 4, 1997 World Series.*

Chapter Two

# THE CHICKEN RAN AT MIDNIGHT

## Coming to Theaters Soon

# MAYBE THERE'S A SEPARATE GOD FOR CHILDREN

RICH DONNELLY

*Rich Donnelly, a native of Steubenville, Ohio has spent his entire adult life as a professional baseball player, coach, and manager. He was a coach with the Florida Marlins (now Miami Marlins) in their World Series winning year in 1997.*

In 1997 the Marlins had Luis Castillo playing second and he was what Jim Leyland, our manager, called an alley player. An alley player was a guy who made a great play but couldn't make a routine play. Castillo would end up throwing the ball all over the place. He was a good player; he just wasn't a Jim Leyland player.

Jim Leyland was called "Hump." Hump is short for Humperdinck. Back in the day, he used to sing in nightclubs and he thought he was Engelbert Humperdinck. Everybody that knows him, calls him Hump.

Jim told our scouts, "Go find me a second baseman." One of our coaches, Bruce Kimm, says, "Hump, last year in Triple-A I saw this kid. He catches the ball, he throws it, and he's solid, not great but he's solid. Jim says, "Who is he?" Bruce said, "Craig Counsell." Jim says, "Who the hell is he?" Bruce says, "He plays for the Rockies, Triple-A team in Colorado Springs. Another reason why you'll like him—(Jim was the biggest Notre Dame fan of all time)—Counsell's from **NOTRE DAME\***." Jim says, "He is? Let's check him out. "They checked him out. The Marlins traded for him in July. Craig Counsell shows up and when he walks in,

---

\*Joe Montana did not start until the fourth game of his junior year at **NOTRE DAME**....Montana was awestruck by Huey Lewis and once sang backup with his band.

he's not real impressive looking. He looks like the paperboy. Jim says, "Okay, let's take him out and work him out."

Counsell goes out for batting practice. I'm pitching batting practice. Jim is behind the cage. Counsell doesn't hit the first ten balls out of the cage, horrible. I can see Jim and he's like, "What the hell is going on here?" Leyland tells Bruce, who we call "Gamer." "Gamer, This kid can't play a lick! If the kid can't play, you're fired!"

Then Jim says, "Take him out to second base. Hit him some balls." Counsell went out to second. We hit him some fungos. Counsell, hell, he couldn't get to the ball. Jim looked at Bruce and goes, "Bruce, you're fired. This guy can't play a lick." The next night, he calls Bruce in. He said, "Gamer, I'll tell you what. I'm going to play that SOB tonight and if he don't do good, I mean it, you're fired! We're trying to win this, we're trying to get in the playoffs, and you send me this guy. He's got no fire, he can't hit and he can't move."

That night, Counsell started, moved a guy over with a bunt and also got a hit—we won. The next night, Jim played Counsell again. Same thing, he gets a couple of hits. He catches the ground balls, makes the plays—end of story. He played every day. We started winning. One time I was coaching third, Jim gave me the bunt sign with two strikes when Counsell was up. This is after he'd played about a month. He got the bunt down. Sacrificed. Somebody got a base hit. We won the game. After the game, Jim goes, "Now that's the kind of an SOB I like. He can't run, he can't throw, he can't hit but he's a winner. He gets things done."

One thing about that bunt sign with two strikes—some batters wouldn't catch it and others might ask me to give it to them again to make sure! Couns did not do that. Then after a while, we were talking about Couns and Jim goes, "Well, hell, he went to **NOTRE DAME\***, he's smart as hell, that's why."

\*Of the 750 players on Major League rosters recently, only 17 were **COLLEGE** graduates.

As the season progressed Counsell pushed Luis Castillo completely out of the picture. Couns was our man. He was our man all the way through. Just as solid as could be. Never made any great plays. Every time there was a ball hit to him in the ninth inning, with the winning or tying run on third, he caught the ball, threw the guy out. When he turned a double play it wasn't real pretty, but the guy was out. Every time we asked him to bunt he got the bunt down. Every time we asked Couns to hit and run, he hit the ball.

We wondered about his goofy stance and how he hit with his hands held extremely high. But, if you watch him close, he starts out with the bat way up high. When he gets into hitting position, his hands are where they are supposed to be. This was a technique, a starter technique, a trigger to get him to where he needed to be. When he swung the bat he brought the bat down, but the initial approach was that real high stance that looked kind of like a chicken. He batted with a regular stance when in college at Notre Dame. I don't know where he come up with this weird stance. Nobody ever asked him.

Later there was something that happened in World Series Game 7 that was an omen that we were going to win and it involved him. The hitter before Counsell was Charles Johnson. Charles Johnson had not hit a ball to right field in his lifetime. He hit a line drive single to right field, toward the line to drive in a run. Here's the kicker—**MANNY RAMIREZ**\* fielded the ball and threw it in. The fans in right field were taunting Manny, so instead of going back to his position, when Counsell came up, which would be right center, (Counsell never

\***MANNY RAMIREZ** grew up in the Washington Heights area of New York. His two sons are both named Manny Ramirez, Jr. Vin Scully also grew up in Washington Heights.

pulled the ball), Manny stood about ten feet from the right field line, taunting the fans.

Counsell came into the box to hit with runners on second and third. We're down a run. It's Game 7. If Counsell hits into a double play, the season is over, and the Cleveland Indians win the World Series. Jose Mesa was pitching—the best reliever in baseball that year. When Counsell came up we were pretty sure he was going to hit the ball. Counsell hit a bullet toward the right field corner. As soon as it was hit I said, "We win the World Series, there's no one there....Oops, what the hell is Manny doing over there?" He was standing there talking with the fans and Counsell hit it right to him. It turned out to be an absolutely vital sacrifice fly. Counsell fought off several pitches that at bat. He hung in there for a long time. It was clutch.

Every time Craig came up you felt like he was going to make an out. He just wasn't a great hitter, but then he got the job done. When he pulled that ball down the line, I said, "We win." And then said, "What the hell is Manny doing there?" As I am looking where the ball was hit, I see they are trying to wave to Manny to get to his position in right center for Counsell. They couldn't get his attention. Counsell hits the ball right to him. Couns could have driven in the winning runs if not for Manny yelling back and forth to the fans.

Here are some stories about Counsell on the road and traveling. We were in Phoenix staying at the Ritz Carlton. There was a church about four blocks from the hotel where I would try to go to Mass when I could. There was a seven o'clock Mass— and this was in 1997. It's getting toward the end of the year. No other player is going to be down there at church so I will just go down by myself. I sit in a pew way in the back so that I can get out early. Mass is going on. It comes to the part in the Mass where you turn around and exchange greetings with the people behind you. I turn around and there is Craig Counsell. I went whoa! Whoa, whoa, whoa! We walked back to the hotel together and I said to myself, "Man, oh, man! What a find we found! Not because he went to church but he was just such a good guy! He really influenced my sons. They always said that they wanted to be like him because he was the consummate, ultimate professional.

I once believed Craig never talked. I didn't know he could talk. He never said a word to anybody about anything. He just did his job and went home. That was it. He was always nice to everybody. He was cordial. You could see he was tough. He was a tough competitor. But he never said a word to anybody. We walked about four blocks together back to our hotel and talked the whole way.

I don't hang around players. I have always been uneasy around players outside of the stadium. I don't go to breakfast or coffee with them. We just walked back and talked. We talked about Phoenix and also about Notre Dame. I always asked him how the Irish are going to be and he'd tell me who they had coming back. He was a serious football fan.

I met his Dad, John, at the World Series and told him what everybody always tells you—what a great kid he had, but the difference is this kid's off the charts. Craig is phenomenal. That's the best thing I can say—and I can say a lot of things about Couns. He was Jim Leyland's type of player. That is the highest compliment you could get.

I will start now at square one with the chicken story. Time to roll with the Chicken Runs at Midnight.

Every summer, my young sons, Mike and Tim would come to whatever team I was coaching. When I was with the **PIRATES**\*

*From 1933 to 1939, the NFL's Pittsburgh Steelers were named the Pittsburgh **PIRATES**. The Pittsburgh Pirates was also the name of the National Hockey League team in the 1920s...In September 2010, Pittsburgh Penguins star Sidney Crosby took batting practice with the Pirates and hit a 370-foot "home run" that almost cleared the park.

they were with me for ten years. They worked in the club-house. Everybody knew them. Barry Bonds was their best friend. They were closer to the players than I was. Everybody knew Tim and Mike.

Craig Counsell grew up in a similar situation. I switch teams to the Florida Marlins and here come Tim and Mike. They were our batboys every night and they would shag balls for us. They were just everywhere. Jim knew them and loved having them around. Then Craig Counsell comes in on a trade. I remember one day, Tim came in and says, "Dad, 'The Chicken' wants to take some BP—batting practice." I went, "What? Who is 'The Chicken'?" Tim said, "Counsell. Chicken—the way he hits and flaps his arms. Me and Mike, we call him 'The Chicken'. Dad we have names for everybody you know. 'The Chicken' wants to take some BP." I said, "You go tell 'The Chicken' I will be right out."

I did not think much of my sons calling him "The Chicken." It was just in passing. I would never, by the way, call him a chicken. I always called him Couns. Everybody called him Couns. My sons called him "Chicken," then they would laugh and run and hide. It was a secret between those two that Coun-sell was "The Chicken." They never said, "Hey, Chicken." No.

We were driving home and Mike would go "Man, 'Chicken' got that bunt down tonight, didn't he, Dad?" I said, "Who?" He said, "Couns." I said, "Oh, yes." It wasn't like that was his nickname, but it was their nickname for him. I never thought anything of it to tell you the truth.

But I am getting ahead of myself here. I also need to tell you about my daughter, Amy. Five years earlier my daughter Amy contracted a brain tumor. Amy was seventeen years old at the time. She called me up on the phone when I was in Spring Train-ing with the Pirates. She said, "Dad I got to tell you something. Don't be mad. I'm sorry, I'm sorry but I have a brain tumor." That buckles you, it just buckles you. I did not know what to say.

I talked to her Mom. We were divorced. I live in Northeast Ohio and she lives in Dallas. Amy went to have an eye test for peripheral vision and there was no peripheral vision on her right side. They were going to have to operate on it to get it out.

I flew from Bradenton to Dallas to Children's Hospital when Amy had the operation. After the operation the doctor came out. Her Mom and I were sitting there and he said he wanted to talk to us in another room. I got the worst feeling that I ever had in my life. I knew this was not going to be good. You never think it's going to come to a healthy seventeen-year-old girl—my daughter!

This happened in the spring of 1992. The doctor came out and he said, "Rich, she has a tumor behind her eye. It is malignant. We tried to get it all. We couldn't get it all." Then he put his head down. I said, 'Tell me straight. Tell me straight." He said, "Rich, the prognosis is she has nine months to live." I got mad. I'm not sure whom I was mad at, but I got mad. It just can't be right—the unfairness. She does not deserve this. I ran out into the parking lot. I didn't know what to do. I was crying, I was screaming and I was mad. For a moment I said, "How can you let this happen to my daughter? Why did you do this?" I blamed God.

It's unfair. "God, why didn't you give me this tumor? Why'd you give it to her?" After a half hour I went back in. My wife and I talked for a while, we hugged and we cried. Then we decided, okay. We know Amy. We are going to fight this thing. We are going to kick this thing. The next day I got to see Amy. When I walked in, I almost walked out. Her head was completely shaved and she had a metal spike right in the middle of her head. I walked out of the room. I went down to the chapel and I stayed there about an hour. I begged for help. I begged God to please help me. Please help Amy. I felt so insignificant as a human being. She was there with a spike in her head, maybe going to die soon. Why am I even living? Why isn't it me? It was very, very hard.

The next day I go in to see her again. She was smiling. "How do you like my new head gear?" I am trying to laugh. She says, "Come here." I got up close and she gave me a hug. She said, "I don't want you to stay here. I want you to get back to Bradenton to the Pirates spring training. I want you to go back and coach third base and get to the World Series." I was overwhelmed. This was the strongest person I had ever met in my life.

She's dying. She's seventeen with a spike in her head, her head cut open. She's telling me to go back and coach third base and try to get to the World Series. I waited five days and I went back. We, of course, communicated every day. We talked every day. The doctor said there's a chance if we find some bone marrow that was her type it could help. We tried that. This goes on all summer. Then later the **MARLINS**\* were in New York. She called us at the suite where Jim and I stayed. She said, "I want you to get in the playoffs because I want to come." Jim said, "You bet your button you're coming." On that day, she said, "Dad, I'm going to kick this thing. If you make the playoffs I want to come to a game."

As time went on, the Pirates made the playoffs. We tried to figure out a date when Amy and Cindy, her best friend, could fly in. I had a dear friend in Fort Worth named Vince. I've known Vince since when I was with the Rangers, he's probably my best friend. He was a millionaire and had a private jet. All the time she was doing better Vince would send a limo over every morning to take Amy and Tim to school. I did not know this. No one ever told me that Vince did that. That's the kind of guy he was. He sent a limo over every day. Amy was going back to school; she was getting her chemo treatments. Amy could only come to Pittsburgh for one night then she had to be back for chemo.

> \*The **MARLINS** retired the number "5" before their first game to honor a person who never played professional baseball: Carl Barger, their President who died before their first season. Barger's favorite player growing up was Joe DiMaggio who wore number 5.

Vince flew Amy, Cindy, and Tim up for the fifth game of the 1992 playoffs. We won that game and took a 3-2 lead. I told Amy, "We are going to win this thing and you are going to the World Series.

We were driving back to the hotel after the game. Tim and Mike were in the front and Cindy and Amy were in the back. She reaches up, grabs me by the neck, gives me a kiss, and she says, "Dad, when you get down in that stance with a guy on third and cup your hands, what are you telling him? The chicken runs at midnight, or what?" I said, "What the heck is 'The chicken runs at midnight'?" Everybody in the car, all the kids are laughing. They were laughing uncontrollably. "What is that one? Where'd you come up with 'The chicken runs at midnight'? What's that mean?" She said, "I don't know, it just came out."

We laughed all the way back to the hotel. It was one of the things that you just can't stop laughing. Every time I looked at her and Cindy, and we go, "Chicken runs at midnight, chicken runs at midnight", everybody just busted up. I don't know why, that's the way it was. That was the birth of it.

Amy goes back to Texas. Back then, of course, no cellphones, no Twitter. She would write me letters, write letters to Mike at school, to Tim, to Bubba, my oldest son, and she would sign them all "The chicken runs at midnight!" Every time the kids talked on the phone I would hear them, "Okay, Amy, chicken runs at midnight, good night, I love you." It became a family motto. During that season, every time I got down in that stance I started laughing, right in the middle of the game. How the hell did she come up with that?

Forward four plus years and it is the summer of 1997 when we acquired Couns. Mike and Tim nicknamed him The Chicken but it never crossed our minds that that was something that Amy said. That was the mystery. Nobody ever said, well there's Couns, he's The Chicken—no. It was not even a thought.

Amy passed in January of 1993. We go to the funeral home. Cindy and I went with her Mom, Peggy. It's awful when they try to sell you a casket, like they are trying to sell you a Mercedes. They tell you how wonderful it is, etc. We said, "We'll take this one." The girl says here are the sayings we can put on the tombstone, "our lovely daughter, with love," …etc. I looked over at Cindy (I remember it like yesterday) and she was shaking her head no. I looked at Bubba, he was shaking his head no. I know what they were thinking and they knew what I was thinking, but we grudgingly said, "Okay, our loving daughter."

We were in a trance. We got in the car and we were driving out. We did not get five seconds down the driveway of the funeral home. I looked over at Cindy and she said, "Turn this sucker around. We are getting 'Chicken runs at midnight' on that tombstone." We go back, walked in and said, "Lady, we were kind of embarrassed to say this, but we are not embarrassed anymore. We wanted "The chicken runs at midnight on that tombstone." Cindy goes, "That's what we want." Cindy was pretty forceful about it.

She said, "I never heard of that!" I said, "I don't care what you heard of. I don't care what you do. If you don't put that on there we are going to another cemetery. She said, "Let me check." She went in and checked with a guy then came back out and said, "Okay, you got it." After that we laughed, we laughed all the way back in the car. When we had the funeral the next morning, that is what was on there.

And still, it made no sense. But all those years after that, **EVERY TIME I COACHED THIRD BASE**\* for the Pirates, every time I got in that stance I thought of Amy.

> \*In 1974 Billy Martin was managing the Texas Rangers and Frank Lucchesi was his **THIRD BASE COACH**. Martin tried using a transistor hook-up to his coaches to relay signals. One game the system was broken, but Martin kept yelling instructions for a suicide squeeze into the microphone. Red Sox pitcher Luis Tiant finally stepped off the mound and yelled: "Frank, Billy said he wanted the suicide squeeze."

A photographer in Miami one night said, "Boy, you coach third different from anybody I have ever seen. You get down in the stance. I said, "I do it as an honor to my daughter. He said, "What do you mean?" Then I told him the story. He took a picture, it's right there, there's the picture. I have it right here in my den. I have the picture that he took. I'm looking at it right now. I told him the story. He thought it was wonderful. I don't know if he printed it or not but he thought it was pretty cool. Every time I go to third, every time I get down in that stance, even today—I just got back from Kingsport, Tennessee—every time I get down in that stance, I think of that night!

Almost five years after Amy died, Craig Counsell was with the Marlins. My kids had nicknamed him "The Chicken." The interaction with my boys and Counsell was unusual. The boys liked Counsell. Batboys don't usually become friends with the players. Tim and Mike were my sons. I told them we have rules. No screwing around; be polite. If the players want something, do it for them. You can't be lost, running around, respect everything, etc. This is not a high school locker room; this is a big league locker room. The kids loved it. Every time I looked out from the coaches' office into the players' locker room, where are my boys? They were sitting on a chair or sitting on the floor in front of Counsell's locker. He was talking to them.

It was the just the way Counsell did everything, his personality. It was just his way. He was a consummate professional. They talked to Craig and he talked to them more than any people in that clubhouse. If he needed a suitcase out of his car, boom, Mike would go get it and Couns would give him ten bucks. If Counsell needed anything, boom! They would hang around him. It wouldn't bother him. He was so nice to them.

Some players would go "Hey, kid, get away from here." They would just hang around and shine his shoes. They adored him, they absolutely adored him. Tim always said, "That's the kind of man I want to be when I grow up. I want to be like Craig Counsell." They never called him "The Chicken." But among themselves, he was "The Chicken." It was just their own little dirty secret—He's "The Chicken," ha, ha, ha.

I never called him "The Chicken." They never connected it with Amy at the time, either.

The Marlins are in the 1997 World Series. It's the seventh game. I flew all our family members and wives and kids to Florida. We had twenty-one people in the house. I have eight kids. When I remarried thirty years ago, my wife had four and I had four so we combined them. My son Bubba and his wife, my son John and his wife and my father-in-law and mother-in-law were there. We had everybody.

This is a pretty neat story. Tim's high school principal let him miss twenty-eight days of school, while we were in the play-offs. Mr. Huizenga, the owner, told Tim he was not going back to high school after the first playoff game. He was going to stay for the whole playoffs and the World Series. He thought Tim was a good luck charm. He told Tim, "You are not going home. You tell your Dad you are not going home." Tim was a junior in high school. I said, "I can't have him miss a week of school." So I call the principal. I said, "My son, Tim, etc." I told him the whole story. "The owner of the Marlins...we are in the World Series." The principal was a baseball fan. He said, "You take as long as you need with Tim. We'll make up the difference. You keep him down there as long as you want to keep him." He let me keep him for twenty-eight days, through the two playoffs with the **GIANTS**\* and the Braves and through the World Series.

When it comes to the World Series I called the principal back. I asked, "Have you ever been to a World Series?" He said, "No, I haven't." I said, "Well, you're going! I am flying you and your wife down here. We have two games and I am flying you down for the first two games of the World Series. I wanted to thank him

\*While in high school in North Carolina, **GIANTS** pitcher Madison Bumgarner dated a girl named Madison Bumgarner, no relation.

for letting my son be here. The principal flew down and stayed two games. I told him this is a thanks for you letting Tim do this. It means the world to him because Tim was closer to Amy than anybody.

All during the playoffs and World Series, Tim was sad. He said he wished Amy could have been here. "She would have loved this!" We had twenty-one people in the house. We had four hotel rooms. We had everybody down there. It was crazy.

(Long pause, sobbing)

Tim would always mention it to me every day, "Dad, I wish Amy was here. Amy would have loved this, she would have loved this."

Now we go to the seventh game. We have a chance to win the World Series. We were down 2-0, when Bobby Bonilla hit a home run to make it 2-1. Soon it's extra innings, Counsell ties it up with a crucial sac fly in the ninth. All the time I am coaching third I am thinking, "Rich, you are in the World Series, your life-long dream. You are in the World Series. There are some twenty million people around the world watching this. There are 75,000 people in the stands. All those times you played out in the alley, when you hit stones and pretended you were in the World Series as a kid—you are there! When you used to watch the Yankees and the Dodgers every World Series and dream about being there. When in 1960, the Pirates won the World Series, **BILL MAZEROSKI*** from right down the road here in Steubenville, Ohio, hit a home run, you were the happiest person in the world. Now thirty-seven years later, you are in that seventh game of the World Series.

Counsell got to third base in the last of the 11th inning. I couldn't remember my name at that point. Edgar Renteria comes to the

*Hall of Fame pitcher Phil Niekro lost one game in high school. The winning pitcher was Hall of Fame second baseman **BILL MAZEROSKI.**

plate, and there's Counsell standing next to me at third base. When runners get around to third there are no big speeches. I don't have to tell him to score on a passed ball. He knows. He's the smartest player on the field, and if you look at the tape, I never went over near him at all. I stayed away from him.

The first pitch was a strike, it was a curve ball. To this day, Jim Leyland thinks that Edgar faked like he was fooled on the pitch so that he would get another curve ball later in the at bat. If you watch the tape of Renteria, Cleveland threw him a curve ball and he ducked, like "whew, it wasn't me." Then the next pitch was another curve ball and that's the one he hit. Jim Leyland thinks to this day that Renteria set the pitcher up.

When I saw the ball go up the middle I lost my mind, I jumped about six feet high (which I cannot normally do). Counsell was in front of me, he jumped eight feet high. Everything you dream about in your lifetime, growing up. I can't believe it's happening to me.

It's over. We are the World Champions!! All the games out in the alleys, all those games in your head when you scored the winning run. How many times have you played that Game 7 in your back yard—a million times—and all of a sudden you're in the middle of it. And suddenly it's over. I saw Counsell leap up in the air, I tried to leap as high as he could; I couldn't make it. He must have made eight feet; I think I got about five. You don't even know what you're doing. All of a sudden, I remember, the whole team fell on top of me. I could not breathe. I thought for a split second, "We just won the World Series and I'm going to die." Twenty-eight players were on top of me, the only thing sticking out was my head. I could not breath.

Devon White saw me and he pulled me out—he saved my life. I had grass stains all over me. I stand up and I still don't know what's going on. I grabbed Jim Eisenreich and picked him up.

I'm looking for my sons, Tim and Mike, where are they? I wanna hug 'em. They were in the dugout. I have the most unique picture in the world. There was a pile on home plate that spilled into the infield. On the top of the pile and you can see it as clear as daylight, there is Mike Donnelly on the stack, number 45. Just to the right of the pile, you see the top of the head of Tim Donnelly, walking, looking; looking for me.

Tim finally found me between first and second. They illuminated the picture of me and Tim hugging. Then he turned me around and he said, "Dad, Dad, look." I said, "What are you talking about?" He was crying, and I said, "What are you crying about? We just won." He said, "Dad, look behind you." I said, "Look where, Tim?" "Look at the clock." I turned around, the clock was 12:02 and he screamed, "Dad, The Chicken ran at midnight."

(Difficulty talking) I did not know what to do. I got down on my knees. I just can't tell you, I never felt like that in my whole life about anything. It was like a thunderbolt from heaven. I tell people I was limp. Every emotion in my body was shot. I thought to myself, "Oh my God." Craig Counsell, The Chicken, scored the winning run at midnight. I just lost it, absolutely lost it. THE CHICKEN RAN AT MIDNIGHT!!!!

It was as if the skies opened up. Like in the movies, where the Lord comes out of the sky, it was like, is this happening? It can't happen, it's impossible. At that moment, the celebration became all about Amy, all about her. I ran around the outfield. And I was screaming like a wild man. I was crying—nobody knew why I was crying. I felt like I was right with her. I felt like she was right there with me during this time as I was running around the outfield, like an idiot by myself.

I go into the clubhouse. I find Mike and Tim. I find my wife Roberta and my other kids and tell them what happened. Everybody turned pale, they couldn't believe it. I was crying my eyes out. Nobody knew what had happened to our family. The media were asking guys to come up to the locker room podium and say something. I prayed to God, please don't ask me to come up there, I was so embarrassed. They were celebrating and I did not want to start bawling—make it look like a funeral. The guys are having fun, please God, do not call me. I'm gonna lose it. Didn't want to ruin it by telling the story because they would have all lost it.

We all celebrated until about four in the morning. All we did all the way home was "talk" to Amy. We just "talked" to her. "Amy, you would have loved this. Amy, this was great." We all actually talked to her.

We had to go ten exits to get home. Amy gave me a note years ago before a game in Atlanta. I kept it on the wall, it's right here. I carry it with me. I had it that night. I told Tim that I feel like I want to pick up the phone and call your sister and tell her, "Amy, The Chicken did run at midnight."

Craig Counsell knew nothing about this until three years later. Tom Sessi, a Notre Dame classmate of John Counsell, said to me, "I heard this story about Craig Counsell is a chicken or something. His dad, John, doesn't know anything about it." I said, "What?" "Craig doesn't know anything about it?"

Craig's father had heard about an article and a show on television. But I never talked to Craig about it. I just didn't think it was important, or that he would be interested. Tom said, "You gotta get a hold of Craig. He doesn't know anything about it." In the spring of 2000, Craig is with Arizona and I'm with the Rockies. He comes over and says, "Am I The Chicken or what, what is going on?" I told him the story. He lost it. That was the first time he heard all about it. Since then, he knows. The kids never called him "The Chicken" except to themselves. He had no clue.

I was too embarrassed to tell the team because I thought it was too hokie. Plus, I did not want it to dampen the fun so I never said anything to anybody.

The boys continued to have interaction with Counsell but they never told him the story. They were sad when we traded him to the Dodgers in '99. We owed six players $80 million and we said if anybody takes this deal, it'll be a miracle. Well, the Dodgers took it. The Marlins traded Counsell, Bobby Bonilla, Charles Johnson and they got rid of all that payroll, every red cent. Huizenga was going to sell the club and he wanted to unload all those salaries before he sold it. He unloaded all good players.

The boys' favorite player was Counsell, for sure. They wanted him to be a Marlin forever, and I just tried to explain to them that is baseball. I don't think the boys have seen Counsell in twenty years.

A writer found out about the story, when I was in Denver with the Rockies, and he wrote a tiny little article. The next day, I got a call from Lifetime cable channel. The lady said, "We heard about your story and want to ask you about it. We have a show called *Beyond Chance* about miracles. There are ten pilot shows and we are going to pick one to be shown on television."

She said, "We have a committee to decide which one, and we'll call you back in about three weeks." The next day, the same lady called, and she's crying. She says, "There will be no study of ten shows. We shared yours with the committee and we all agreed this is the show that's going on." So, they put it on *Beyond Chance* and it tells the whole story.

They put it on Lifetime and then we did an interview for a Catholic publication. The story started to explode. We are right in the middle of a movie deal right now.

I was the coach for the World Baseball Classic two years ago when I get a call down in Florida. A good friend, Denny Neagle, called. He was in the Pirates organization when all this happened with Amy. He says, "Rich, I got two buddies here, the Nicotero brothers from Pittsburgh. They heard your story and they want to do a movie, they are serious. "Well, wait until I get home." I get home and the brothers flew to Steubenville,

Ohio. We signed a three-year option to do the movie. They said, "Rich, this is the best story we have ever seen." They are the producers of *The Walking Dead,* by the way. We signed the three-year deal. They've been trying to get it into production and if they don't they have two choices: they can drop it or renew the contract. I got a call the other day from writer/ friend Tom Friend who said there are six other studios that are ready to pick up the option if the Nicotero brothers don't.

A movie would be a great tribute to Amy and our family. Everything we're doing here is a testament to Amy; the way she was, the way she was in the hospital, the way she bought bicycles for all the terminally ill kids in Dallas before she died. All she cared about was Dad going to the World Series, not about her brain tumor. The way she cared about her brothers. The way she cared about her mother and stepmother. In nine months she taught me how to live and how to die. Everything I do in my life right now, I think, if Amy can do that, I can do this. And that's the way I approach life.

## Letter from Amy

Dad,

Will you teach me how to hit a home run?

All the boys in school talk about home runs. They call them dingers, jacks, taters, round-trippers, bombs, grand salamis . . . Gosh, I'd love to hit one of those.

Okay, whenever you get back home, let's talk about it.

Love,

Amy

At midnight during Game 7 of the World Series, God answered my questions as to why this had happened to Amy. I was born and raised a strict Catholic, strict as you could be—altar boy, pontifical server, sixteen years of Catholic education and I was just mad. I was upset. It was a spur of the moment thing. I didn't know who to yell at. I didn't know who to reach out for. Who the heck are you going to yell at? Somebody else? Are you going to get mad at your daughter? God was the logical one. After I calmed down and saw everything as it transpired over the last twenty-seven years since Amy died. It's been one of the most wonderful things in my life. We have been able to do so much good for a lot of people. All because of this story, all because of Amy.

Amy's death meant so much to people, too. Mike and Amy, of course they were close. Tim was their baby, though. When Tim was a little boy Amy carried him around. She was the mom. Amy was the mom. Timmy was her baby. That's the way it worked. Amy and Mike were a little older. We called them both pistols. They were always fighting but it was good-natured.

The letters that Amy wrote, most of them were to Mike, because he had some trouble. He had all As in high school, but was always in trouble. He was the kicker on our football team but always in trouble. Then he got out and went to Cumberland College as a kicker; smart with good grades. He was an artist. He could do anything. If you asked anybody in our family, "Who do you want to spend a day with?" Everybody would pick Mike. He was hilarious, a comedian but always in trouble. Later on he got into drugs, met bad people. He spent time in jail, bad stuff—stealing cars. It was terrible because he was the most talented one in the whole family.

Two years ago, Tim went home to Texas for Christmas. He said, "Dad, Mike's doing well, he's being nice now. I think he has finally figured it out." A month later Tim called me one night and said, "Dad, I have bad news." I said, "What's that?" He said, "Mike was killed last night." When I heard killed, I thought somebody had shot him. Then he told me the story. In fact, the Highway Patrol in Dallas called me from Texas and said, "Rich, your son is a hero." They said, "He pulled over to the side of the road at midnight to help a pedestrian."

A girl and her boyfriend were pushing a car across the road because it had been in a wreck. A car came around the bend, Mike grabbed the girl and instinctively threw her out of the way, shielded her and he got hit at 65 mph. When I heard that, it sounds crazy, but all the trouble he gave us, all the stuff went away. My son gave his life to save a total stranger.

That girl's name is Lindsay Longoria Ramirez. She called me the day after the accident. She said, "Mr. Donnelly, your son saved my life. He didn't even know me. He shielded me and he got hit." A few years ago she had a baby and she named him Michael Donnelly Ramirez. You are supposed to be the hero to your kids. My kids, my kids have become my heroes.

Michael gave his life; he gave his life. There is no other sacrifice you can give. You can give all your money to charity but when you give your life, to save another's life, that is the ultimate.

Now what happened next? My two living daughters, Tiffany and LeeAnn went to that Las Vegas concert where 58 people were killed in 2017. They were standing near the stage when a bullet went between them and hit a lady in the face in front of them. Her name is Natalie Grummond, a total stranger. She falls to the ground, blood everywhere. People don't know what is going on. Tiffany and LeeAnn took off their blouses, tied it around her face to help stop the bleeding. The girls lay on top of her through fifteen minutes of shooting until the shooting had stopped and the paramedics came. That girl, Natalie Grummond, who has had eight surgeries since, called me. She said, "Mr. Donnelly, your daughters could have run like everybody else did. But they didn't. They stayed on top of me and shielded me from bullets for fifteen minutes and saved my life."

My children are heroes to me. I don't care what they do. I know what they did. They saved other people's lives. When the time came down to decisions that you should make—look what they did. Look what they did! It sounds crazy. It's been a wonderful journey with my children. I lost two of them, and I almost lost two other ones. Amy bought bicycles for all the kids in Children's Hospital before she died. She left a check in her drawer. "Dad, when I'm gone please buy wagons, not bicycles, buy wagons for all these terminally ill kids." She cared about everybody else. Michael saved a total stranger. Tiffany and LeeAnn laying on top of a girl for fifteen minutes when they could have run; they didn't. I asked the girls, "Why did you do that? Why didn't you run?" They said, "Dad, something inside of us told us to do the right thing."

## Letter to Amy

Amy,

I took your check, and I bought more red wagons. The hospital has them. You should've seen the kids' faces. Then again, maybe you did.

Amazing, huh?

Love you . . . the chicken runs at midnight,

Dad

We were blessed to have them in our lives. Our kids drove us crazy sometimes. But I tell them, "I don't care what you did in high school or college. You are special; you are so special to us." It has helped our family. To me, I tell the story in all my talks; it has helped so many other people around the world. A guy called me, "Mr. Donnelly, I heard about The Chicken Runs at Midnight and I was going to commit suicide. I changed my mind. I have about twenty of those.

Getting back to Craig, he has the perfect temperament. He had the knowledge way back when he played. He is perfect. If you would have asked—Who on this team would be a good manager? We would have all picked Craig. No doubt about it.

He was just way ahead of the game. He is doing a great job, fantastic! Managing nowadays is very hard. You got people coming at you from the front office, people from the media, fans, then you got your players; it's a different era. It's very hard to manage. You are going to get criticized unless you win the World Series. What he has done in Milwaukee is unbelievable. He's a Wisconsin kid. It's just natural. He runs the game great and he's one of the best managers in the game. It's not a surprise!

Craig wore that uniform shirt—"The Chicken". You get to wear your nickname on your uniform one weekend a year. He wore "The Chicken." He said, "That's not my nickname, but in honor of the Donnelly family and that story; I am wearing it." This year he took it one step further. The Brewers have a lot of Latin players, so they put El Pollo on his shirt. They asked Craig Counsell about it because the players said, "Who's The Chicken?" They did not know anything about it. So he tells the story. So many players know the story in the big leagues. It's great! It's unbelievable!

Sandy Alomar, the **CATCHER**\* on that '97 Cleveland World Series team, once said, "Why didn't you tell me we had no chance to win the World Series?" I said, "What are you talking about, Sandy?" He answered, "Why didn't you tell me that story? We would have given you the game!"

---

\*Brent Musburger was the home plate umpire when **TIM MCCARVER** made his pro baseball debut for Keokuk, Iowa, in the Midwest League in 1959.

I last saw Craig, probably four years ago. Once in awhile I'll text him about something. ESPN did a piece. I texted Couns, "Could ESPN call you?" They came in and interviewed Craig and he did a great job.

The players had tremendous admiration for Counsell all around baseball. In his playing days, he was probably the most respected player when he was done. You could just hear players talk about him. "He's a winner! He's got two World Championships. He played the game the right way; never disrespected anybody." And he didn't do it with a great amount of ability. He did it the old fashioned way—hard work, ground it out. That's what most people respected about him. He respected the game and he played the game the right way.

My final thoughts on Craig Counsell—I have five sons and three daughters. I would be honored; I'd be humbled to call him my sixth son. That's the truth. I think of him as my son now, I really do. I would be honored to be his father. I know John is his father but he could be my son any day of the week.

The Chicken Ran at Midnight and it changed our lives forever!

# CRAIG COUNSELL WAS JUST A REGULAR GUY WHO SOME DAYS WORE A CAPE

TIM DONNELLY

*Tim Donnelly and his late brother Mike were young clubhouse workers for the Florida Marlins (now the Miami Marlins) in the late 90s. Donnelly attended high school in Arlington, Texas and graduated from Hardin-Simmons. He is assistant baseball coach at Southeastern Louisiana University.*

The first time we heard Craig Counsell was coming into the Marlins clubhouse and joining the team was in the summer of '97. We didn't know much about him other than my Dad told us he went to Notre Dame. Growing up, my Dad and his friends, and my oldest brother were big Notre Dame fans.

In Miami, kids-wise, we really did not know anybody, other than the clubhouse guys because they were all about my age or a couple of years older. They were the only kids we knew down there at that time. We were from Eastern Ohio, but lived in Dallas.

The very first day, Craig got to the clubhouse, he didn't look like a player. We thought he was a clubhouse worker. We were looking for a different looking guy, a bigger guy. When we found out who he was, my first thought was that since I was an undersized kid, I might get a chance to make it in professional baseball. He was there early so my brother and I were able to talk to him. From then on, being undersized and being from Notre Dame, he was already one of our favorites. We had not even seen him play a game, but if he made it to that point, we knew he was going to be a good player.

As the summer went on, he was always out for early work. That was also when my brother and I could get out there and work out; get ground balls, etc. before the whole team got out there. We were limited to shagging balls for batting practice. Since he was always out early, we could talk to him. Most of the time was just "How you guys doing?" Not too much crazy conversation. Over time, he was a guy we got to talk to a lot and we really looked up to him. The more he played; it was easier to become a fan of his.

My brother Mike's interactions with Counsell were similar. My brother was more outgoing.

Soon we were able to watch his play, see how good he was; there was nothing flashy about him; nothing stood out but he was really consistent. Growing up with my Dad, his big thing was not striking out. Craig hardly ever struck out. We could look up to him and really think we could make it one day as long as we worked our butts off like he did. He really didn't give us too many tips, he just kept working and letting us know and encouraging us. We probably realized he was better than we thought when we saw him playing more, and it was nothing outstanding. He was funny and quirky and just got the job done. His being in the lineup and being consistent changed the Marlins.

The first time my brother and I saw him play, we noticed his stance was different. We called it quirky. We would be sitting there talking, just the two of us. I said to Mike, "Man, just kind of like chicken wings" and we started laughing. We would imitate it like we would do for some of the other batters' stances. We did this where Craig couldn't see us; we didn't want to make fun of him. It just came to be that we would call him "chicken". He didn't know it. We were scared to death to talk to him about that. It was just between us. We weren't in the business of making fun of these guys. They were in the big leagues for a reason. Some guys had different nicknames for different reasons, but we were just the coaches' kids and batboys;

maybe it would be different if we were players and in the dugout. He used a normal bat, probably a little lighter; definitely not a heavy bat.

You see this guy who comes along, just a little guy to be here. We've seen plenty of players, we didn't know if he was going to make it. Sure enough, he's consistent throughout the year; did the little things right. Manager Jim Leyland loved that. He stuck him in there a lot. It was fun watching him succeed at the highest level.

With him, nothing was too big for the moment, that's what I saw. You got this guy, undersized, and everybody just looks at him like he's eighteen. He's fitting right in. You just don't notice him too much. He's not flashy, just getting it done every single day. That was the big thing we took away from it. He became the team favorite, both with coaches, players and fans. They knew he was consistent and would get the job done. All the guys were really rooting for him and everybody wanted him to succeed. I don't remember which players he might have been close to; we didn't see him off the field, other than during the World Series on the plane. He interacted often with Kurt Abbott, the second baseman. Kurt was the older guy, the veteran. They talked a lot and joked around.

When the playoffs approached, the Marlins were playing pretty good, looked like they were going to get the Wild Card. My Dad told me, "We are going to make the playoffs. I'm going to fly you down for the series at home even if you miss a few days of school". I was there for the opening couple of games they won; they were in Miami and then I was planning on going back to school. The owner, Wayne Huizenga, was in the clubhouse and he heard I was leaving; he wanted to know where I was going and I told him I was going back to school. He said, "Oh no, we just won two games. You're good luck, you have to go with us." I was the only kid that was on the team charter flight to San Francisco. The Marlins played one game out there and won it; clinched it to go to the next round versus

Atlanta. They wouldn't let me leave. I was fine with it. Leyland, the manager, told my Dad I wasn't going anywhere. My Dad had to call the principal; they were fine with it—a once in a lifetime opportunity. I ended up missing a whole month of school. I was really lucky to be there every day and got to see Counsell, the playoffs, the World Series.

The playoff run was wild. He came up big in a couple of moments and he was able to hit a sac fly to tie the final game of the World Series. Then the eleventh and final inning, never have seen a bunch of men act like it's a high school game; yelling like little kids. Yelling at every pitch, at the ump, at each other, etc. It was crazy. Never saw anything like that. Most of the time a major league game is pretty quiet. There's a force out at home, so Counsell goes to third. Renteria comes up; bases loaded, two outs, Game 7, game goes on forever. Where I was sitting, down the first base line, I could see the clock. I peeked up and it was midnight!. That was the first time I thought to myself, the "The Chicken Runs at Midnight."

Before every game throughout the whole World Series, whenever my Dad flew me out there, it was really for my late sister Amy. Because back in '92, we thought the Donnellys were going to the World Series. The team was up 2-0 and blew it to the Braves. That was the last game Amy got to see Dad coach. Her big thing was she was going to go to the World Series. She never got to go. Dad told me that I was with her, that I was with her and that me in the dugout, being there (Tim trails off). I started to think about all of these things once I saw the clock. It's a little after midnight; not too many games are played into midnight. It was crazy. I am thinking, wow it's midnight. Not a lot of time to think about it other than it was midnight. That's all I was really thinking about: my sister, the "Chicken Ran at Midnight," not really anything about Counsell at the moment. But then, Renteria singles up the middle and Counsell is on third, heading for home. We just took off out of the dugout; we were going crazy. I am running around with a bunch of grown men jumping around with me. I don't know where the heck to go. I'm looking for my Dad. There's a pile at home plate, there's a pile at first base. If you watch the video, I'm running right in the middle of both piles and finally veered off.

I started running out toward home plate when I actually saw Counsell running home with his hands up. At that moment it hit me. We used to call him "The Chicken". At that moment, it just hit me; the guy we called "The Chicken" scored a run at midnight; the "Chicken Runs at Midnight." It was a whole other level of excitement. I was crying and looking for my Dad, trying to find him. "Hey Dad." He says, "Why are you crying?" He can hardly hear me. I say, "The Chicken ran at midnight." And he lost it; we gave each other a big hug. It's one of those moments in life that I just can't believe. I still have no words to really say how it happened, why Amy had ever said it.

Amy was sixteen when she got diagnosed and I was twelve. At the time, my parents were divorced. My Dad lived in Ohio; my Mom lived in Texas. Amy and I lived in Texas. My two brothers lived with my Dad in Ohio. It was really just Amy and I down there for a few years. When that happened, my parents kept the severity of her illness away from me. They knew it was going to be bad. They wanted to protect me. I had seen her in surgery; had seen that she was miserable. You see what cancer does to people. It makes you hate it. It was so different; you hated to see her go through it. My Mom told me one time that Amy grabbed me, like I was her baby. It was really hard! I always thought Amy was going to pull through, even when she was in a coma. Amy's very last night on Earth, they told me to go in, give her a kiss, and tell her I loved her. I had no idea that was going to be the last night. It was tough. It wore on me for a long time. It wasn't very easy. Amy died at seventeen and I was thirteen.

Really after it all came together there were a couple of articles in the paper a few days later. It was neat to see people that were close to my Dad and in the media be able to share that story.

Later, I was a sophomore in college and my Dad called me and said a TV program *Beyond Chance* was going to feature the story on the Lifetime Network. I thought that would be a good way to honor Amy. They flew me up to Colorado and we shot most of it there at Coors Field. It was hard to watch. But it was nice to keep her memory alive. If you go to YouTube and type in "the chicken runs at midnight," ESPN will pop up. Melissa Etheridge was the host and I was a mess. I never met her. She was just doing the voice. The ESPN story was fourteen years later.

A lot of people may not have seen Lifetime back then. Some people contacted my Dad with a similar story; people who had a son or daughter who passed from cancer. That's probably when my Dad knew he had a platform to help people. Not a lot of people saw her story on Lifetime, but ESPN was going to do its own version. I was shocked that they were going to do the story and Amy's memory was still going to be out there. Craig probably found out not too long after the World Series. There was a big story in some papers not too long afterwards.

As a young boy it was pretty cool being in the dugout during the playoffs and the World Series. Obviously, one in a hundred million kids get to do that. Most of my close friends knew I was in the dugout during the year. Once the playoffs came along more people got to see it and tune in. When I got back to school it was pretty neat. They were all really happy for my Dad and asking about how it was.

Moving on, brother Mike gets in the accident and passes away. It was tough, for me mentally, after losing one sibling already, going through that again. With Amy, there was a whole period where I didn't know how to deal with it; I kept a lot inside. I wasn't able to talk to anybody; I didn't care to talk to anybody about it. It was my personal pain and I let it probably wear on me too long. Finally I made some good friends in college and got out of my funk. When my brother passed away it was easier to deal with. It was a lot easier to deal with because I had dealt with it before; I was a little older. But it sucked no doubt about it, it sucked. I know I'm never going to see him again on this earth. There was a lot of thinking about all the good times we had and trying not to think about the bad times. Trying to celebrate his life instead of thinking about how tragic it was. In my mind, if you think about that everyday, your own personal life is going to suffer for it. Just think about the good times, and just keep living. That's the only thing we can do.

My mother has had a tough go of it. She's the strongest woman I have ever met. I can't imagine any mom or dad losing their kids, especially with me about to have my second child. She was always tough; she always worked hard. It was really tough on her. She and my Dad were divorced long before all that; she's by herself, definitely tough on her.

At the same time whenever I go see Mom, she's laughing. Every time my oldest brother and I get together there are a lot of stories and laughter. Mom has probably hid all of her pain a little bit but no matter how she's feeling she always laughs along with everybody else she's talking to.

Once I knew Craig was going to start managing I thought, on the field side of it, he would be a Jim Leyland type manager. Obviously not smoking in the dugout like Leyland, but as far as knowing the game and getting the best out of his guys. That's how he played and that's how he went about his business. He was going to be successful. I hold him in the highest regard; I always wish he'd be on top when it's all said and done with his career.

He's an amazing guy; not everybody talked to us clubhouse kids, let alone helped us out, hit ground balls, whatever. He was always there willing to say "hi," willing to talk.

Any town would be lucky to have a guy like Craig Counsell as manager. He's never going to give you any reasons to say anything bad about him. He's going to do everything the right way and push everybody. If he wants to stay there in Milwaukee for the rest of his career, I hope that's able to happen for him. I know how it is, you have to get players and they've got to give you players. Hopefully they keep putting money into it and they will help him be successful.

Craig Counsell is a wonderful human being and has had a profound and positive force in my life.

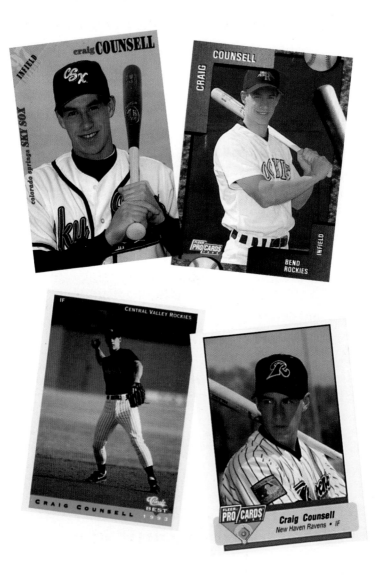

# Chapter Three

# WHEN WE WERE YOUNG AND OUR WORLD WAS NEW

## 12 Years Old Forever

# HAVING CRAIG COUNSELL FOR A FRIEND IS LIKE PLAYING HOOKY FROM LIFE

BRAD PARKINS

*Parkins was a grade school and high school classmate of Craig Counsell in Whitefish Bay, Wisconsin. He is a graduate of Wisconsin-***EAU CLAIRE***\*. Parkins is Director of Marketing at Pearson Education in Chicago and lives with his family in Hinsdale, Illinois.*

I met Craig in grade school when the Counsell family moved from the South Bend area to Whitefish Bay. We had a pretty good soccer team in that little suburb of Milwaukee. We saw that Craig was an athlete and we worked really hard to convince him to play **SOCCER**\*. He did play soccer and he was good. We were convinced that we were going to have him be a soccer player and help our team. He obviously stopped playing soccer and focused in on baseball. We almost screwed up his career by trying to peer pressure him into soccer. He did play goalie for a while and then hung up his cleats for a different set of cleats.

In high school there were a few of us that were small, we didn't grow right away and Craig was one of them. Then all of a sudden, junior and senior years he became just a fantastic baseball

\*Hank Aaron's first minor league team at age 18 was **EAU CLAIRE** in the Class C Northern League. Aaron hit .336 in 1952.

\*More American youth play **SOCCER** than any other sport. There are some who say the reason is so they don't have to watch it.

player at the high school level. He was our high school Athlete of the Year for two consecutive years.

After the Marlins 1997 World Series, Craig came back to Chicago and was sharing an apartment with Michelle and a couple of other people. He had to go back to Florida to an autograph signing. They offered him a couple thousand dollars to hop down and do that. My name is Brad but he always calls me "Homer" because I always root for the home team, "Do you want to come with me, **HOMER**\*?" I figured what better things do I have to do besides hang with Craig in Florida so I said sure.

We got to Florida and went out with some of Craig's friends the night before and maybe, just maybe, stayed out a little late. The next day we drove from Craig's apartment to a shopping mall. I dropped him off at the front door and told him I would meet him at the Food Court when he was done. We were late getting there and no lie, there was a line of people wrapped around the shopping center. We were about five minutes late. When we saw that line, Craig said that there is no way that line could be to get an autograph from him!

When we got there, security directed us to a back entrance where there was more security. They had been waiting for him. They stated that they needed to rush him in. I went to the Food Court to wait. Security comes and tells me to meet Craig back where I dropped him. I said, "Just have him come to the Food Court because he is probably starving. We can get lunch." This person said, "You don't understand, the line will not stop. We need to get him out the back entrance."

Craig stayed for more autographs; but when he did come out the back entrance, people ran to the car. They were trying to jump on the car to get access to Craig. We had to slowly drive

\*Ten players named **HOMER** have played in the majors, but only four hit a home run.

away. The mall got security and had security actually drive around the car and bring us out back to the on-ramp to get on the freeway to leave. It was amazing. The fans loved him. It was a surreal experience that neither one of us had expected would happen.

When we got in the car to leave, I had the windows open, enjoying my moment of fame and Craig's, but I had to close the windows. People were trying to literally jump in the car; but we were trying to be as nice about it as possible. There was no harm but we had to get out of there because it was crazy. We both just laughed about it because it was nothing either of us would ever imagine could've happened. Reflecting on it now, it is just so exciting to know this was a friend of mine that I grew up with and people wanted to see him because he scored the winning run in Game 7 of the World Series.

Next we tried to get an earlier flight back to Chicago. This was pre-9/11 so getting in and out of airports was so much smoother. We walked up to the counter and asked if we could get on the next flight. They told us it was sold out. Craig and I looked at each other and I asked him if he didn't mind, that I'd like to try something. He said sure. I said to the counter persons, "Would you two people happen to know who Craig Counsell is?" Craig would never use his own name to get advantage in anything. They said, "Yes." Then I said, "Do you think this guy looks like Craig Counsel!?" They said "He does." I told them that we were just at an autograph signing and we had some extra merchandise. We asked if Craig would personalize a few things for them, their family and friends, was it possible we could get on that flight?

We got on that flight! We got on the early flight with a few autographs. Craig will go to the grave saying it was 100 percent my doing, but no one wanted my autograph, they most certainly wanted his. That was a surreal experience. Going to Florida for the autographs, a crowd bigger than we could have ever imagined and somewhat leveraging that to get on an earlier flight home was pretty cool. Craig was against doing all of this; but he was willing to do it to get home. He said that I had to do the entire thing because there is no way that he would ever walk up to someone and ask a favor like that. I had the little box of extra glossies that he had left over after the signing. The people at the counter couldn't have been happier. At that time there weren't really a lot of mobile phones. No one was there snapping pictures with their phones because back then, phones just made phone calls. It was a simple time compared to now. Craig was a little uncomfortable; but we were both happy to get on the flight.

My father-in-law, **A DIEHARD CUBS**\* fan, has these phenomenal seats at Wrigley Field. They are literally front row behind the visitors' dugout. Once when the Cubs were playing the Diamondbacks my father-in-law gave me his two seats. At this time, Craig was with the Arizona Diamondbacks. Our friend Jeff Margolis came in from Minneapolis so we could go to the game and see Craig play. We went out before the game in the Wrigley Field area and enjoyed ourselves, had a little liquid fortification against the unknown.

Then it started raining. It wasn't going to stop raining. It was just pouring and pouring. Jeff said "Let's text Craig and see if he actually checks his phone. Maybe we could at least go into Wrigley early and say hi to him". Lo and behold, Craig picks up the text. He told us to come over and go to a particular door. We went to this little door where there was a security guard. Craig was waiting on the other side of the door for us. Craig walks us through this tunnel under Wrigley Field. We came out in the dugout.

We sat in the visitors' dugout with Craig and Jerry Colangelo who was the primary owner of the Diamondbacks and the Phoenix Suns. We had had a few beers, we were soaking wet

\*When Chicagoan Joe Davita, 78, died in 2001 his obituary read: "Memorials to **CUBS** so they can acquire a qualified relief pitcher."

and Craig was trying to introduce us. But the best part of this story, Craig the Baseball Historian, made us stop while we were entering. He said that we needed to pause, look around and take this in. He said this, "First of all, this is a classic stadium and you have to remember the names of the baseball greats that have walked where you are walking today."

Craig was all in on just going down the history of the players that have gone through **WRIGLEY FIELD**\* and sat in the visitors' dugout. Craig also pointed out a urinal. It's a little known fact that there is a urinal right behind the dugout in the walkway to the locker room. Just think of all the famous ball players that went to the bathroom right there. It was unbelievable to have the history of Wrigley Field and to be able to sit for a multiple hour rain delay in the visitors' dugout with Craig and the owner of the team, Jerry Colangelo, just to hang out with our friend. Jerry Colangelo was a Chicago summer youth baseball teammate of the late Jim Bouton and a basketball teammate of Wilt Chamberlain at Kansas. When Wilt joined the Harlem Globetrotters, Colangelo transferred to Illinois. Wilt claimed he slept with 20,000 women. I don't know any man who has even peed that many times.

We've lead a charmed life knowing Craig. The boring stuff is that this has not changed him at all. He is still that same guy we've known forever. When the Diamondbacks played the Yankees in the 2001 World Series the Diamondbacks won the first two games in Arizona, a number of us made the road trip out to New York to hopefully see the Diamondbacks win in New York. Unfortunately in New York they lost three heartbreaking games. Jeff Margolis and I got to travel on the Diamondback's family bus. The family bus took us from the hotel in Manhattan to the

\*More NFL games were played at **WRIGLEY FIELD** than at any other stadium in the country until The Meadowlands in New Jersey set a new record in 2003. Mile High Stadium in Denver was in second place until demolished in 2001.

Bronx. That in itself was fantastic to be with all the family and friends of players and to get the police escort and the motorcade that just burns through Manhattan.

The game ends in a heartbreaking loss. We get back on the bus and owner Jerry Colangelo gets on the bus and addresses everyone. He is talking about how heartbreaking this is and his speech is from the heart. It is a nice speech; but it is sad because he is disappointed. At this point the liquid fortitude was flowing and I just yelled, "Here we go Diamondbacks, here we go!" and did the two claps. And not a thing, literally crickets. I do it again, crickets. I do it again and out of pity a couple of the players family members clap. Then the whole bus just starts rocking! We get all fired up because we think that we are going to go back to Arizona and win the World Series. And they do.

Colangelo was on the Jim Rome show after the World Series talking about that speech. He said that one of Counsell's friends, who had been having a good time, interrupted him with this chant and fired up the fan base again. When Craig heard about that story after the fact, he put his head in his hands and said, "I really can't let you go anywhere".

I have a more sentimental story from the night after the Marlins won the 1997 World Series. The team went out and had a good late night and the next day we were all catching up. I was talking to Craig and Michelle and I asked Michelle what happened right after the game. I didn't go to Game 7. When Michelle went into the locker room to be part of the celebration, the very first thing that Craig said to Michelle was "We did it." And he gave her a big hug and kiss. It was Michelle who had been with him all of those years. To see him grow from the kid in high school to the guy at Notre Dame to the one who struggled through A ball, Double A and Triple A. He knew that she was his soul mate. They weren't married at the time. They were still dating; but they were going to get married. That just spoke to the person that he is. It wasn't that he just scored the winning run, or that his team won. It was that Michelle was with him all the way.

When Craig went to play for the AAA Colorado Sky Sox in 1997 I drove his car out to Colorado Springs for him. I even drove through a tornado on the way. Craig is such a quiet guy that when I got out there, we didn't know what to do.

When Craig got called up to the majors, I was actually being a stand-in for him at a wedding that Michelle went to for one of the people that Craig and Michelle knew in Chicago. I went to the wedding ceremony with Michelle. It was so hot that the stain on the pews was bleeding onto peoples outfits in the church. We found out right after the wedding that Craig had gotten the official call up to the Major Leagues. We were buzzing with excitement. He got called up to the Rockies and then got traded to the Marlins pretty much right after that.

The excitement of having a friend in the big leagues, just took over. He got out of the gates hot. He was swinging a really hot bat. There was one game when the Marlins came to County Stadium, pre-Miller Park, and like a bunch of buffoons we got together with construction paper and made a sign that said "Counsell MVP." It took us a few tries to get it spelled right once we were lining up in the outfield so it would show in the Marlins broadcast.

Another early game was when the Marlins went to Wrigley and a group of us sat together close to the visitors' dugout. The Sunshine Network from Florida came over to interview us because we had more Counsell signs there. They asked us how we knew Craig and if we had any messages. We told them we grew up with Craig and we loved to see him play. Somebody in the group made fun of **JIMMY JOHNSON**\* since it was the Sun-

---

*Coach **JIMMY JOHNSON** and Janis Joplin were high school classmates at Thomas Jefferson High School in Port Arthur, Texas. Jimmy Johnson didn't know she sang. They hated each other. She called him "Scarhead" and he called her "Beat Weeds."

shine Network. We said the Packers were going to crush the Dolphins later that year.

Another road trip to Miami was right after Craig got hit in the jaw with a ball and his mouth was wired shut. Four of us went down to cheer him up. He had a pretty cool apartment right on the beach at the time. We had planned to go see him play but since he wasn't playing he had arranged for us to sit in the owner's box. The **MARLINS**\* were playing the Dodgers. Before we walk in, Craig tells us that other people are going to be in the owner's box so we have to act somewhat civilized. Lo and behold, Tommy Lasorda is sitting in the room. We are like, this is great! Tommy Lasorda is a great storyteller.

To all of us Tommy Lasorda was a moment from the movie *Fletch*. We all grew up loving that Chevy Chase movie. Tommy was indirectly in that movie. There is a scene where Chevy Chase is in jail and he is talking to the police chief. Chevy sees a picture of Tommy Lasorda on the chief's wall and asks him if he likes Tommy Lasorda. The police chief says "Yes" and Chevy Chase (Fletch) punches Tommy Lasorda's picture and says, "I hate Tommy Lasorda." Tommy Lasorda asked us if we remember the scene in the movie where Kareem Abdul-Jabbar and Chevy Chase are playing for the Lakers. We, of course, knew that scene.

Tommy told us that there was another scene where Chevy Chase is a pitcher for him on the Dodgers. Chevy is trying to strike out someone who is not that tall and he can't throw the ball into the strike zone and gets really frustrated. "They cut out that scene, and that is why I hate the movie *Fletch*!" Tommy said. We just had so much fun in the owner's box with Craig, trying to lift his spirits; but we were all just absorbing

\*The first player to ever represent the **MARLINS** in professional baseball was John Lynch, the current General Manager of the San Francisco 49-ers and former All-Pro NFL linebacker. He was the starting pitcher in the Marlins first minor league game…two years before the MLB team debuted.

the stories. Tommy could literally sit there and talk to you about every baseball player who was out there. He knew their strengths, weaknesses and knew what was going to happen and was pretty much right every time. We shook Lasorda's hand, and someone asked If they could have his World Series ring. He said "No." He was great. He doesn't really have a filter... much shorter than you think.

Craig and Michelle are now back in Whitefish Bay, the town we grew up in. It is like an open door at their house. Everyone is welcome. For three of the last four years they have had a 3rd of July party at their house for kids and friends and family. If Craig is in town he is there. If he is not, Michelle is the host. John and Jan are there and Craig's sister comes into town with her kids. It's pretty neat. We always do a picture of all the friends and their spouses, and then we weave all the children into the picture. It's wonderful to see how many kids we all have now...just to see that we've been friends since grade school and we continue to be super close friends. Craig is really kind and opens his door for everyone. He is still very humble, but he obviously has a competitive fire that is on display from time to time. But besides being famous, there is no change in who Craig Counsell is and that is the best part of it.

*Brad Parkins, the sausage on the left, flashes his slowness at Miller Park. He managed to finish in the top five.*

Every home game at Miller Park there are five people dressed up in oversized sausage costumes and they race. They are about 8-feet tall and start in left field and run all the way down behind home plate and sprint past the home dugout. I thought if I got in this race there is a good chance I could win.

I did leverage my relationship with Craig and Michelle to be one of the racing sausages in Miller Park. One year I got to be Stosh, the Polish Sausage. For years I have always let Craig and Michelle know that I was costume friendly and I felt that I would be a good ambassador for the Sausage Race. Finally at one of those 3rd of July parties I told them at some point we have to make this happen. That was after some good amount of beverages. It was really more Michelle. I got the call from Michelle and she told me that there was one open date for the year. I told her I'd be there.

I had to check in at a special desk at Miller Park, and then they walk you down to get dressed. I could bring my wife and son. In my mind I was going to win. I was in good shape for my age and I am a **RUNNER**\*. I turn the corner and I see two chiseled, young athletes. They look like wide receivers on a college football team. I was like "oh, no." Then there are two professional sausage racers there who work for Miller Park. Sometimes these sausages are amateurs and sometimes these sausage spots are filled through charitable auctions. In this case, there happened to be an opening so I was a last minute fill. Other times they may use Miller Park employees that specialize in this race. As we were getting ready I mentioned to the Miller Park employees that I assume they would let those of us that were guests battle it out for first place. Those Miller Park employees, told me that since I was a friend of Craig's that it

*The late Buzzy Bavasi, when G.M. of the Dodgers, once offered his pitchers $25 if they would **RUN** a mile. Don Drysdale said he would do it right after Jesse Owens won twenty games....Drysdale once said that his most important pitch was his second knockdown pitch. "That way the batter knew the first one wasn't an accident."

was their job to shame me out on the field. So I was surrounded by these two guys who are chiseled and two guys who say they are going to shame me.

Now I'm nervous because I have family and friends who changed their plans at the last minute to come to Miller Park. And of course before the run, my friends are like, you can't do this without a beer, so I have a beer, maybe a couple, to carb load. I get all ready and let's just say I finished. I ran my heart out. I ran as fast as I could. It was literally one of my favorite sporting experiences. I was so excited I called Craig after the game and asked him what he thought of my performance. He said, "Homer, it was such a close game against the Dodgers. I knew you went right past me, but I didn't see it at all."

Craig was so focused on beating the Dodgers that he didn't even see me. In the costume I was wearing, you can't see a thing except straight ahead. You have no peripheral vision. You can only see out of the mouth of the sausage costume. They really stress that you can't fall down because they would have to get the sausage cleaned by the next day and that is expensive. There is a lot of pressure being a sausage. Coming in fifth was a shock to the ego; but it was a great experience and that was because of Michelle Counsell. My friends and family said it was awesome and worth the price of admission. They will always make fun of me for being last. My friends knew which sausage I was because I had my phone with me. They let me ham it up with the crowd before the race and high-five the kids. A lot of people can have children but not everybody can be a racing sausage.

With Christian Yelich going down in early September, 2019 that could have been a bottom out moment for the team. I sent Craig a text. I knew he'd be getting a lot of texts that would say how terrible that was; but I sent him a note along the lines of, "you got this". He's like, "Homer, it's a sad night, we are going to pick ourselves up and we are going to go win this thing. It's in our DNA." That was his approach. He loves Christian Yelich, the

whole city does; but he loves his team and they had an opportunity. He knew their pitching was getting better and healthy.

They were getting fresh arms and the team was going to rally
for Yelich. We didn't know what they were going to do in the
post-season; but for them to do what they did shows that Craig
was able to rally a team that could've gone south really quickly.
They had a tough schedule with the **CARDINALS**\*. Tough schedule with the Cubs and they crushed them in key series. They
were battling to be the number one Wild Card team. His management style is we are going pick ourselves up, we are going
to do this, we don't let things get in our way, it is in our DNA to
finish strong and we are going to win. I WILL! I CAN! REPEAT!

I find myself getting defensive for Craig when I hear criticism
about him. I won't respond because I don't want to cause a
storm. I get frustrated when I hear things like, "Is Craig Counsell the right one to manage the team and is he managing the
bullpen the right way?" I don't think it's justified. With social
media, people can be really bold and hide behind their names.
I believe that Craig is probably on the short list for any manager job that opens up. He knows how to get the most out of
people. The everyday baseball fan, they can have their opinion; but my opinion when they criticize him, is that they are
wrong. He is doing a great job. He is doing this on a team pay
scale that pales in comparison to what the Cubs pay. Craig is
getting a lot out of his talent and he is being creative in how to
use his pitchers down the stretch.

I never dreamed he'd be managing our hometown baseball
team. When he played A ball he was good but things weren't
jumping off the charts. Then when he got into Triple-A, one

\*In late 1953 the **CARDINALS** chose Jack Buck for play-by-play
over Chick Hearn from Peoria, Illinois. Buck got the job because
he had done excellent Budweiser commercials that summer while
broadcasting the Rochester Red Wings, the Cardinals' AAA team in
New York. The Cardinals had just been purchased by Anheuser-Busch.

could start to think that he deserves a chance the way he was hitting. When he signed with the Brewers as a free agent, that was incredible. We knew the mind he had and he was well read. He studies the game. He knows the game like the catcher. When he got the front office job, we thought Craig could be groomed to become Commissioner or be the overall representative for the players' union because he is so well spoken and even tempered. Then he became the manager of the Brewers and wow!

We live in Chicago so we don't get to see all the Brewers games. My son and I will literally watch phone updates on MLB.com or **ESPN***, pitch by pitch to see how the Brewers are doing. There is no chance I would do that if Craig wasn't involved. Baseball on a phone when it's not even a game, it's just updates, it's crazy. We do it because of Craig. The last couple of years Craig has brought the passion of baseball back to Milwaukee. The city loves baseball and for a long time wasn't able to celebrate baseball because it was terrible. Craig is part of that renaissance of sports of Milwaukee and darn humble about the whole thing all the time.

Michelle and Craig are great complements to one another. They are perfect for each other. They started dating in Craig's senior year in high school. They dated on and off through college. Then after college they got together and it's been perfect. There was a beautiful snow storm on the eve of their wedding. His wedding party was made up of friends he grew up with, friends he played baseball with and everybody got along. Michelle and Craig's kids are kind. Michelle and Craig know they are fortunate and they are giving. We see each other as often as we can. During the baseball season we give Craig a little breathing room and communicate more with Michelle. It's strange to say but they are the ideal couple.

***ESPN** debuted September 7, 1979. ESPN2 debuted October 1, 1993. *ESPN The Magazine* made its first appearance on March 11, 1998.

My neighbors can't stand me regarding sports; but they think it is cool that I know Craig. And most people like him as a manager because he was a great player to watch. People in the Chicago area have nothing but respect for Craig as a manager. They have less respect for me as a Packer and Brewer fan; but that is just part of the banter of the neighbors.

*President George Bush, Craig, John, and Laura Bush, Little League on the White House Lawn, 2002.*

# THE TWIN CITIES:
# HALF AS GOOD AS THE QUAD CITIES

JEFF MARGOLIS

*Jeff Margolis was part of the Gang of Six at Whitefish Bay High School. A grad of the University of Arizona, Margolis has lived the last 26 years in Minneapolis and worked as a sales star in the digital arena with a company called Equals 3 and an artificial intelligence-powered knowledge management system.*

We became friends because Craig is just a good Midwest kid. We have a really close-knit group of friends. There are six of us who are still close and in touch to this day. We're all turning fifty. This friendship goes back forty years, and some of us even longer before Craig moved to Whitefish Bay. We are all still very close. We're trying to figure out a way to get together for our 50th birthdays. It's pretty unique that we have such a close friendship after all those years. Craig was a pretty quiet soft-spoken kid. He fit in well with our group.

We went to Richards grade school together. One of the memories of growing up with Craig—he was a great athlete. I would never say he was the greatest baseball player ever. He was a very good baseball player, but we never dreamed what would happen. He was always a good athlete. You always wanted him on your **BASKETBALL**\* team. He could go pick up some golf clubs and go shoot a better score than any of us. He was just a good all-around athlete. I do have a vivid memory of him

---

\*When Steve Alford was a senior in high school in 1983 in New Castle, Indiana, his high school team averaged more people in attendance per game than the **INDIANA PACERS**.

growing up in the summers back then. We'd hop on our bikes and be in the neighborhood. He lived two houses away from Richards school, and we used to play this game called Strike Out. Strike Out is basically a two-person baseball game. It could be more than two, but all you needed was two people. You needed a pitcher and a batter because the backstop was the brick wall at the school. You'd spray paint a catcher's mitt, or a box on the back wall of the school. We'd go out there for hours. I'd pitch, and he hit, and he'd pitch, and I hit, and he beat me about 21-2 every time. I wasn't that good. He would always crush me. He would hit **HOME RUNS**\* over the fence that would end up in his yard. Literally he hit home runs that would end up two houses in. There was an alley there. We'd have to go chase the tennis balls pretty much in his backyard. We did that for hours in the summer. I was a glutton for punishment. He'd always crush me, but it was a fun way to spend some outdoor time and get a little exercise and have a lot of laughs.

We broke windows even though we used tennis balls. More often than not, it was just more of dodging cars and finding the balls in the trees.

I've seen the movie, *The Sandlot*. It totally reminded me of my youth. There are a lot of similarities there. We grew up in a nice area, a nice suburban area, a pretty simple area. It was a simpler time back then without cellphones and Internet. You were hanging out on bikes and walking and going to play basketball at school or going at the park playing Strike Out against the wall. That's what we did, hours on end until our parents told us to come home.

Craig was a good basketball player. He was a really good all-around athlete. Craig was just a smart player. He had a good

\*During the Seattle Mariners' first year in 1977, the **DISTANCE TO THE FENCES** was measured in fathoms. A fathom is 6 feet. For instance, whereas one park might have a sign that denotes 360 feet, the Kingdome sign would have the number 60…

shot. He was athletic. He was a **LITTLE GUY\***. Even when he played baseball, he looked like the batboy. He looked young. He just was a smart player and athletic enough and talented enough to make shots and make plays.

We didn't get into a lot of trouble. In high school, maybe I threw a few parties. I was the third boy of three sons. I had a little more leeway with the parents. I lived three blocks from Craig. I threw a few parties here and there at my house in high school, having a few beers, and that type of thing. The funny thing is his wife, Michelle, went to high school with us. She was a year younger than us. My father was a lawyer, and so was Michelle's father. One day at court, they ran into each other. Mike McClone is Michelle's father. Mike is like, "Mark (my dad), my daughter said she had a great time at your house last Saturday night." My dad had no idea. It got me in big trouble quickly there.

Michelle was popular. She was just a good, good person. Everybody wanted to be friends with her. She was just a very popular girl, good friends with all of us. We were a year older than them, but we hung out with her and her friends in that grade quite a bit in high school. Even though she ended up marrying Craig, she was good friends with me and Jamie and the rest of the guys. We're all cool friends. I text Michelle much like I text Craig. It's not like she's just a wife of Craig. She's a friend of mine.

We had a big 30th high school reunion a couple of summers ago. It was in Whitefish Bay at a restaurant. We had a tent outside in back. What I found really cool was that the Brewers had a game that day. Craig had many excuses not to show. Not only did he show up, he really showed up. I didn't bother talking to him. I let other people talk to him. I see him all the time. When

*Mark McGwire's brother, Dan McGwire, a former #1 pick of the Seahawks, is the tallest NFL QB ever at 6'8". Former Boston Celtic and Toronto Blue Jay Danny Ainge is the **TALLEST** second baseman in Major League history.

I'm home in Milwaukee for Thanksgiving or Fourth of July, my morning run is I'll run Lake Drive, and I'll stop at Craig and Michelle's house to say "Hi." That's just what I do. I see him plenty and travel to see him play and spend time with him.

He was talking with people at the reunion who really were excited to talk with him, who were proud that they were friends and went to high school with Craig, even if they were not close friends. He spent time with all of them, just a normal kid, talking to old colleagues and old, not even friends, more acquaintances, acquaintances and friends. He spent time with them. He took pictures with them. He was just having a good time and being a nice Midwest kid, no attitude, really just being a regular guy.

I can't say enough about that. He's one of us. He's one of all of the Midwest kids. He's not any better just because he's the hometown manager and has two World Series rings. That night, I saw him talking to people when he suddenly whips his phone out. I saw he got a phone call. He rushed out. He walked down the block. It was a call from the general manager because they were working on a trade. Here he is at the reunion, literally going out to talk to the general manager about a trade that just happened.

I saw him play in the minors. I was in Tucson at the University of Arizona when Craig was with the Colorado Rockies. The Rockies spring training was in Tucson in those days. We're the same age, but I was on the five-year plan at Arizona. That's what you do. You're not going to want to rush out of there.

He came to Tucson five days early and and stayed at my apartment. I took him out to a nearby park, just a random small little park and did the soft toss where I'd throw the ball up in the air, and he'd hit it into the fence. I was out there working him out before he goes to his first spring training ever as a major leaguer or a minor leaguer as a drafted rookie. We'd do a little warmups. We'd go out and have fun. He probably had a good time also, but he was focused, and I did my little part to make sure he was ready for that spring training.

I went out to Hi Corbett Field in Tucson. I'd go out to his hotel and drive him to the ballpark. Later I'd pick him up and go to dinner. Some nights we'd go to a sports bar and watch an NCAA tourney basketball game. I'd take him back and forth to the hotel. There wasn't Uber back then. There was maybe a hotel shuttle or a cab, but I was his Uber before there was Uber. I was so proud of him.

When he was in the minors he had so many chances to give up. He had injury after injury—a broken leg, a freak accident, a broken shin. He had a lot of things happen in the minors. He had several injuries in the minors that many people would have been derailed and never would have made it to the big leagues, but he plugged on in A ball to AA to AAA, a couple of injuries. He hung in there. Lo and behold, he's in AAA, and he makes the AAA 1997 All-Star Game in Des Moines, Iowa, home of the Iowa Cubs. He got called up to the big leagues a month later. Four of us buddies from high school drove to Des Moines to go see our buddy play in the AAA All-Star game. We thought that was the pinnacle. This is the greatest thing ever.

We thought this is it. This is the top. Lo and behold, it was not the top, but at the time, we thought it was. We drive to Des Moines, get a hotel, go to the AAA game. We ended up sitting in a box with some other players' wives. Michelle was there with us. Michelle Counsell, Michelle McClone at the time. They weren't married. We go to the game. We go to the postgame afterwards. There was a party that we went to with Craig. People like Jerry Colangelo were there—the Arizona Diamondbacks president was at the party. There were some famous people there. We were wide-eyed. We couldn't believe we were at this party. Here we are, mid-twenties, and seeing our buddy play in the AAA All-Star game. We thought that was the coolest thing ever.

Then probably three weeks later, he gets a call up to the big leagues. It's like almost out of a movie. It's like *Major League* or one of those baseball movies. I get a call from Craig at 11:00 at night saying, "I'm going to the show." Literally, that's what happened. It was straight out of a movie. I don't know if I was more excited than he was. He was super excited, all that hard work and all that time and injuries. He was never the most talented player growing up. I'll say he got the most out of his talent than anybody in the big leagues ever. The career he's had is truly fascinating. It is a little bit like a real-life *Rudy* except for **BASEBALL**\*.

The field that our high school played on, Cahill Field was just horrendous. It was just a dump. Now Craig has donated a bunch of money, and that field is absolutely spectacular. That would be really cool to get a picture of Cahill when he played on it versus what it looks like today. That would be a great photo.

We grew up playing Little League at a place called Water Tower Park. That is now Craig Counsell Park. That's where we played Little League. I was not a very good player.

When he got called up by the Rockies for his first game, we went to a Minneapolis bar called Old Chicago, a pizza place. We went, got that game on their TV and saw our buddy in his first time. He got on base for sure that first night. It was a pretty special night, being in a bar in downtown Minneapolis, watching Craig in the majors for the first time.

When the Marlins won the World Series in '97, I went down for Games 1 and 2 in Miami. I was there with Craig's parents, his sister Jennifer, and Michelle. We all hung out, had a great time. I went to Games 1 and 2. His sister Jen, Jennifer, flew back from Australia that night. We celebrated at the hotel. One of my biggest regrets in life is I didn't make it to Game 7. My parents

---

\***Charles Schultz drew almost 18,000 Peanuts strips and almost 2,000 dealt with BASEBALL.**

were visiting me in Minneapolis. I was selling my condo. The time didn't work out. I did not go to Game 7, and as you know, he scored the winning run of the **WORLD SERIES\***. His cleats are in the Hall of Fame, and I would have been in the clubhouse. It would have been just an epic, memorable night. I'm very, very upset with myself that I didn't figure out a way to get there for Game 7, but I didn't.

With that happening, I told myself, "If this ever happens again, I will not make the same mistake twice." When he made the World Series with the Diamondbacks after 9/11, I went to Games 4 and 5 in New York. I'd never been to **YANKEE STADIUM\***. I went out there and took the family and friends in a box with Michelle and my friends Brad and Tony. We took a team bus with family and friends to the Bronx, the first time ever. It was right after 9/11. It was November. It was delayed.

The Dbacks lost both games in the last of the 9th. Tough losses! We were on the bus ride going back to the hotel. We were all depressed after losing those games. Jerry Colangelo, the owner of the Diamondbacks, gets on the bus and does a little pep talk. He says, "Okay, guys, that was tough, but we're going back to Arizona for 6 and 7. We're going to win this thing. Keep your heads up."

All of a sudden, my friend, Brad Parkins, starts, [sings a melody], "Go Dbacks, go!" It was just quiet. He gets the whole bus roaring after these depressing two losses, after they lost on last-second home runs.

*The last **WORLD SERIES** game played during the daytime was in 1983.

*In the **YANKEE** locker room, on the day of DON LARSEN's perfect game, Larsen was served divorce papers....Years later Don Larsen threw out the first pitch the same day David Cone threw his perfect Yankee game....Larsen and David Wells, another Yankee with a perfect game, graduated from the same high school in San Diego, Point Loma.

After the New York games, I flew back to Minneapolis for three hours. I got some shorts and T-shirts, and I fly to Arizona for 6 and 7. I told you, I was not going to miss them winning Game 7 and not being in the clubhouse if they won again. They won Game 6 big, and then they won Game 7 in extra innings. Craig was on base again. He got hit by a pitch. He was on first base when Luis Gonzalez hit the game-winning hit. He was an integral part of both of those World Series.

I was in the clubhouse after Game 7. When I walked in, Rudy Giuliani was walking out. At the time, he was the king of the world basically because of New York City and 9/11. I shake his hand, and I go in. Craig's in there and all of the players. I'm pouring a beer over Craig, literally pouring a beer over him while he's getting interviewed by Biff Henderson from **DAVID LETTERMAN**\*.

Craig's a pretty quiet kid. He's not going to try to make it on Letterman's show. He's not going to say anything too exciting like Mark Grace would. He's pretty understated. I'm pouring a beer on him. I'm thinking that maybe that would get him on TV. It did not, but I tried.

It was really special to sit with Craig's family in the postseason games. They're close family friends. My mom considers Craig a fourth son. I'm sure the Counsells think of me the same way. I was Craig's best man at his wedding, Craig and Michelle's best man. We're close friends. The funny thing with John, the dad, is he would pace. He would never sit there. He would walk around

\*On January 4, 2000, Kurt Warner was on the Late Show With **DAVID LETTERMAN**. Letterman asked Warner what it felt like to be cut by the Green Bay Packers. Warner said, "Well, I was a little disappointed." Letterman responded, "It made you feel cheap! It made you feel cheap and dirty and like a loser, didn't it?" Both Warner and the audience roared.

Other QBs with the Packers at that time were Brett Favre, Ty Detmer, and Mark Brunell.

the stadium. You wouldn't see him for innings. He couldn't sit there with us. We were having fun. Jennifer and I were having a beer and trying to keep our nerves calm. Jan is a teacher, a little quieter. John, he'd be gone for innings at a time.

I watched the 1997 World Series game when he scored the winning run for the Marlins Game 7. I was actually at a friend's condo. I kept the champagne bottle that we cracked after they won. I literally ran out of the house. Bob Costas was the announcer. One of the key things of that game that people don't talk about a lot, Craig came up in the ninth inning, and they were down a run. He came up in the ninth with runners on first and third, and one out against the Indians. If he hits into a **DOUBLE PLAY\***, the World Series is over. The Indians win the World Series. It was against Jose Mesa, the best closer in baseball. Craig hit the ball—I'm telling you I've never seen him hit a better ball. When he hit it, we thought it was a three-run homer to win the World Series. It ended up being a sacrifice fly at deep right field which tied the game to force extra innings. But that hit, that sac fly, that RBI was just as big as him scoring the winning run, and people forget about that. To do that off of Jose Mesa at that time, rookie Craig, that was unbelievable, and then he scored the winning run. We were running around like crazy in St. Paul, running out of the house and yelling and popping champagne.

Mesa was very tough. Craig had two strikes. He kept fouling off pitches against a very tough pitcher. That was amazing, the World Series, and then the World Series again in 2001.

---

\*In April of 1957, Don Hoak of the Reds was on second base and Gus Bell was on first when Wally Post hit a **DOUBLE-PLAY** ground ball. Hoak fielded the ball with his bare hands and tossed the ball to Johnny Logan. Hoak was automatically out for interference—but not the batter—and Hoak thereby avoided an easy double-play. The Reds did that three times that year before the rule was changed...After Johnny Logan's major league career was over, he played in Japan.

ALL IT TAKES IS ALL YA GOT

We went down to see Craig when he broke his jaw. We stayed with him. We went to a Dodgers game and were in a suite with him. He's got his mouth wired shut.

That broken jaw was bad. We were in South Beach, Miami at the time. We would go out to lunch. We would want to go to a bar and grill and have fun. We'd have to give him something in a blender. He had to eat his food through a straw. It was pretty bad, but we were there to support him.

That was unbelievable when Craig came home to play for the Brewers. What a dream come true for everybody, to be part of a team that was struggling and to help them become relevant again. I lived in Minneapolis at the time. The Brewers would come up here, and every time the Brewers were in town, I'd go see him play. We would go down to the bowels after the game and hang out with family and see Craig. We would bring my son down there for a picture in the hallway. He was always great about that. Before the game, I'd bring my son and his friend down for a signed baseball down by the dugout. Always doing that. Now he comes to town, we get together for dinner or coffee or both. Every time he's in town, we're spending quality time together. Usually it's dinner and coffee the next morning, just hanging out and catching up, just small stuff.

When he became manager of the Brewers, that was amazing. The Brewers had created a front office job for him. They created a job as the special assistant to the GM. We started a joke, "He's the George Costanza of the Brewers." As much as he was good at that, he was very good at what he did, he belongs on the field wearing a baseball uniform, not a suit. He did that job as assistant GM for the Brewers. He learned a lot on the baseball side. He's a very smart guy. He has a finance degree from Notre Dame, was a player's union representative, talking to people like Bud Selig.

**BUD SELIG**\* was the commissioner of baseball, also a former Brewers owner. He was one of my dad's very close friends. Bud was always very complimentary to my dad about Craig. He knew that we were close. Craig had a very smart analysis of the game, for the front office. When the Brewers fired their manager a month into the 2015 season and they hired Craig, Craig had never coached one baseball game in his life, nothing professional, nothing in the minors. The only thing he had coached was his kids' teams. That was it. He coached his sons' baseball or basketball teams. That was his coaching experience when he got the job as the Brewers's manager. He's just been amazing.

As a player, you hear over the years every announcer saying, "Someday, Craig Counsell is going to be a manager. Coaches love him. Someday he'll be a manager." I pay Direct TV a lot of money so I can watch his games. Every time the announcers would always say, "Craig will be a manager someday," and he's doing a great job. He's a players' coach. He learned a lot from people like Jim Leyland and Bob Melvin. He's seen it all, but also having that finance degree and having a four-year college degree as well, not just a baseball player.

I think most Brewers fans appreciate what Craig is doing. They've had some serious injuries over his years. Most of the fans in Milwaukee love him as a player and as a person. They know he's homegrown, but more than that, he's a really smart baseball guy. If he was homegrown and wasn't very good, they would kick him out. They know he's good.

Craig is just a good, good egg. He's really a down-to-earth Midwest kid. He's done well, and he's earned it, for sure. It's all hard work and dedication.

Good guys do finish first.

*\*BUD SELIG first tried to buy the White Sox in 1969 before taking the Seattle franchise in a purchase approved by a Seattle bankruptcy court. He became the largest shareholder in the Brewers by the time he was 29.*

# A DRIVER WITH CONCENTRATION

JAMIE GLINBERG

*For the last 13 years, Glinberg has been a marketing consultant for ESPN-Wisconsin. He was a classmate of Craig Counsell for eight years in Whitefish Bay.*

I met Craig when he first came to Whitefish Bay to start the fiifth grade. He was wearing a red hoodie, he was a new kid, and he was supposed to be real fast. The way we met is we raced after school on the blacktop. He beat me. From then on, we became very good friends

I did play Little League baseball against him. He was on the Tigers. I was actually on the Brewers, the name of our team. Everyone played against each other. We were all friends. We played and practiced together.

Truthfully, I didn't think Craig was going to be a professional baseball player. I don't think he even thought that or his parents. In grade school, he wasn't a big standout. Even in high school early on, he wasn't a big kid. His house growing up was next to our grade school where there was a baseball field. His dad used to hit us grounders and throw us pitches.

In school, Craig was one of the guys in a group of five or six guys. We all were like a little gang together. He was more shy. In high school, he dated a girl named Mary Ellen, freshman, sophomore. He may have gone to a prom or a homecoming with her. It's funny. I have a picture of him and Mary Ellen together, and then at our 30th high school reunion, Mary Ellen was there, and I recreated the picture with him and her together. I did like a then and now. I have those pictures of

him and Mary Ellen in high school and him and Mary Ellen
from last year. I've got great pictures of Craig. He was a funny-
looking kid.

Then he started dating a gal a year younger than us, Michelle
McClone, also one of my dear friends. They started dating
junior and through college. She's his wife today of many years
with four kids.

Michelle was one of the popular girls, very cute. Dating a girl
a year younger in high school is a big deal. Michelle was great,
very popular, a cute girl, very bubbly. That's her personality.
Craig's much more quiet. He doesn't need to be the center of
attention, although he always is.

I went to college at the University of Minnesota. Once Craig got
drafted, me and some guys, we'd follow him around when he
was in A ball. Then AA ball was the New Haven Ravens. We used
to follow him around once he got into the system. I've seen hundreds of baseball games. I was fortunate enough to see one of his
first games. I was at both World Series, in 1997 with him when he
scored the winning run. I was in Arizona in 2001 in the clubhouse
when they won the World Series, holding on to the trophy with
champagne being poured over our heads. I was lucky enough.
He brought me down with a couple of other guys, and we got in
the clubhouse with him when they were celebrating.

It was like cool for us to see him. That was his job. We all have
jobs out of college, and he's playing baseball for the Rockies
system, never thinking that not only was he going to go to the
Majors, but he was going to win the World Series, be the MVP
Playoffs and be a manager of our hometown team.

The people who went with me to the games were Jeff Margolis,
Mike Hoffman who lives in Minneapolis, and Brad Parkins, all
still good friends to this day.

Our high school gang would travel to watch him play in the
minor leagues. We went to New Haven, CT and Colorado

Springs. These parks were like schlocky little parks. The players lived in motels. They'd take little city buses. It didn't seem big time at all. It was kind of cool for us, but it wasn't anything glamorous, not the way it is today. It was definitely not a glamorous life, but it was fun for us to see our friend playing baseball.

When Craig got called up to the major leagues in Denver in 1995 for three games, I sent him a telegram. There are no telegrams anymore. I was in Minnesota. I sent him a telegram and had it delivered to his dugout.

He got called up to the majors again in '97. That was the year the Marlins won the World Series. That was exciting, "Oh, my god, our buddy." I used to look at *USA Today* and the box score every day just to see his name printed in *USA Today*. "Oh, my god, my best friend is in *USA Today* in the box score nationally. That's the coolest thing in the world!"

We went to Miami for the World Series. He had an old car. The night he scored the winning run in the series I was driving his car as we left the ballpark. Craig was in the back seat. Fans are chasing the car, trying to push the car over, shaking it because Craig Counsell scored the winning run. He was in the back seat saying, "Just drive! Just drive!" and I'm driving the car. I'm like, "This is awesome. Let's slow down." He was yelling at me to drive the car faster.

When we were in Miami, leaving the ballpark after the '97 World Series, fans knew where the players' cars were parked. I remember girls would lift up their shirts and press their bare chests against the car. As a young single guy, I'm saying, "This is fantastic!" These girls are like, "Sign my boobs!" Craig is like, "Just keep driving. Keep driving!" He's huddled down in the back seat. If this is how the **BEATLES**\* felt, I think I understood it. This was crazy. The girls are chasing the car. He's like, "Just

---

\*The **BEATLES** final concert together was at Candlestick Park in San Francisco in 1970.

go! Just go!" He just wanted to get out of there. I remember driving his car. It was a dumpy little junky car that he had in college. It wasn't his sister's car. It was his.

In Arizona, at the 2001 World Series we were seated down on the third base line. I was with this girl who eventually became my wife. I remember him walking on the field and pointing up at me. A couple of security guards came to get me. I told Amy, this woman I was with, "I've got to go. They're bringing me on the field." I didn't have a cellphone.

I went down on the field with Craig. The Diamondbacks had already had the big scrum on the mound. After that, Security ushered everybody into the dugout toward the clubhouse. Craig said, "If they ask anything, just say you're my cousin." We walked in. There was the plastic sheeting and racks and racks of beer and champagne. We just walked in and started grabbing stuff and spraying everybody. Once you're in there, nobody really cares. They just won the World Series. What do they care, who I am?

For someone that didn't play, with all of the champagne and everyone's jumping around....There's champagne being sprayed everywhere, and talking to Craig and giving him a big hug. People are just dumping champagne on his head. I remember asking Craig, "How is your hand?" He said, "What do you mean?" In that game, he got hit. He's lefthanded, and his right hand got hit. He said, "I don't even remember." I said, "Yeah, you got hit. That's how you got on base and eventually got to second base when Luis Gonzalez hit the ball, and then Jay Bell scored the winning run to win it."

He didn't remember getting hit. I just remember we were like drinking and jumping around. In '01, this was before cellphones were so prevalent. People had them, but no reception, we were trying to call people, like other friends of ours. We couldn't get a signal out because the clubhouse is underneath. It wasn't like it is today when you can get a cell signal anywhere. No one's cellphones could work. We couldn't call anybody.

Being in the clubhouse was one of the neatest things that can happen to you.

There's stuff that he's done that people don't realize. When he was a player for the Brewers, he would—and it's not easy—he would bike to the ballpark. Most players take their fancy cars and their fancy parking. He would ride a bicycle. He would bike through the city, through the inner city, to Miller Park. And you picture, "Hey, does this kid have a backpack with his mitt and his ball cap and a bat sticking out?" He would bike, not all the time, but he did it for exercise, and he would just do it for fun. He would bike to the ballpark. I'm not saying every game, but he would take his bicycle from his house in Whitefish Bay and say, "Bye, I'm going to work," and he would bike to the ballpark, and then he'd be playing in a major league game.

He didn't bike home. Michelle had an SUV, and after the game they put the bike in the back of the SUV, and he'd drive home.

Another good funny story is years ago, players used to make fun of Craig because he enjoyed mowing his lawn. What ball-player mows his own lawn? Pitcher Trevor Hoffman bid on a beautiful riding lawnmower at an auction. It was a Brewers logo lawnmower that he still has today. All the players signed it with a silver Sharpie. It was blue with a big Brewers logo, a big riding mower, and Trevor gave it to Craig as a gift. You'd see him on the front yard on his riding mower, mowing the lawn. He'd mow the neighbor's lawn. He'd be like, "Why not?" He still has it. It's a Brewers blue-and-silver riding lawnmower.

# DOCTOR, DOCTOR TELL ME THE NEWS HOW CRAIG COUNSELL PAID HIS DUES

## DR. JOE REGAN

*Michigan alumnus Joe Regan is the leader and the best as Medical Director for Ascension Columbia-St. Mary's Milwaukee Bariatric Center. Regan has been a close friend of Craig Counsell his entire life.*

My first memory of Craig is probably playing Strike Out at the grade school. He and I grew up in Whitefish Bay, but we went to different grade schools. There were two grade schools in our community. We had painted a strike zone on the side of his school building, and we typically had a hitter, a pitcher, and an outfielder. We played Strike Out with a tennis ball. I have very fond memories of those days.

I was lefthanded. Craig hit lefthanded. I used to always think he couldn't hit my curveball, but, of course, that's not true. He hit it like a rope. Back in the day before there were cellphones and computers, going to the playground and playing baseball was what it was all about. Hours were spent that way.

If someone had said then that in the future this field would be Craig Counsell Park, we would have laughed. Craig always had a love of baseball and an incredible knowledge of baseball. He was very well versed in major league players and statistics related to baseball.

We would have picnics for the baseball teams at the end of the season, and Craig's father used to always bring the Secret

Stadium Sauce from the old **COUNTY STADIUM**\* where the Brewers played. That was always such a special thing as a kid to have Secret Stadium Sauce at our Little League picnic, even though now I think that was just half ketchup and half barbecue sauce. That was the secret behind it. That was always my memory of his father at the Little League picnics.

I don't know that I ever thought at that point that Craig was going to evolve into what he is today and have such a successful career. You could start to tell that he was turning into a pretty special player. He always hit line drives. He was an incredible player at defense. Nothing could get by him. He had a great arm. In high school you started to think maybe this was going to turn into something.

In the game of Strike Out, you can play with just two players, which was the benefit. You could spend quite a bit of time just with two people playing baseball. You didn't need to gather a whole team. You didn't need to reserve a ball field. Yet you could spend hours playing baseball. That was how it started.

We learned over time that you had to use tennis balls, and not because that was good for your arm by any means, but there were windows in the area. There were homes in the area. You had to be a little careful. I think I'll leave it at that. We learned a **TENNIS**\* ball was the most appropriate ball to use in those circumstances.

> \*Milwaukee **COUNTY STADIUM** cost five million dollars and had 35,000 seats and 9,500 parking spaces when it opened in 1953. It took only 13 home games for the Braves to exceed the club's entire 1952 Boston attendance of 300,000. The Braves drew over 1,800,000 that first year.

> \*In what sport was Chris Evert the leading money winner in 1974? The answer: Horse racing. The owner, Carl Rosen, named his horses after **TENNIS** players. The horse named Chris Evert won $551,063 with five wins in eight starts.

When we'd break a window, there would be a little bit of scattering, not sure what to do sort of thing, and then some investigation. Losing a ball was a big deal back then. Today people come out with buckets of them, but we had a limited supply back then. It wasn't a complete scattering. There would be some investigation. I think that we often played at the same places. The neighbors got to know us. We may have helped with fixing a window periodically. The tennis ball and Strike Out was the way to go.

Craig and I were both Little League teammates and opponents. We played on some of the same teams together and also competed against each other at the Little League level.

A light blue shirt was the uniform, not the nice materials of today's uniforms, that's for sure, kind of a mesh weave. You usually had a sponsor on the back. Well-used uniforms. They were not a single-season uniform. You didn't get to keep it at the end of the year. It was passed down year to year.

My memory of Craig in those years was just consistency. He was always so levelheaded. He was consistent. He was focused even at that young an age. He's a reserved guy. He always has been, even in those days. That was where he was at.

I was always amazed, particularly in high school, of his knowledge of the statistics and the names of players, even players that were still moving up the chain. It was quite remarkable. It was amazing. I guess it was a signal that he was going to end up where he is today.

It was a big deal that Craig's dad worked for the Brewers. It was something we were all aware of. I certainly have a memory of meeting him and being impressed that he worked there. That was definitely a big deal.

I went to games with Craig. We would go to some games at the old ballpark. The core group of friends that he developed over time, there were games that we attended. That was definitely part of it.

Obviously getting to the playoffs or getting to the World Series in the early eighties was huge. I still have a piece of the outfield turf from when the Brewers won the pennant that year. Everybody was allowed on the field for some reason. I'm not sure why. We filed out, and I was able to pick up a little piece of turf. I have it stored in a bottle. I remember I touched Rollie Fingers on the shoulder. All the players were mingling with all the fans on the field. That was certainly a big memory for me as a kid. I was twelve when that occurred.

Since I was lefthanded, I pretended I was Teddy Higuera and other lefthanded players. They were your idols back then. There was a lot of pretending, that's for sure. I played first base. So I pretended to be Cecil Cooper. I'm not sure who Craig pretended to be. He was closer with the team and with the organization because of his father and had met the players and been in the clubhouse. Those were heady times.

We went to the same high school, Whitefish Bay High School. We played on several different teams. The rules were different back then. We played on the high school team, but there also were a couple of different teams that we played on, local teams. We played on different teams at the same time through the summer season. Basically it was not a spring sport back then. You could play on multiple teams. We would often play two or three games a day in the summer.

We lived and breathed baseball. That was all we did because we played so frequently. We would often play a game during the day for the high school, and then we would have a **DOUBLE-HEADER**\* at night on another field. That was how we spent our summer days and evenings. We played a lot of baseball.

The team became close. We were friends because of that. I like to say that at first base, I scooped all of Craig's bad throws from

\*In 1943 the Chicago White Sox played forty-four **DOUBLEHEADERS**. Last year they played one.

shortstop, but he rarely had bad throws, if ever. He really was an incredible fielder. He had great range, a great arm. He was really a leader on the team because of his understated consistency and manner. As has been seen in how he carried himself today, it was the same way. That was how he operated. He was a great hitter. He always hit line drives. Back then we had no outfield fence. It was just an open field. They used it for other sports, for soccer. It was an ice-skating rink in the winter. If you hit a line drive in the gap, it rolled forever. It was a guaranteed home run, especially by August when the ground was hard. The dry weather had hit. You hit one in the gap, and it rolled forever. Now that's a turf field with a fence and drainage. That's changed dramatically since those days.

I've seen the movie "The Sandlot" multiple times. Many of the scenes reminded me of my youth. The group getting together that was very close. I spent more time with those friends, those players than my family members. It was a great way to grow up. It was a ton of fun, and it kept you out of trouble. I have very fond memories of my teammates and the seasons that we were able to have.

Growing up in Whitefish Bay, we were somewhat protected. It's a relatively affluent community, very solid schools with a large majority heading on to the next level to go to college... with very competitive sports throughout the North Shore of Milwaukee. As a teenager and as a high schooler, it was just a very exciting place to grow up and to participate in sports.

Times have changed. It's different now. Kids are just focusing on a single sport. There are junior teams and select teams. You pay thousands of dollars to participate in those teams. Back then, it was a lot more of three and four sport athletes. You moved on to the next season. You really had a very different environment than that you have today. Not to say that all of that is bad, but the memories are just fabulous, the togetherness and the idea of teammates and the team. Every day was just about baseball and summertime. That's something that I still think about today.

Our high school baseball coach was Frank Klode. Coach and I sometimes work out at the same gym together. He's still involved in baseball locally. He thinks the world of Craig. He loves to talk about baseball.

Frank Klode was a great guy. He related to all the kids. He obviously gave a lot of his time to helping us grow as players and young men. He was one of the guys. I wouldn't say that he was a strict disciplinarian by any means. He was somebody that everybody really related to, listened to, and got along with. He created a nice environment for a baseball team. I still enjoy seeing him. He really hasn't changed a bit. He's just like he was back then.

We progressed a little bit into the tournaments, but we did not get to a level of championships. We would play several dozen games a summer, if you included the multiple teams that we played on. Again, it was nice back then when it was a summer sport because school was out. The focus was just on baseball. You weren't going to practice or to games after the school day. The weather in Milwaukee can be rough in the springtime in terms of cold and wet. So having it be focused on just a summer season, it was a great time for baseball.

Craig and I worked hard in school and got good grades. Craig went on to Notre Dame, which is a challenging school to get into. I went to Michigan. He and I shared a little bit of a competitive edge there with that as we moved into the college years. We were really a close group of friends, a core group. Craig was a private guy. He kept things close, but he also had a really strong group of friends. That even carried on until today. It's hard to stay in touch with people, as people move to different locations and get into different things and have kids and whatnot. Craig, even as busy as he is, has still kept close with his core group of friends from high school.

I drive by Craig Counsell Park with my six kids. Craig Counsell Park! Imagine that! My three boys are older now and have moved beyond Little League. The park is very close to my house so I do drive by it quite frequently. It's changed a lot. It's quite a busy place during the summer.

When we were in college, Craig and I traded some football games when I was at Michigan. His schedule was busier than mine obviously with sports. He had better seats than I did, that's for sure. The Michigan-Notre Dame rivalry is strong. It was then. It is now. It's fun to participate in that. I've even gone to a game more recently where some of our kids came with us, and his roommate from Notre Dame as well, who's a surgeon in Milwaukee. His name is Chris Fox. I think he was Craig's roommate at Notre Dame for all four years.

Craig dated Michelle in high school. She was a year younger. She was fabulous. I've always loved her. She's just a great individual. I see her more than I see Craig now because he's gone so much. She's always been great. I think that's a tough road when some-body's going up through the farm system and trying to have a relationship when you're traveling around. Those are difficult times. They're difficult to keep relationships together. They've done great. Their kids are great. They're just a fabulous family.

In the later years of Notre Dame, I thought Craig would get drafted and play. There was that possibility. It's a long road in baseball. There are very few that jump right into it, but he clearly had significant talents. Also I think he had the work ethic to make it happen. He's a smart guy. He graduated from college, which is really unusual in the baseball ranks. He had the smarts. He had the discipline, and he was willing to put in the work. Those things were what made you feel that it was going to be possible.

When Craig first made the major leagues, it was so exciting, the hometown kid. It's such a long road to get there and to finally make it, that's fabulous. It's so exciting, the local con-nection. It's good stuff.

When I first heard Craig was going to play with the Brewers, I thought he was coming home to play. What more could you want? Again, those memories we talked about from growing up come full circle when you can be part of that at a later generation. It was very exciting. What he did in that play-off run for Arizona, that was just really exciting. Those were some great games, fun to watch on TV, very exciting. That's good stuff.

What he did in the '97 World Series was amazing.

I knew that Craig would do something more in baseball after he retired as a player. It was clear that general manager, manager, that something was going to happen. That just goes to his talent and his intelligence regarding baseball. You knew that that was going to continue. He had too much to give to not continue to contribute. I wasn't exactly sure what piece it was going to be or what position it was going to be, but there was a strong feeling that there was going to be another step up.

Craig's done a really nice job as the manager of the Brewers. A lot of these players are young guys from all over the world. Some of them don't speak great English. There are a lot of egos involved. We're a small market team with a low payroll compared to some of the big ones. What he's been able to do with that, how he's been able to manage that, the number of injuries every year has been unbelievable, particularly in the pitching area. Baseball has changed a lot with all of the shifts and the starting pitching just going a few innings, but he's adapted to that and really done amazing things. The pennant runs in 2018 and 2019 were really exciting for the city. It was electric inside that stadium for those games!. It's been a long time since we had seen that. When you can introduce that energy and that excitement for baseball, that means you're doing something right. He's done a great job! He's done an amazing job every year of dealing with the adversity of the season.

I don't think the fans in Milwaukee expect too much given the current talent level of the team. Milwaukee is a little more understanding. In Boston, they have a really short memory. Craig is a Milwaukee guy. The organization has shown at all levels that they're willing to take some risks and make moves, some for the short term, some for the long term, to try and bring the postseason to Milwaukee. That's really exciting. It's not always about LA and New York and Boston. It's a lot of fun to insert Milwaukee into those situations. The Cubs spend an awful lot of money. It's a lot of fun to compete with them, given the short distance between the two places.

Craig's boys are solid players. Craig's an athletic guy, and his wife is athletic, and his kids are the same way. They're good athletes. Soccer teams wanted them to play because they were good athletes. They could do whatever sport they want, but they were drawn to baseball for obvious reasons. They're good players. They've had good success to this point. They have a batting cage in their backyard, and it gets all kinds of use, even in the early mornings and late evenings. I think they're carrying on the tradition there.

It's been a fun ride, knowing Craig. He's been fun to associate with on the playground, in Little League, in high school, and now into adulthood and raising kids and leading a major league ball team. It's fun to see him on TV every night. It's fun to read about him in the paper. It's amazing what he's been able to achieve. The end is not here yet. There's still a lot more to be written.

# PUT ME IN COACH

FRANK KLODE

*Frank Klode, 80, was Craig Counsell's coach at Whitefish Bay High School. Klode was an outstanding Milwaukee high school athlete and played college ball at Florida Southern. He was a very successful sales rep in the furniture business in the Upper Midwest.*

I took over as head coach in 1987 when Craig was then a junior. I moved him to shortstop because he had a better arm. We could tell in drills that he just had a better arm. He didn't make a mistake. He moved well. Because of the league we were in, players were not restricted by the state as to how many games a kid could play. Craig was playing sixty games in the summer. for three teams. He was playing all the time. He just got to the point where he was so much better than anybody else as a fielder. He knew what was going on, and he could hit. He just plain flat could hit. He didn't hit for power though. There were other guys on the team that were bigger and stronger but he was just—he just didn't make a mistake.

He laughed at me one time. We were down one run with a runner on third.We used to squeeze a lot, and I didn't let him squeeze. He made an out, and he came up to me later and said, "Coach, I thought you were going to give me the sign to squeeze." I said, "Craig, the way you hit, I'm not going to squeeze you." That's how much confidence we had in him. He was that good. And as a senior, he was that much better. He was a Captain both years, all conference, the whole nine yards. Then, as you know, he went on to Notre Dame, and played for his current bench coach.

Craig outworked everybody. Sometimes in February, he'd be out catching fly balls over at the Jewish Center. He and a buddy of his would be working out. He just outworked everybody. He was well schooled coming in, and he was extremely intelligent.

He had it all. He was not one of these guys who boasted. He was very reserved and very quiet. Michelle, his wife, has been very good for him, too. She's outgoing. She runs marathons. They've got four dogs, four kids. She's very protective of him in his job and managing the kids and everything else.

She didn't come around to the high school games at that time. It was typical high school. They dated and broke up a couple of times. They were going together, but I think they were on again, off again. You know how that is in high school.

I was not sure if Craig would be good enough to play at Notre Dame. I knew how good the Notre Dame program was, how strong it is. We're not talking Division 3 here. We're talking Division 1, but he had no problem.

When I was down at Notre Dame, John took me through their indoor baseball practice facility. That is quite a facility, the whole thing. That's years ago. I'm sure it's even better now. They've got it all.

I was amazed. I got a chance to walk around the Notre Dame campus. The campus itself is not as big as I thought it might be. It was gorgeous. It was phenomenal. What a great place to go to school.

The fundamentals. It's not the same game. Everybody swings for the fences, but it is what it is.

Baseball unfortunately is entertainment. The average fan, the average young person goes to the game to drink beer and watch home runs and look at their cellphone. They could be watching water polo. They don't have any conception of what in the heck is going on. It's crazy.

I would say if you look at Craig intelligence wise, a lot of that has to do with John. His dad is the main influence of his success. When we got him, he was almost a finished product for a high school kid.

We were all excited when we found out Craig was going to get drafted and play pro ball. I was still coaching at Whitefish Bay. Everybody was happy for him and excited. It was a great thing. We had never, ever really had anybody from Whitefish Bay, to my knowledge, get drafted. Usually most kids, once they get out of high school, that's about it. A few go on and play at a small college. The majority of them don't go on, or don't go on to a major university to play and/or get drafted. We have had two drafted since Craig.

The first big league game I ever saw with Craig playing, I took myself and a couple of coaches and the AD down to Wrigley. Craig got us tickets. I'd never been one to ever abuse that. We drove down to Wrigley and one of the guys was yelling out the window, "The **BEARS**\* suck!" I was like, "Would you keep your mouth shut? We're going to get killed. Do you want my car to be rocked? They're very passionate down here. Be quiet."

We parked the car in this guy's garage for fifty bucks. The guy put a cardboard box holder between the two cars. When the guy opened the door, it didn't hit the other car, which I thought was interesting. We parked about three blocks away.

We went to Murphy's, the bar across the street with all of Craig's high school buddies. They all came up and said, "Hey, Coach, how are you doing?" You know how kids change? They get older; they get heavier, whatever. I didn't recognize half of them. It was amazing. Craig had about ten of his friends there and he was playing.

*The Chicago **BEARS** wear blue and orange because those are the colors that team founder George Halas wore when he played for the University of Illinois.

It was great when the **MILWAUKEE BRAVES**\* came to town. That was phenomenal. Milwaukee was at that time pretty much a very small market. The Milwaukee Brewers were a AAA club at Orchard Field. Then the Braves came from Boston. It was fantastic. When they won the World Series, the town went nuts. Milwaukee led or was up at the top for attendance for four years—for a Milwaukee size of a town, the attendance was phenomenal.

It was nice when Craig came back to play for the Brewers. It was nice for him to come home. What worries me is that managing is not always a long-term job. It's not always the manager's fault. All you've got to do is look at **MIKE MATHENY**\* with St. Louis. For whatever reason, they pushed him out. If you last seven, eight years, nine years, you're really pushing the button. They don't normally last quite that long. I'm not saying that that's going to happen to Craig, but that's not a job you're going to have for twenty years.

I could see him moving into the front office. The owner really likes him. I don't see that being a problem. At some point, and it's not only the manager's fault, you can't fire the players. You can only fire one guy, and usually it's the manager. You always wonder in that scenario—there aren't too many Bruce Bochys who are going to last twenty years, if you know what I mean.

No matter what you do in sports, there's always going to be somebody who doesn't like you. I had a guy the other day at my gym say, "Why the heck didn't Counsell do this?" I said, "Basically, analyze what the situation was." I tried to explain it

---

\*Besides being the only Brave to play for the team in Boston and Milwaukee and Atlanta, Eddie Mathews also played minor league baseball for the **BRAVES** in both Milwaukee and Atlanta.

---

\***MIKE MATHENY**'s son was a popular player for the Madison Mallards in the Northwoods College League.

to him, but he didn't want to listen to me. The manager can't play for the players. Craig even told me when he was playing, "You know, Frank, the manager makes up the lineup. He expects once he makes the lineup up, the players have to perform, but they can't always perform for whatever reason."

The Brewers don't have any prospects down on the farm. They traded away their whole farm system. Every other time, you've got a crap shoot in the bullpen. You really do. Your starting pitching, at best they're young. They have great potential, but they're average at best. Craig is doing it with baling wire and toothpicks.

Channel 6 came out and talked to me when Craig was named manager of the Brewers. I said, "He's been successful at everything he's ever done. Why won't he be successful as a manager? He's been successful as a student, as a college ballplayer, as a minor leaguer, as a big league ballplayer. He was in the front office. Why won't he be successful as a manager? He's got the right demeanor. He's played the game. He's got two World Series rings. What do you want?"

The girl who was interviewing me didn't know beans about baseball. She was very nice. We did the interview out on my front yard. I said, "Have you ever been to a game?" She said, "No, I've never been to a Brewers game." I said, "Who do you normally interview? Gardeners?" We had a nice time. Anyway, I said, "You're not taking some guy off the street here. Craig's been doing this his whole life. He's going to be successful, and he's extremely intelligent. He's very quiet. He doesn't say a lot."

I'll give you one quick story about Craig. One day I had some old high school pictures. I drove over to the house and just stopped. I figured he was probably home. He came out. I said, "Come here. I want to give you some pictures." He looked at them. He knew every single kid that he played with and where they were working, right down the line. "This guy's over at the airport. He's a guard now. This guy's doing…"—What a memory!

He has a very good memory. That's very important in baseball, what you feel they can do, their positives and negatives, what these guys are capable of.

Craig's got it all, but he's very understated. He's not one to boast. You can sit there with him. He's very quiet. He doesn't talk a lot. Michelle is much more outgoing than he is, nothing wrong with that. I'm somewhat the same way. If I go to a ballgame, I'm relatively quiet. I've got friends of mine that have played that I'll go to a game with. There are friends of mine that I will not go to a game with because all they do is yip, and I hate that. I don't mean to be nasty to people, but I don't want to go with somebody who just talks all the time.

Craig does well against the Cardinals, as a player and as a manager. I don't know much about the current manager of the Cardinals who took over from Matheny. He's been managing in the minors and then moved into the manager's job. He's doing a pretty good job, but certainly not good enough to beat Craig out for Manager of the Year award in 2019. Craig should have won that award in '18 and '19!

*Head Coach Frank Klode, Craig, and Assistant Coach after a Whitefish Bay High School game, 1988.*

What I respect about Craig is he doesn't boast about himself. Some people in the limelight start to feel a little full of themselves.

When I was still coaching, I asked Craig a couple times if he would come over and talk to my high school team. It was interesting. He would not talk about himself. He would answer questions. He would say, "Frank, I'm not going to talk about myself. You can have the kids ask me questions," or I'd ask a question to get him going. I brought him over to the Dominican High School because I was there for two years. It was interesting. I asked a question. The kids were sitting there in awe with their mouths open. Here's a major league ballplayer walking down our high school hallways. Once I asked, "Who were your best friends playing college ball?" I knew what the answer would be. You know what the answer was. He said, "My best friends were on the ball club. That's all we did. I went to class. I played baseball. I went to class. I played baseball. My best friends were on the baseball team." He would not talk about himself.

He'd probably be embarrassed about a book about himself. He's not one for a lot of fluff. He's not one of these guys that is at all full of himself. He's very understated. He doesn't stand out. He doesn't wear designer clothes. He doesn't drive a Bentley. He doesn't wear an expensive watch on the field. He's just a normal guy. He walks up with his family to watch a Whitefish Bay football game because it's six blocks away. They watch the game, and they come home. He's got a hitting cage in his backyard. I guess he's the hit of the family. [laughs] All the kids come over.

He's done a lot for people. He's done a lot for his mom. I know he's helped her set up some stuff for her financially, John told me. He's done a lot of stuff on the side that you just don't know about. He helped put money in the field there. He donated some money up at the Little League field. Quiet stuff. You just don't hear about it. He just doesn't talk about it. Never "I gave

$20,000 to the baseball team to put that field together." It's a gorgeous field. It's really first class for a high school program.

Craig was never a really high average, but he was able to be very difficult to pitch against under pressure when you had to win a game or get a guy over. That's how you judge an athlete, how you play under pressure, no matter what you're doing. He's always graded out extremely well. He once told me, "Frank, in an at-bat, you only get one pitch maybe that you can hit." Larry Hisle works out at WAC. He played for the Brewers. He said the same thing. He said, "You may only get one pitch that you think you can hit, and you'd better be ready for it. You hope the pitcher makes a mistake, but he may not. You get one pitch maybe in an at-bat. You may only get one pitch in a whole series, but you'd better make sure you hit it. Craig did that, and that pretty much separates him from a lot of these guys that are just flailing away.

I didn't retire until I was seventy-seven, almost seventy-eight. I've been retired for about two years. You get on the roads today. It's like the Indianapolis 500. It's crazy, but it is what it is.

If you know any of the Counsell family, you know how solid they are. The Counsells are the best.

Chapter Four

# SHAKE DOWN THE THUNDER

## Under the Golden Dome

# MURPHY'S LAW

PAT MURPHY

*Upstate New York native Pat Murphy was the youngest college head baseball coach to win 500 games. He became the head coach at Notre Dame in 1987, where an early recruit was Craig Counsell. After seven years at Notre Dame, he became head coach at Arizona State and led the Sun Devils to three College World Series titles in fifteen years. He left Arizona State in a controversial fashion amid allegations of recruiting violations, all of which he was proven innocent of upon investigation. He then joined the San Diego Padres as a minor league and then interim major league manager and in late 2015, he became the bench coach and right-hand man to Craig Counsell at the Milwaukee Brewers.*

It was late August 1987, and Notre Dame classes had started. I was super, super busy. I didn't get a chance to recruit for that first year. I was just trying to get my feet on the ground and understand how we could turn their program into something special. The power of Notre Dame is incredible. The money for assistance and the money for recruiting wasn't as powerful.

Roger Valdiserri, the sports information director, walked in my office and said, "Hey, Murph, a former Notre Dame player and coach, John Counsell, has a son in Milwaukee. He's a fine baseball player. They're part of a workout that will be at Milwaukee County Stadium this weekend. If you want to go up and take a look, I'm friends with Sal Bando. You can have dinner with Sal. You can meet John and his wife Jan and watch their son Craig work out."

I said okay. I got in the car that day, a nice drive to Milwaukee, not knowing fast forward thirty plus years what was to be. I got to the ballpark early. There are kids working out. I saw which one Craig was and which one Sal Bando, Jr. was. Sal Bando, Jr. was more physically developed, a bigger, stronger kid. Craig was this fair-skinned, 145-pound infielder. I watched him take balls.

Craig was impressive in that he was very steady. I watch Craig's son, Brady, these days. Brady is taller than Craig was, but just as slightly built. I watch him take balls, and it reminds me of his Dad's workout at County Stadium.

Craig played sixteen years in the big leagues with that swing. It didn't change all that much. In 1987, he was a weak kid who was just starting his senior year in high school, but he had a knack for putting the bat on the ball. At that point, we probably had $6,000 total in scholarship money left to give out to as many kids as I could get for the 1988 year. You're talking about a nominal scholarship in order to get not one but six kids to come to school. I wanted to give $1,000 here and there, $500, $1,000, $750. We were trying to get six kids. As it turns out, it was a pretty good deal. Those six kids won a lot of games the next four years of my life.

I met with John and Jan in Milwaukee that day long ago. I knew what kind of people they were. I'm like, "This fits." Craig was a great student. He had a baseball aptitude, from a Notre Dame family, and had a burning desire to play at the highest level. He knew he had to improve. It was a great fit. It was easy, but I don't always like easy recruitments. It was the right fit.

If I didn't go that day, I'm not sure if Craig would have ended up at Notre Dame. Baseball was important to him. He wanted to go to Notre Dame, but he certainly wanted me to see him play and be a kid that was wanted by the university. He understood that with the type of skill level he had, he wasn't going to jump out at you like a big time prospect. You had to understand how important aptitude, the types of players I wanted at the base of the program. He fit the description. It might not have happened if a different team had come over and looked at him or if we were at a different spot. He came in and played as a freshman at Notre Dame.

When I saw him, I wasn't disappointed in his size or any level of his play. I was excited that he wasn't that big, and he wasn't as physical as he came to be because then you might lose him in the draft, or you might lose him to Wisconsin in Madison. He was a Midwestern kid that had Notre Dame bloodlines. I didn't say more than a hello to him that day.

The things that I emphasize in baseball, the aptitude, understand base running, understand playing defense, throwing the ball accurately, knowing how to control the bat, strike the ball, understanding strike ball discernment, understanding how to conduct an at-bat, Craig just had a knack for it from Day One. When you looked around the diamond, we had football players on the team. We had some big, strong kids, but they didn't really know how to play baseball. The type of competition we were going to play early in the season were college baseball powerhouses: Miami and Texas and LSU. You have to be equipped with guys that understand when the game is going to deal you a walk, you take a walk. When the game is going to deal you a fast ball down the middle, you're ready to hit it. He was both of those things. He just had a nice feel for the game. He helped us win as a freshman.

I said Craig's senior year that he would be the next big leaguer from Notre Dame. I was popping off a little bit, like I had a tendency of doing. I was just pretty certain he was a pretty special player. His junior and senior years were really magnificent as shortstop. He made every play. He hit the best pitching, and he hit consistently, and he hit with power.

The other kids that came with Craig that freshman year are all successful: a head coach at Toledo, a gynecologist, an engineer in Houston, Texas.

Notre Dame can win at any sport. There's something different about the kids they attract. You either get it, or you don't. If you get it, you use it. It empowers you to do things above and beyond whatever you could think you could do because you have the power of Notre Dame, the power of your team, the power of what that place represents. There's no question.

His sophomore year, he moved from left field into the infield. It was a tougher transition because he hadn't really fully matured yet, physically. He played third base, some at shortstop. By the end of his sophomore year, he was showing signs of "This kid's a really good player." By his junior year, he was an established shortstop. Without many scholarships, Notre Dame was in the NCAA Sweet 16 three straight years. He was a huge part of it.

By his senior year, it was no doubt this kid was a real baseball player, not a kid that was going to be drafted high, but a kid that just understands how to play. He showed power. Now, it was aluminum bats. They're a little lively. He didn't lose his command of the strike zone. He wasn't a swing-and-miss guy. He was an ultimate team guy. He could understand what the game called for.

He was never vocal, but he was a leader nonetheless by the way he went about his business. When practice was over, you knew Counsell was going to hang around and take ground balls, and he was going to hit extra on his own. He didn't care who was looking. This guy defines work when no one is looking. He still had that same baseball character when no one was looking. He adjusted at every level.

I was lucky enough to continue a conversation with him for the next twenty years after he graduated. We just talked baseball. It's a terrific baseball story.

When Craig showed up at Notre Dame, he did not have that odd batting stance. He had a very conventional stance, much like his Dad. His Dad used to come back for the alumni games and was the best hitter in the ballpark, including our team, until he was well over fifty-five years old.

I saw John and Jan when Craig was a player here. They came down from Milwaukee all the time. I loved talking baseball with John. I loved Jan's perspective. Craig was a great mixture of both of them. He didn't talk much. He didn't like his coach—me. I wasn't his favorite guy. I was very tough on him. Sometimes I now think I was inappropriate. Sophomore year, he's trying to become an infielder. I'm this brash coach who thinks Craig should just stay in the outfield and could never see him being a major league infielder. He worked and worked and worked. He's at third base. We're on old Jake Kline Field. To say the least, it wasn't manicured. I hit a ground ball. It took a bad hop and hit him right in the nose. His nose, which is bigger than the average sized nose, was then literally closer to his ear than it was his mouth. It was displaced, and blood was just spewing out. He went to the hospital with the trainer. He was back an hour and fifteen minutes later, and he wanted to take more ground balls, no face mask, no nothing, just "Hit me some more ground balls." Most kids not only wouldn't come back to practice but wouldn't be eager to jump back in there right away, but he was, and he did. He took some more ground balls.

He literally played his senior year for about a week and a half with two sprained ankles wrapped. His ankles were as big as his oversized calves. It was the weirdest looking thing. He could barely run, but he still played effectively. At the University of Detroit, he hit lead-off home runs in both games of a doubleheader. He could hardly make it around the bases. The kid played in great pain.

I realized he could play pro ball in his junior year. Most kids that are playing at that level will play for the LSUs or the Miamis or the Texases. To play in the big leagues, I wasn't quite sure.

After the Miami Regional, famed Miami coach Ron Frazier came to me and said, "That shortstop of yours, he's the real deal." I'm like, "Wow, everybody notices it."

Craig didn't change his stance at Notre Dame. He changed it in pro ball. The way he tells it, he was just trying to find a way to get going, trying to find something different that could keep his hands back and get him through the baseball. It wasn't the swing, it was more the set-up.

When I first saw that stance, I was like, "Why?" I thought about an old Notre Dame player, **CARL YASTRZEMSKI**\*. "Maybe he's trying to be like Yaz and drive the ball more." I'm not sure. I knew there had to be something to it.

As a coach, one of the biggest thrills you have is when one of your players makes it to the major leagues. You're so darn proud. There's nothing better in coaching than seeing one of the guys where you were a part of their career in some way, go on and be so successful. It's really cool.

When Craig was in pro ball, we stayed in constant contact. We got closer as he became older. When he got with the Diamondbacks in '99 and I was coaching Arizona State, we got real close. He was dating Michelle at the time, later his wife. We'd pretty much get together once a week or once every couple of weeks and have dinner.

I don't know if he ever said, "Now I understand why you were so tough on me," it was just understood. We had so many good conversations. I always tell him I was maybe inappropriately tough on him. I was really bothered that a guy that played like

---

\*The bat that Jack Torrance (Jack Nicholson) wielded in *The Shining* was a **CARL YASTRZEMSKI** model Louisville Slugger.

him wouldn't speak up more and wouldn't talk more on the field. I used to make him do it. I used to force him to do it. Sometimes I think I was a little off base being so tough on him, but he made the most of it.

Craig tried to hire me as a coach when he first got the Brewers job, but the Padres actually named me the interim manager for ninety games. The minute my season was over with the Padres, he called me that day and said, "If you're not going to stay with the Padres, I've got a job for you here. I'd like you to talk to my general manager." It was actually the first day after the season was over.

When I went to the Brewers, that was a story, the mentor thing. Craig did so much in baseball beyond my time with him at Notre Dame. It was more that Craig thought I could bring something totally different to the Brewers. I'm a totally different personality than him. We think alike about how to win games.

In the dugout, we disagree all the time. That's why I'm there. It's not like we don't understand each other. We talk all the time. I have a feel for what he wants and likes and what he believes in. We have a good system.

I don't think anybody would ever categorize me as a "yes" man. I've learned a lot from Craig. I've learned a ton. He has different ways of doing things, things I wouldn't do. Over time, I've realized how effective he really is. I may not agree with how he does it, but I've learned, "You know what? I would have blown that up. It would have created more problems, and he handled it really good." I've learned a ton. He'd never managed before. It's pretty amazing. It's wonderful.

# OF MIKES AND MEN

MIKE ROONEY

*When he's not doing analysis on college base-ball for ESPN, Mike Rooney is the Director of Sales Training and Education for a huge pharmaceutical company in Arizona. Rooney was a four-year teammate of Craig Counsell at Notre Dame.*

I only do college baseball with ESPN so I won't work until late March when they transition from basketball to baseball. During the College World Series in the last few years I've been the dugout reporter for the day games.

Couns and I were in the same class at Notre Dame and our fathers had both gone there. I was a pure walk-on. Back then we had hardly any scholarships. I had always heard the story that Couns was on $500/year scholarship. We show up and I went through the walk-on trial. Coach Pat Murphy doesn't have any idea who I am. I was so convinced I wasn't going to make the baseball team that I actually was going to inter-hall football practice at night, because if I got cut from baseball I still wanted to play in the interhall football team with Keenan Hall.

Murph was only 28 when we got there. Our freshman year was Murph's second year. There wasn't a lot of recruiting that had been able to take place. There were 28 of us from the class of '92 that were a part of the program at one point and we would start to play inter-squad games. The walk-ons would be on one side of the field and the recruits would be on the other end. It was very easy to tell who Couns was. He was a thin guy; I bet he was 150 pounds as a freshman. A left-handed hitter, you could sense his baseball instincts were really strong. He played left field for us as a freshman. Couns was very quiet but he was always in the right place at the right time on the baseball field; which is how his career played out as well. We used wood bats. My wood bat had K-Mart written on it and Craig's wood bat had Robin Yount, or Paul Molitor on it. His Dad was working for the Brewers so he was able to scrounge up some of those bats. That's how we got started. It was an awesome wild time. Murph was super young and energetic, just building the program. He was going a million miles an hour. I didn't know whether I was kicking off or receiving.

He was one of the freshmen that played right away. He was our starting left fielder, your vintage two-hole, nine-hole hitter. He didn't have a lot of physical strength yet, but one thing that was very clear early, was that he had planted the seeds that, "Hey, I am going to play baseball at the highest level." A lot of the rest of us, honestly, I know I am speaking for myself, I was there to go to school; I was just hanging on for dear life in baseball. Couns played as a freshman. It was a really neat year. It was a team that made an NCAA tournament. We had to go through the loser's bracket of the MAC tournament.

Murph asked us all to stay that next summer in South Bend and weight lift and workout.

After sophomore year, Couns went to the Jayhawk League and we stayed in South Bend. After junior year he played in Alaska. We lifted weights and took summer classes. It was good in that regard. When Couns went to Kansas it was a little bit of a wow factor. College summer leagues were not a big deal for me back then so it was a big deal for him to go play in a league of that caliber.

The Central Illinois Collegiate League was still around but not great. The Cape Cod League was a really big deal, the Jayhawk League and Alaska were each a big deal. When he came back after that fall, he was a different dude. He was more confident, stronger. He really dedicated himself to the weight room; to strength and conditioning. That was the year Couns broke his nose taking grounders at Jake Kline Field.

One day, Murph just got sick of Counsell being so quiet. We were taking fungos and Murph said to Couns, "Every ground ball that's hit to you, you need to call that ground ball." Couns was mortified, I'm sure. But every ground ball during fungos, "Mine, mine, mine", he's screaming. At the end of that drill Murph hits a laser of a ground ball at him. Jake Kline Field was not exactly a major league surface. It kicks up and hits Couns in the nose and breaks his nose. I don't think breaking his nose was what Murph had in mind when he was trying to teach this lesson.

Craig did not take long to recover from the injury. Honestly, I think he might even have finished the practice. One thing about Notre Dame was toughness, there was such a premium on that. Murph breathed toughness into us. There was a mentality in the program where someone is going to have to pull you off the field because it was very competitive. It was a neat thing in that you were going to see what you have inside yourself. It wasn't easy.

Back then we were on the road a lot. Almost every year we spent the first seven weekends on the road. It was a neat time. Murph was a very aggressive scheduler. We played on the road in Miami, on the road in Texas. We would go anywhere and play anybody and won a lot of those games. It was neat in that the road trips were fairly Spartan back then. We stayed with a lot of host families when we traveled. That was a unique Notre Dame experience. Couns was a quiet dude. He really got into music and he'd have his headphones on. It was amazing to see his level of focus at that age. I'm sure there was nobody telling him, "Hey, you're going to play sixteen years in the big leagues." As he got older, junior and senior years in the program, you started to see Couns' personality more and more. He really does have an awesome sense of humor with a very dry, sarcastic sense of humor that he seldom used back then.

By the time we were seniors he was really fun and you could count on him for a good laugh.

Couns never was kicked out of a game, nothing as egregious as that. Junior year he really started to emerge. He was our shortstop and our three-hole hitter. He was not drafted after junior year and that surprised all of us. We were fairly naïve to all those things; we had a really neat year our senior year. We went to the Miami regional literally one game away from Omaha. We were playing University of Miami, in the last game of the regional—winner goes to the College World Series. We had already beaten them once and South Carolina had beaten us. Couns was just a monster at that point. If we need a home run, he had sixteen home runs; he could do it. He had turned himself into an outrageously good shortstop. I don't know who the most outstanding player in that regional was, but it certainly should have been Couns. There were five of us that had stayed all four years. We had been through so much together. We had gotten all the way to that final game of the regional and we had a ton of fun all the way.

I will never forget, I was always a utility player, but my last two years I was primarily an outfielder. We were playing Michigan during finals and you know Notre Dame. They are not rescheduling a finals test for a baseball game. So I am going to have to start at second base, because our second baseman is taking his final. I hadn't played second base in two years.

During the anthem and warm-ups, Couns is sitting next to me. I turned to him and said, "I have no idea. I haven't played second base in years." Couns looks at me like, "Shut your mouth, what are you talking about?" I'm like, "Alright, I'm just kidding", but I am not totally kidding! I am sort of kidding. He basically carried me through that game. It was just another one of those things, where his baseball instincts—he never had to think about baseball, it was so hard-wired in his brain. He was so bright, so instinctive of a player. It always amazed me to watch him play.

Of course we followed him in the minor leagues, but at that age we didn't have any perspective of what a big leaguer looks like. Following his big league career has been the most incredible experience. You feel like it's a family member. You play four years of college baseball with somebody; you spend a lot of time with them. You are so proud to see who he was as a player and what he did—the two World Series. I lived in Arizona during that 2001 amazing World Series. As thrilling as that was, watching Couns in his press conferences with the Brewers—just so good! Not giving canned responses, actually saying real things without missing that delicate line between saying something meaningful that's worth hearing but not painting yourself into a corner. I just thought he was tremendous!

Sixteen years in the big leagues? If somebody had told me that, I think I would have said, "I wouldn't put anything past him, but that would be an amazing accomplishment!" Nobody would have accused any of us of being world-class athletes.

When he became the player he became, I thought that managing would be a possibility. He is so good with people, so bright and so conscientious. That is a heck of a commitment. The Brewers are like family to him. I go to a lot of college games in my role. I was at a college game where Kyle Schwarber was playing for University of Indiana. Schwarber was going to be a first round pick. I don't even notice when someone sits down next to me. I turn, and there sits Couns right there. He had taken an Assistant General Manager job with the Brewers.

I had a Wichita State game later in that year and one of the Gillespie brothers is playing in that game. The next day Couns gives me a call and says, "Hey, I heard that broadcast." First he starts giving me a hard time about my hyperbole, then he says, "But what do you think of the kid? How would you compare him to Mike Conforto and Schwarber?" He has always been a very focused, very conscientious person. I guess that's one of the reasons why none of us are surprised at the success he has had.

In college Craig's batting stance was normal. I would say his hands were high, maybe higher than most. But not anything like what he had with the D-backs. In today's world we don't really teach kids to progress as hitters, we have gotten in the mode of going—break a launch angle and drop off.

Couns was the classic hitter, when we were freshmen he couldn't have hit a ball out of the yard if he hit it twice. But he got hits. He just wore out the five-six-hole. And then the next year some of those balls are drilled in the gap. And in the last two years you couldn't give him the wrong pitch on the wrong count; he'd run one out of the yard on you. He had great hitting skills when we were freshmen and he just grew into a better, a stronger athlete. Our senior year he was a monster. There wasn't a day where he wasn't the best player on our team senior year.

We didn't have great perspective on the **DRAFT**\* in college. Our freshman year there was a kid named Dan Pelletier who was a third round pick, but he was a freak athlete. Pelletier was 6'2", 225 pounds, a left-handed hitter, ran like a deer and looked like an NFL player. In our mind, if that's what a third round pick looks like, Couns is a better player but he doesn't look like that. It was hard to know. After his junior year when he wasn't drafted I remember thinking, "with a bazillion rounds, if Couns isn't good enough to get drafted, I don't know what a draft pick looks like."

I thought his stance was the perfect embodiment of who Couns is. He is very bright and reserved but he is also aware enough that, hey sometimes, maybe this comes from our time with Murph. Sometimes you just have to do some things that are a little out of the box if you want to get to the place that you want to get to. If there is one thing that I would say about Craig

*During WWII, the NFL did not refer to the teams' selections of college players as a **DRAFT**. It was termed the "preferred negotiation list."

is he just has a great ability to be aware of what is needed to be successful.

Craig is not one of those people that would say, "Hey, I'm quiet, so that's just who I am." He's one of those people who have enough awareness to say, "Well, quiet is what is comfortable for me, but if I have to be noisier to get where I want to go, then I guess I have to be a little bit noisier." When I have talked with him about the stance, which I am sure everyone has, I remember, it's like a lot of major league hitters. It's not where your hands start; it's a mental key. It's something that's triggering the right mindset before you hit. It's definitely not to get attention, he's someone who loathes attention, but he took on something like that because getting the job done was more important than being comfortable.

It was hard for me to know if it would work for him. He had been released at that time; he had that run with the Marlins and he ended up with the Dodgers and then was released. I didn't think of it in those terms. I remember thinking of it as "Boy, being a major league player is a fragile deal. This is tough." I went to see Couns play at a AAA game one time. I remember thinking the problem for Couns his abilities don't really work on a losing team. His skill set is really only applicable for teams that are in "win now" mode. More than anything else you worried for him that if he doesn't end up with a team that values winning now, it's probably not going to work out for him. Sure enough, he ended up in the right spots and it did work out.

If you are going to Notre Dame you have super academic aptitude. But I always looked at Couns as a baseball player, not as a Notre Dame student. We both were accounting majors at Notre Dame. He really is an extremely bright person. When Craig got the job as manager of the Brewers, he eventually hires Murph as his bench coach. Murph is like family to me. He has done so much in my life for my wife and me. I owe a lot to Murph.

But Murph's a lightning rod; he's a controversial guy. Even though they shared incredible friendships and a million shared experiences, he and Couns are extremely different personalities. I asked Couns, "Why Murph as your bench coach?" Murph had some major league managing experience. Of course, Murph had been at AAA, but he had not been a big league bench coach yet. Couns' answer was just beautiful. He basically said, "Pat Murphy and I have been in a baseball conversation that has lasted twenty-five years." The first part of that just struck me—that is so Couns; to nail it like that! It's so true. We've all been talking about baseball with Murph for decades.

Murph is not one of those guys that have been teaching hitting the same way for thirty-five years. Murph has always been someone to challenge his own thought processes; challenging us to look at things differently. The other thing that Couns said about hiring Murph as his bench coach was, "I know what my thoughts are. I don't need nine more people with the same thinking that I have. I need something different. I need people who will challenge and test the way I think." It's really cliché to say that. Every leader says that, "I don't want 'yes' men." And then guess what do they do? They hire a bunch of "yes" men. Talk about a courageous move. It's your first time getting to be a major league manager, and you make an out of the box hire because you want to be challenged; you want some uncomfortable conversations. I thought that showed tremendous confidence and tremendous vision. Sure enough, they have had a phenomenal run there in Milwaukee.

We both were accounting majors. Couns was over a 3.0. We shared a lot of classes together; I don't know how many I attended. Between baseball and social life I was fairly busy in college. My goal at Notre Dame was to graduate in eight semesters and I accomplished that. Couns was a little more conscientious on that side than I was. I do remember giving Couns a hard time when I found out his grades were better than mine, "Couns, we have this messed up. You're the one that's probably going to play baseball and I'm the one that needs better grades in accounting. I think we have this backwards."

I was an accountant for exactly ten working days, so my accounting degree has not been maximized. Back then between St. Mary's and Notre Dame, there were half as many women, if not less, than men; now there are more women than men. It would be hard enough to date women at Notre Dame just because the numbers are not in your favor. But then the other problem is that every one of your classmates has twelve varsity letters, was president of the student body in high school and has a GPA of 4.0.

Couns lived on the North Quad; maybe it was Cavanaugh Hall, next to Zahm. We became really friendly. One of his roommates was Korey Wrobleski who was on the team with us and then Chris Fox was another one of his roommates. Chris is a surgeon up in Milwaukee. Chris' son Luke just verbally committed to **DUKE**\* to play baseball.

We all hung out a little bit, not like parties and such, but in the dorms. We were close to Korey Wrobleski, whose son, Ryan is a sophomore at Dallas Baptist University and is on scholarship there for baseball. We all became, and still are friends. When I moved off campus as a junior to our apartment we had more festivities. Couns and his guys would come over at times. Couns was more focused. He would definitely go out and have fun on occasion but he was super locked in on what he was trying to accomplish with baseball. I never met his wife, Michelle, at Notre Dame.

\*The Rose Parade originally had nothing to do with the Rose Bowl football game. It was a celebration in Pasadena for the ripening of the oranges....The 1942 Rose Bowl game between Oregon State and **DUKE** was played in Durham, North Carolina because of fears that the Rose Bowl in Pasadena could be attacked like Pearl Harbor was three weeks earlier....The Rose Bowl has been sold out every year since 1947.

Counsell was an incredibly regular, humble, self-aware guy who has gone on to do incredible things. Let's be honest, Couns is a famous person. For those of us that aren't famous, even though you know the person forever, it's a little bit awkward or anxious when you see that person. And Couns has always been the guy that makes you feel, "Thank God you came up to me so I can get some normalcy in my life." Not only he never makes you feel that you were burdening him, or that he was too busy, but he made you feel, "I am so pumped that we caught up."

The coolest compliment you could ever give someone that has gone on to do incredible things is that he hasn't changed. Couns has been the same dude all the way through. I know that I speak for our whole group from Notre Dame. We are so proud of what he has done. It is so neat to see the things he has accomplished and the way he has gone about his business.

My experience at Notre Dame and playing baseball was incredible. All of the baseball opportunities I have had in my life have come down to making the team as a walk-on, the success we had in those four years, and being exposed to people like Pat Murphy and Craig Counsell. It was really challenging to try to balance school and baseball there. I was over my skis. I was just a three-star kid in high school. I had no idea that the level of baseball that we played at Notre Dame was something I could even participate in, in any way shape or form.

It was awesome. We won a ton of games. We worked our tails off. We always felt like we were going to win because we worked so hard. It was important life lessons that you take with you for your whole life. As far as what do I need to do— who I am today is not going to be good enough to last through this experience. What do I need to do to draw out the very best I have in me. Murph taught us that the way the program was going to work is that we were going to do things at the highest level and we were going to take pride in it. It wasn't going to be the easy way but it was going to be the winning way.

I never forgot those lessons—figure it out, find a way. If you want something great to happen, hope is not a strategy. You have to go get it done. I have incredibly fond memories. It was a tough experience but it was worth every bit of it. Really proud of what we did; I'm proud of what all of us have accomplished individually. Those are not coincidental. It does trace back to that special experience of playing baseball at Notre Dame.

*Craig Counsell on third base with Notre Dame Head Coach Pat Murphy at Duke University, 1989...Murphy became Counsell's Bench Coach with the Brewers 28 years later.*

# A ROOMIE WITH A VIEW

## KOREY WROBLESKI

*Korey Wrobleski was a catcher at LaPorte, **INDIANA*** High School for Ken Schreiber, one of the winningest high school coaches in the country. Wrobleski played baseball at Notre Dame where he roomed with Craig Counsell. Wrobleski is a Regional Sales Manager in Minneapolis for Verint Corporation.*

What is important to me is that Craig Counsell is a really good guy. He has always been very gracious to me and my kids. We go see him when he is in town and he always takes time to see my kids and give them access to batting practice, in the dugout, and the club house. I remember we went to see those guys in Milwaukee, stayed with Michelle and the kids, and after the game we went out on the field and hit. We got to park in the players' parking lot and he gave us the big league experience. My kids had a blast. With all of Craig's success as a player and now a manager, he has always been my friend.

Craig and I ended up as roommates at Notre Dame. The coaches put me with Craig and two others who were regular students. We meshed pretty quickly. Our two other roommates were both from Waukesha, Wisconsin. We weren't there to go to parties and do the college scene; we were very focused on studies and baseball. Some students probably called that boring, but it was what we needed to do. Dorms would have dances and we would go to some, but no serious dating. Craig

*In the 1976 Ohio State-Indiana Game, **INDIANA** scored on the first play of the second quarter to take a 7-6 lead. Indiana coach, Lee Corso, called a timeout. During the timeout, Corso had his team pose for a group picture with the scoreboard—showing Indiana leading Ohio State 7-6—clearly visible in the background. Corso featured the picture on the cover of the 1977 Indiana recruiting brochure. Ohio State won the game 47-7.

and Michelle were in a long distance relationship in college. She would drive down a couple times a year with some friend for a football game. When Craig got into pro ball is when they got serious.

Pat Murphy, who is now Craig's bench coach, wanted to build ND back into a national competitive baseball program. The first couple years we really did not have a lot of free time; there was practice, studying, lifting weights. Murph did not give us a lot of time to get in trouble: not a whole lot of craziness to be honest. Murph was a good leader in the world we were operating in. He was operating on a shoestring, not a lot of scholarships or support from the college, but he loved ND. He found the right kind of guys to join his journey. He knew how to handle kids who were fighting for notoriety and fighting for their place. He gave us vision and hope. He had a fighter's mentality.

Craig had been a pretty good high school shortstop, but he was not that physically strong when he arrived at ND. He needed a lot of development, all of us did. His baseball IQ was off the charts compared to anyone else on the team. There were plenty of times he would get down on himself. I remember he came in after he made some errors and told me his glove didn't work. It just didn't work anymore. He was just in a bad run. Nothing traumatic, just the normal ups and downs of the game.

I majored in business administration so we had some classes together since he was an accounting major. At Notre Dame, even for football players, there is no hiding academically. There is no easy way to get your degree. They don't have football degrees or baseball degrees. We spent many nights studying like everybody else and we went to class like everybody else. The way Murph ran the baseball program there were long days of practice so we were studying into the wee hours of the night. We were on the road a lot playing all over the country and we didn't have laptops, no online courses. There were many times we were in the computer lab at 12 o'clock at night typing out papers because that was the only time we had to get our work done. The professors were not forgiving if we showed up late to class because we had to deal with Murph or do a presser.

Craig and I look back and wonder how we did it. We played against Paul Wilson from Florida State before he played for the Mets. Andy Benes from Evansville threw a really heavy ball. It was like a two-seamer, but the ball was really heavy. A two-seamer is different than a 4-seamer fastball. A two-seamer, especially for a right-handed hitter, runs in to your hands; it gets you inside more times than not. For a left-hander, it's running away; it gets you on the end of the bat; consequently it is hard to square those kind of guys up. You are not getting it on a good spot on the barrel of the bat.

Craig was single-minded and focused that he was going to play in the big leagues. It did not seem that far away for him. He grew up knowing Robin Yount, and Paul Molitor. In fact his sister used to **BABYSIT\*** for the Molitors. Being a big leaguer for him did not seem that far out of the realm of possibilities. His perspective was different than a kid like me who grew up in northwest Indiana. Nobody in my family went to college. For me, I wanted to be a big leaguer but it seemed like a long distance opportunity. Craig, he could see it and he was close to it. I believed him. He was not a top prospect from a physical aspect, but he had it in his mind's eye and it was real for him.

Craig loved his time at Notre Dame. He loved the work, he loved the preparation, loved to play. He knew more than anybody else that he was good. Nobody else could figure it out at that point. He was not this top prospect coming out of high school, but he was good at it. He had that demeanor of "I just do my work, I get it done."

*A young Martha Stewart was the Berra family **BABYSITTER** when Yogi played for the Yankees.

Craig got picked up by the Rockies. We kept in touch all the time. One day I was on a work trip and eating at a sports bar, watching the Braves play the Marlins. At the time I did not know Craig got traded. But I did know how he played. I was sitting at dinner and I see the ball hit to second and the guy picks it up and throws to first for the third out and they went to commercial. I was sitting there thinking that looks like Craig, the way he threw. There was no close-up; it just cut to commercial. I'm watching and all the sudden Craig gets up to bat. I am going "holy crap, he got traded to the Marlins."

I went to Cleveland for the 1997 World Series. It was awesome. I have never been in an environment like that. I have been to big football games. Plus, Notre Dame was one step from going to the College World Series in '92. When I went to that game in Cleveland, it was electric, unbelievable. Watching Craig was like watching your brother,. He made it and it was awesome.

I knew Craig wanted to stay involved after he retired but he had four kids and his wife, Michelle. I don't think he wanted to go through the normal progression: single A- manager, double-A, triple-A route, you know, that grind and lifestyle for his family. He had it in him but there is this rite of passage—to be a big league manager, you need to start in the minors. Once he got the front office job it gave him a different perspective on how big league teams run and how to manage, which gave him a different path to get there.

Today's managers have a different set of requirements with all the Sabermetrics and algorithms. Craig is very intelligent and he knows how to put things together.

# IOWA? IT'S ON ALL THE MAPS NOW

DICK FOX

*Dick Fox is a native of Lost Nation, Iowa and was a classmate and baseball teammate of Craig Counsell's dad John at Notre Dame. They have remained friends for many years even though Fox has lived in Scottsdale, Arizona for 44 years and the Counsells have lived in Ft. Myers, Florida since the early 90's.*

The sea was angry that day my friend, oh wait that's from another book. Actually it was a cold and windy March day in Notre Dame, Indiana when the Irish freshman baseball team had their first workout. Along about an hour into it some kid in right field threw a bullet to third base. In the inning before he'd hit a line shot that had been caught by the second basemen, but after the throw everyone said, "Who is that kid and where's he from?" Somebody said, "I don't know what his name is but he's from a town called Oh, Come On and Walk, Wisconsin." Oh, Come On and Walk? What kind of town is that? Must be an Indian town. We found out later it was Oconomowoc and his name was John Counsell.

We came to know John very well during those four years. He was a non-scholarship player with a beautiful swing and a rifle arm, except he looked like he was 12-years-old. He later became captain of the team; he and his son Craig are the only father and son captains in the history of Notre Dame sports. He had a sweet swing and at the estimation of all his teammates, would've made the big leagues, except he had allergy problems. Sometimes his eyes would get so swollen he could hardly see depending on the day.

I remember one game at Ohio University where John went 3 for 4. The next day he could not see the ball because of the pollen. The problem at Notre Dame in those days was the coach Jake Kline. The field we played on later became Jake Kline Field.

Jake Kline should have retired 20 years before we got there. I think he was an ND student back when the earth was still cooling. In fact, we had a teammate named Shaun Fitzmaurice who was maybe the best player in the country his junior year and played baseball in the '64 Olympics in Tokyo where he was MVP. There was no baseball in the Olympics those days, but they had it that year as a demonstration sport. The United States won and Fitzmaurice was the star of the team.

The reason I mention his name is, in his final game at Notre Dame, he thought he was given the bunt sign. Because he was such a strong hitter it was the first time he had ever been given the bunt sign. To be doubly sure that he had seen the bunt sign he walked over to the dugout as if to get a different bat. He was really asking Coach Kline what the bunt sign was and if he'd just put the bunt sign on. When he got to the dugout Kline was asleep, sound asleep during the game!

When Shaun came back from Tokyo he signed a big bonus with the **NEW YORK METS**\* and was invited to major league Spring Training the very next spring. He thought he was given the bunt sign his third time at bat in Spring Training but he wasn't sure so he did the same thing. He walked back to the dugout as if he was switching bats to ask Casey Stengel, the Mets manager, if indeed he'd given him the bunt sign. He gets to the Mets dugout and Casey Stengel's sound asleep.

That's the way it was at Notre Dame even though the roster was very talented. One year we went 15-15 yet had 4 pitchers from that team make the Major Leagues. Of course, Fitzmaurice was one of the position players that made the big leagues. So John Counsell from Oconomowoc was playing in pretty good company. There was no draft until the year after we graduated, but the Minnesota Twins signed John as a free agent. A

---

\*After the **NEW YORK METS** had played their first nine games in their inaugural 1962 season, they were 9½ games out of first place.

year later my wife and I went to a Midwest League game in Clinton, Iowa, my home county. The Clinton team was playing Wisconsin Rapids and John Counsell was a star player for the Wisconsin Rapids team along with Graig Nettles.

That night John was 4 for 4 when he came up for his final at bat. He hit a shot to the right of the second basemen who got a glove on it. He was lucky to knock it down. But the scorekeeper gave him an error. I went up to the **PRESS BOX**\* and talked to the official scorekeeper. I talked him into changing it to a hit so John Counsell did go 5 for 5 in a professional game.

In 1998 I was having Easter Brunch at another classmate's house in Portland, Oregon. His name is Jon Spoelstra and he played freshman basketball at Notre Dame. He worked for me three years after college, and later became president or general manager of 3 different NBA teams. After brunch we were sitting in Spoelstra's living room and wife Lisa said to me, "Dick, you have the greatest memory of anybody I've ever known. What did you do to train it?" I broke out laughing and said, "Train it? I've never done anything to train my memory." Her husband Jon is sitting on the sofa and he said, "I can tell you exactly what he did to train it." I said, "Jon, you can tell me exactly what I did to train my memory when I never trained my memory?" He said, "You trained your memory and just didn't know it. "I said, "What are you talking about?" He said, "Name at least two people we both know that have exceptional memories." Which I did, and he said, "You're right. What do the three of you have in common?" I said, "I don't know." and he said, "When you were young all three of you memorized baseball cards. Any kid who memorizes baseball cards grows up to have an incredible memory as an adult. I don't know

---

\*The **PUBLIC ADDRESS ANNOUNCER** for the Houston Colt '45s (later the Astros) in their 1962 inaugural season was Dan Rather, later the CBS anchor....The P.A. announcer for the Brooklyn Dodgers in 1936 and 1937 was John Forsythe, later a TV and movie star.

how it happens, but when I find a person with an exceptional memory I ask them, did you study baseball cards when you were younger, and almost every single one of them says 'yes.' Furthermore, kids that memorized baseball cards are geography experts and good at math. The latter because they learn how to do earned run averages (ERA) and batting average, geography because they memorize 500 U.S. towns."

The other thing that I remember from that day was Jon was smoking while he was on the sofa. This was 1998, and I said, "Jon, it's really none of my business and it doesn't bother me, but I'm really surprised that you're smoking. Nobody smokes anymore. I gave it up two years ago." He said," Dick, let me tell you something. You can smoke or not smoke, you can diet or not diet, you can drink or not drink, you can worry or not worry, but unless you're in an accident you're going to live to be five years older than your father." I laughed at him but that was years ago and over that period of time I've been watching carefully and basically he was right. Which explains why Craig Counsell and his dad look like teenagers. It's all in the genes.

We flash ahead to when John Counsell was the assistant baseball coach at Notre Dame. He had already been an assistant for a few years. All of us were really, really excited because we felt John was going to become the head baseball coach when Jake Kline would soon retire. Well, John was there for over six years and Kline never retired! Kline was older then God's dog and yet he never retired. So John moved on from South Bend and went back to his home state of Wisconsin. In 1974 John was still in South Bend*, when my wife and I were visiting the Counsells. Little Craig Counsell was 4-years-old and had memorized all 500 of Topps baseball cards that year. He was in his bedroom when I peeked in and I started asking him questions to see if he really knew all the cards and he did. He had it all memorized except I phrased a question in an unusual way and he answered the question with the name Sparky Anderson. I said, "No, it's not Sparky Anderson it's Sparky Lyle." He got so mad he started crying and he threw down his baseball cards. He was very upset.

That was in 1974 and 24 years later I'm at Wrigley Field where I'm down on the field with Chip Caray. I look into the visitors' dugout right in front of me and who do I see there but Craig Counsell. I'd seen him play a couple times at Notre Dame but he didn't really know me well. So I yelled into the dugout, "Hey number 30! Do you know the difference between Sparky Lyle and Sparky Anderson yet?" He gave me a look like you wouldn't believe. Craig Counsell has a great memory probably because he memorized baseball cards. It helps him tremendously during game strategy sessions.

Spoelstra was right about genes too. I'm going to tell you something right now that not many people know. That is John Counsell and his son Craig did some kind of Faustian deal with the Devil so that they will remain looking young forever. When John was a freshman that day at Notre Dame he looked like he was 12 years old. If you look at a picture of Craig when he was at Notre Dame, he may not even look that old. That's where the genes come in; Craig was blessed with super genes from his father John in conjunction with an intercession by the Devil.

In 1975 the year after the incident with the Sparkys, John was my partner in a member-guest golf tournament at Crow Valley Country Club in Bettendorf, Iowa. John and Jan got there a day early and John and I played lights out in a practice round. I said, "John we have to buy the other half of our team in the Calcutta tonight. We're going to win this thing, we're both playing great." That night was pretty expensive, but we bought 100% of our team. Now the first day of the 2-day member-guest tournament is completed and I'm not going to tell you what we shot. I will tell you that we finished long before the cutoff time for turning in your scorecard. We turned it in barely in time because when we came off the course we sat by the swimming pool with our wives for over an hour since we wanted to be the last ones to turn in our card.

The next day we played much better and had the low score of the day. The pro at that country club in Bettendorf, Iowa was Butch Harmon. Butch is probably the most famous teaching pro in the last 50 years. At the banquet the final night John and I won a nice prize for low score of that day. As Butch Harmon handed the prize to us he said "I know exactly how you guys felt yesterday."

What's even more amazing is, Butch Harmon got fired at that country club because some of the wealthier members wanted him, the son of the 1948 Masters Champion Claude Harmon Sr., to play **GOLF\*** with them every day. Butch kept saying, "I'd love to. There's nothing I'd rather do, except I have a pro shop to run and a ton of lessons to give. If I can get that out of the way I'll come and play with you." That's why Butch Harmon got fired.

That same year, my wife and I moved to Scottsdale, Arizona and a few years after that John and Jan Counsell moved to Ft. Myers, Florida. All I can say about the relationship with the Counsells is if you meet any nicer people let me know. John is different than Craig in that John is very outgoing, great sense of humor, always laughing, and always smiling. Doesn't make Craig a bad person; it just shows how different they are.

My biggest fear with Craig is that if the Brewers have a couple of bad years many of the fans will turn on him. I'm a huge St. Louis Cardinals fan. I think Whitey Herzog was the best manager in my lifetime. But when the Cardinals had a down year or two you could hear the rumblings from the fans. I was

---

\*The Professional **CADDIES** Association (PCA) has 2,800 members and is headquartered in Palm Coast, Florida. Until 2002, the PCA's Hall of Fame was located in founder Dennis Cone's Winnebago.

thinking how stupid those fans were. How ungrateful are they? Do they not realize what they have?

John and I usually go to a Brewers Spring Training game or two in Arizona. Every spring I say, "John, the talent on the Brewers is substantially less than what the Cubs or Cardinals have. How's he going to compete this year?" Almost every year, at the end of the season, the Brewers are ahead of either the Cubs or Cardinals. Some years the Brewers are ahead of them both.

I just don't understand it, it's unbelievable the job that Craig Counsell has done there. I don't mind reminding John of it every time I see him, and I'm really happy for Craig. I do hope that Brewer fans realize what kind of man they have running the team, what kind of manager they have running the team. He reflects well on Milwaukee and the Brewers around the National League and around baseball circles. It has been a real pleasure and a real highlight of my life knowing the Counsell family.

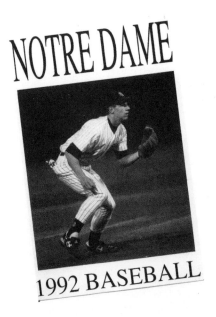

# NOTRE DAME NEEDS A HALFBACK, A FULLBACK AND ROCKNE BACK

CAPPY GAGNON

*Cappy Gagnon is nearing legendary status at Notre Dame. Recently retired as the security honcho for the football and basketball facilities, he wrote the authoritative book:* Notre Dame Baseball From Anson to Yastrzemski. *Gagnon was an early member of The Society For American Baseball Research (SABRE) and twice served as its President.*

I was living in the Seattle area, in 1995. I got a call from John Counsell, telling me that he was coming to town to see Craig play short for the Colorado Springs Sky Sox against the Tacoma Rainiers. Oh, by the way, Tacoma also featured a pretty good young shortstop, named Alex Rodriguez. At this time, Craig was approaching 25 years of age, which was about the final age that anyone might be expected to make their first trip to the majors. Craig was having a nice season and according to John would be pleased to be a lifetime Minor Leaguer, except that the pay was terrible, compared to what a Notre Dame grad could earn, because Major League teams kept churning out more prospects and pushed out those who did not break in.

From his earliest days, Craig was the complete package both as a player and a person. The question in the summer of 1995 was whether Craig would ever make the bigs, with the parent Colorado Rockies, or whether he would soon be putting his Notre Dame Accounting Degree to work. I moved back to

South Bend, to work for Notre Dame, on August 15, 1995. On September 17th, I saw Craig's name in a box score and I could add him to my list of Notre Dame Major Leaguers. Shameless plug—I'm happy to have him included in my book, Notre Dame Baseball Greats.

A few years ago, I drove up Milwaukee and was able to chat with Craig before a Brewers game. One of my prized possessions is a photo of Craig and me next to the steps of the dugout. Even though Craig was in his 40's, he still looked like the batboy, with his boyish good looks and excellent fitness. I bumped into Craig outside Soldier Field, October 6, 2012, when Notre Dame Football played a night game against the Miami Hurricanes (ND 41, Miami-3). He called me "Mr. Gagnon". I said "Craig...you're a big league manager; call me Cappy". I expected him to reply, "Yes, Mr. Gagnon". John and Jan did a marvelous job in raising Craig.

*Graduation from Notre Dame, 1992*

Chapter Five

# FLORIDA MARLINS

Pro Player filled to capacity once Craig
Counsell (completing a double play
over David Justice in Game 2) and the
Marlins made it to the Fall Classic.

## It Was a Ball

# IT WAS MAGIC, I TELLS YA

### JIM LEYLAND

*Craig Counsell was the spark that propelled Manager Jim Leyland to the 1997 World Series title. Leyland managed the Pirates, Marlins, ROCKIES\*, and Tigers, and was three times Manager of the Year. He was a second string catcher at Perrysburg High School near Toledo. The starting catcher was Jerry Glanville, later an NFL head coach.*

The acquiring of Craig Counsell by the Marlins in 1997 was one of the best jobs our scouts were involved in. They described him to a T. They said this guy is really a good player and he can help us. He does all the little things right. He is a very good solid player. He is a very intelligent player. At the time we had had Luis Castillo, who was a very talented player and went on to have a heck of a career; but at that point he wasn't quite ready yet. So we brought in Craig and pretty much the rest is history. He did a great job for us. Craig was one of the most fundamentally solid players I ever had.

Craig was exactly who the scouts told me he would be. I am not sure who the scouts were but I think Dick Egan was one of them and maybe Jim Olander. I respected my scouts and it didn't take me long to figure out that Craig knew what he was doing. I could tell that he going to fit in the clubhouse well and fit on the team well and contribute. We weren't expecting him

*\*At **COORS FIELD** in Denver, in the upper deck, there is one row of purple seats that encircle the stadium designating the "mile high" level.*

to hit home runs, or knock in all the big runs; but we knew that if we needed to put a ball in play he was going to do it. If we needed a bunt, he could do it. If there was a big double play situation he wasn't going to panic. Craig didn't **HIT GREAT**\*. He didn't tear it up but he was consistent. He was the guy that could keep an inning going. If a situation came up that we need something done, with the exception of a home run, Craig was the guy who could get it done.

Craig had a couple of extremely crucial at bats in the 1997 World Series. He knocked in a tying run in the ninth inning with a sacrifice fly. I was surprised that Manny Ramirez got that ball because he was playing the pole. When Craig first hit that ball I thought it was going to be a double and we were going to win the game. Craig always figured out how to get it done. He was facing Jose Mesa. Mesa was a really nasty pitcher with some really nasty stuff. Mesa was an excellent closer and Craig just kept fighting and fighting him tooth and nail until he got a pitch and drove it to the outfield. That is just the kind of player he was, he had determination and he wasn't going to give in. Craig was just a real treat. We went on to win the game and Craig is the player that actually scored the winning run.

That World Series team had some stars. We had Gary Shef-field, Moises Alou, Darren Daulton, Al Leiter, Alex Fernandez, Kevin Brown, Edgar Renteria. When you think of Craig Coun-sell, you don't really think of him as a star; but he was one of our most contributing players. We wouldn't have won the World Series without Darren Daulton or Craig Counsell. Craig was just what the doctor ordered at the time. Luis Castillo needed a little more seasoning and Counsell just fit in like a glove. He was a Steady Eddie. He wasn't the prospect that Luis

\*The difference between .250 **HITTER** and a .300 hitter is one hit a week.

was at the time, physically, talent wise, in my opinion; but he a perfect glove to put on a hand. You can only have so many star players. Complementary players and players that fit in to that with those players are very important in putting your team together.

I've always believed that a manager's biggest and toughest job is knowing how to put a team together. You have to have some star players, but also some contributing players and some role players. General managers that do that are great. That is the toughest job. Dave Dombrowski told our scouts what they needed to be looking for and they came up with Craig Counsell.

I didn't think about Craig being a good manager; but it came as no shock that he's become a very good manager. We knew he was a student of the game and he was a college player. He has a good feel for people and he is a very bright guy but yet he has plenty of personality to relax everybody. He has got enough personality to jump on them if he needs to. If I would've analyzed that and sat down and thought about it I would've said, "Yeah, this guy is a good candidate to be a manager." You never know for sure that somebody is going to be a big success.

We never worried about Craig. He came to the park the same every day, ready to play and ready to perform. I used to say about guys like that they are maybe not the prettiest; but they are like an old shoe, they are comfortable. He was like an old shoe. He was very comfortable for me as a player. I didn't have to worry about him. I knew he was going to do things right. I just made sure he was fine and healthy and let him play.

There is no question that Craig has done a very good job in Milwaukee. Making the 2018 and 2019 playoffs was an incredible managing job. You have to be careful not to go overboard with your bullpen. But Craig has done a great job. You can tell that he is the manager and the players respect him. You can tell when their team plays they have the utmost respect for him and they are going to give him everything they have. Craig is just one of those guys that is a perfect fit for a managerial position.

Craig has decent talent to work with but the depth of their starting pitching has not been as good other teams like the Cubs or **CARDINALS\***. They have one great bullpen guy with Hader and some other guys have done some great jobs for him. Overall their team is pretty good. They do have Yelich, the MVP and they have Braun who has been a great player.

As a manager you expect that people are not always going to agree with your decisions and they will find flaws when you don't win. He is a perfect fit for that town. He is a blue collar guy and a perfect fit for that city. He is very well respected there. As a manager you have to have thick skin. You can't worry every time somebody doesn't agree with whether you bunted, hit and run or pulled your pitcher. Craig is a bright, solid, intellectual guy. He is not going to panic. He is going to do what good managers do; he will put his players in a position where they will do their best and have some success. He will do that as long as he is manager. Some years are better than others. In Craig's case, you don't win every year because its hard; but I don't think anybody is going to jump ship on him if they don't make it.

There are more analytics today. But analytics is just a more sophisticated word for what we had for a long time. Its information which I think is good for any manager. I enjoyed that kind of information when I was manager. When we got the computer we put all the information in the computer the same way. The computer just spits the information out faster. You don't get any different information. You only get out of it

*All six games of the 1944 World Series were played at Sportsman's Park in St. Louis. The rival managers—Luke Sewell of the Browns andBilly Southworth of the Cardinals—shared a one-bedroom apartment...never expecting that both teams would be in town at the same time.

what you put into it. Information is good but they are making sabermetrics sound like a more modern thing. It's probably exaggerated a bit. I'm a big believer in information but you have to be careful to sort out the information and don't lose track of the player.

When you are managing a player, you cannot always do statistically or analytically what the computer might say you should do. If you have a star player and he doesn't hit a particular pitcher and you want to give him a day off you should look down the road to see when you are playing that pitcher and that might be the time you give him off. Generally speaking you are not going to take your star out of the lineup. Be careful not to get swallowed up with so much information that you lose track of the player.

Call it whatever you want sabermetrics, analytics, I think information is great. I always wanted information. I have never met a manager yet that didn't want information that would do one of three things: help him win a game, help him get his players better, or find better players. Information is great but there has to be some type of balance where you still know the temperature of the player in the dugout at a particular time and sometimes that information can't give that.

I don't think there will be any issues with Craig managing a former teammate like Ryan Braun. Craig is very respected and Ryan Braun understands what Craig's responsibilities are. It might be an issue in the minor leagues or below. That happened to me one year. I ended up managing a bunch of guys I played with and I didn't do a very good job. They were friends of mine so it was difficult.

I think the world of Craig. I've chatted with him a couple of times every year. I'm so happy he got an opportunity and he is running with it.

Craig Counsell is laid back but aggressive, consistent, very intelligent, very instinctive. A great guy!

*Game 7 of the 1997 World Series was the largest World Series crowd since 1963.*

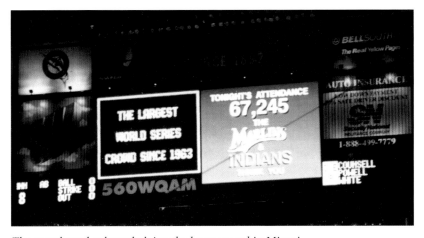

*The scoreboard acknowledging the large crowd in Miami.*

# A WRITER AND A FRIEND

TOM FRIEND

*Tom Friend, 58, is a native of Rockville, Maryland, and a graduate of the University of Missouri School of Journalism. He reported for* ESPN the Magazine *for twenty years and has written sports for forty years. He now lives in the San Diego area, where he is a freelance writer and wrote the wonderful book,* The Chicken Runs at Midnight *that turned into a bestseller in late 2018.*

When I was at ESPN, I came across the story of "The Chicken Runs at Midnight." The story had been told before, but I had never heard it. This was February of 2016. It hadn't been told nationally. I mean, it had been told, but I didn't know about it. I saw a blurb on it. I told my editor at ESPN, "We should do a TV version of this. It would be a great TV piece." Lifetime did it, but it wasn't very good. It was good, but we could do it better. ESPN could do a great job.

We decided to do it. It was supposed to be a Father's Day piece, and it turned out so good that it ran as a Sports Center feature, they called them SC Feature. It ran on a Sunday night. It blew people away. We got nominated for an Emmy for the piece. It was just tremendous, the TV version of "The Chicken Runs at Midnight."

When that happened, I knew there was more to the story than we told in the TV piece. You can only get into so much in ten minutes. I decided I'll ask Rich Donnelly if we should do this book. We had to sell it. Zondervan Publishing were the ones that were really interested. Harper Collins is really the owner of it. They're the ones who wanted it.

We did the book for Harper Collins and Zondervan. It turned out really good. I'm really happy with it, proud of it. I interviewed Craig for it. I interviewed John Counsell for it. I know John. He's a great guy. That's how it all started.

Craig Counsell is so popular because he's everyman. He had that weird batting stance, which led to "The Chicken Runs at Midnight." If you read the book, you read how Rich Donnelly's kids just fell in love with him right away. One of his sons, Tim, is now the recruiting coordinator and third base coach at Northeast Louisiana. He said, "Oh, my gosh, he gave me hope that I could make it, too."

Craig just looks like your average next-door neighbor guy, the guy next door. He didn't have a great body. He didn't have great speed. He didn't have a great amount of power, but he just got it done. He was fundamentally sound and knew how to play the game the right way. He's popular because people can relate to him, and he's a nice guy. He's got a great smile. I just feel like he's just everyman. That's how I felt.

The way that Craig found out about "The chicken runs at midnight," was Rich's sons were batboys that summer of '97. When Craig gets traded at the trade deadline from the Rockies. Usually at the trade deadline, you trade for a veteran. The Marlins identified him as a AAA kind of a guy they were trading for who they felt could play in the big leagues. As you know, he goes over there. One day, he goes to the clubhouse. He tries to drive his car in there, and they think he's a batboy. They won't let him in. They don't think he's real. He has to get a guy to vouch for him. He looks like he's twelve-years-old.

The other thing, he was driving his sister's car. His sister was overseas when he was traded. It was some mundane car. Everybody else was driving Lamborghinis or Porsches or BMWs, and he's driving this rickety old car into the players parking lot. This is his rookie year. He's just loving it.

Those genuine, salt-of-the earth stories are my favorite about him. Those are the ones that I remember when I was doing the book. I wanted to paint him as a guy who was very likable because he was, and those were the stories that John gave me and Craig talked about.

With all the Marlins' weapons, they just wanted reliability, a role player. "We didn't need another all-star," Dave Dombrowski says. So, on July 27th, 1997, when the Rockies asked for just journeyman pitcher Mark Hutton in return, Craig Counsell became a Marlin.

It was an unorthodox trade. Usually at the trade deadline, contending teams use minor leaguers to acquire veterans, but this was the polar opposite—Florida had traded a veteran for a no-name. Manager Jim Leyland thought he was done with low-budget rookies. Coach Rich Donnelly remembers Leyland telling Coach Bruce Kimm, "If this guy can't play, you're fired."

Counsell walked into the Florida clubhouse on July 28th, looking all of 18 years old. Tim Donnelly and Mike Donnelly thought he might be the newest clubhouse attendant, certainly not a prized second baseman. Leyland, who can be gruff at first sight, waved Counsell over to his office and said, "Tell me about yourself." Counsell, unable to tell a lie, was blunt:

"It's not always going to look pretty," Counsell told him. "But I'll get the job done for you."

A wary Leyland told Counsell to meet him at the batting cage. On his way there, Leyland—unimpressed with Counsell's physique—stuck his head in the coach's room and grumbled, "I ain't gonna put him in the lineup today. This guy might just be a utility guy. But let's check him out."

"So after two rounds," Counsell remembers, "Leyland says to me, 'Hey, don't ever come out here again. If I have to watch you hit, you're never going to play.'"

But just to spite Kimm and everyone else, Leyland wrote Counsell into the lineup the next night. "You wanted him, you got him. He's starting today," Leyland told Kimm.

"Well, you don't have to start him," Kimm answered.

"Well, he's startin'," Leyland snapped. "But I'm batting him eighth. I don't want to see too much of him, so I'm battin' him down at the end."

Counsell trotted out there and did what he'd always done at every level—performed. He had his first major league hit and turned a double play into a Marlins victory over the **REDS\***. Two games later, Leyland reinserted him against the rival Braves to see if it was a fluke. But Counsell had another hit and turned a key 9th inning double play into a 1-0 victory.

"I told ya," Kimm gloated to Leyland. "I told ya he can play."

"We'll see how good he is," Leyland shot back. "We get Greg Maddux tomorrow."

Twenty-four hours later, Leyland started him against the future Hall of Famer Greg Maddux. Counsell flailed at Maddux's pitches, went 0-for-2 with an error. Leyland scolded Kimm again. The manager was going to give the kid one more shot in the series finale against the Braves on August 3rd. All Counsell did was go 1-for-3 again in an 8-4 victory. "Jim started scratchin' his head," Rich says.

The whole clubhouse was picking up on Counsell's vibe. The team won eight of its first nine games after the trade—and the one they lost was Counsell's day off. Nothing fazed the kid. He wasn't intimidated by the Sheffields, the Browns and the

---

*Don Hutson, the all-time NFL receiver or the Packers, played two seasons in the Cincinnati **REDS** organization before focusing exclusively on his football career.

Bonillas. He acted like he'd been there before. And in a poignant sort of way, he had been.

He was the son of former Twins minor leaguer John Counsell, who had gone on to work as video coordinator and community relations director for Craig's hometown Milwaukee Brewers. John would bring his young son to the clubhouse, where Craig learned how to blend in, how to be seen and not heard. "He was a classic, one-word, two-word, three-word answer guy," John says of Craig. "But huge at soaking up the information."

Craig was in the clubhouse during the 1982 Brewers' World Series run and studied how the players conducted themselves. He would tag along on community service appearances, where he'd get to spend quality time at the houses of the Brewers' two star players, Paul Molitor and Robin Yount.

That self-aware side of Counsell is why he became one Leyland's favorite players. And it's also why he caught the eyes of young Tim and Mike Donnelly—because he would've fit in with them in the clubhouse. Counsell looked about their age and was about as bony as they were, as well. They figured if he could make it to the big leagues, so could they. "It gave me hope," Tim says. "I said, 'Man, I've got a shot to get to the Majors.'" But most of all, Counsell was the nicest, most sincere, most unassuming player they'd come across.

In fact, the day the boys knew Counsell was special was the day he showed up at the Marlins stadium driving a black, faded, dinged up 1991 Nissan Altima—a four-door family car. It belonged to his sister, Jennifer, who was living abroad in Australia temporarily. The first time Counsell tried pulling it into the team parking lot—amid all of the BMW's and Mercedes' and Lamborghini's—he was denied entry.

"Where you going?" said the parking lot's security guard.

"I'm a player," Counsell said.

"Yeah, you wish," said the guard.

For 10 minutes, Counsell tried arguing his way in—although arguing wasn't his forte. Eventually, a clubhouse attendant came out to rescue him, and from then on, Tim and Mike were sold on Counsell. He was everyman; he was them. Then, when Counsell let them hang out at his locker, when he hit them fly balls and ground balls before home games, Counsell became their No. 1.

"I might have talked to his boys more than I talked to Rich," Counsell says. "They were just good kids hanging out with their dad like I had hung out with my dad. They were baseball kids. I felt I'd lived a similar life, for sure. So I respected that. That they were just there because they wanted to share time with their dad more than anything."

Tim and Mike just admired how "normal" Counsell was, how unpretentious. Counsell earned a minimum rookie salary and stayed at a local AmeriSuites motel for $40 a night. Tim particularly considered him his role model. One day, Counsell—who liked the way Tim fielded a baseball—asked him if he wanted to play for Notre Dame someday. Tim answered, 'Heck, yeah." If he could've, Tim would've followed Counsell around all day—particularly to the batting cage.

Shortly after he joined the Marlins, Rich Donnelly went to an early Sunday mass in Phoenix where he ran into Counsell. They walked back to the hotel together, never once discussing their faith or Counsell's secret nickname, the Chicken. The truth was, Counsell was somewhat like Rich—he wasn't constantly in church, but found himself drawn there at times. Counsell considered himself "a little more than an Easter-Christmas Catholic, but not much." Like most young boys, he had struggled with the meaning of religion and was in church that Sunday to continue his education.

"I probably questioned it more than I believed in it, to tell you the truth" Counsell says. "As a kid, I remember going to ask a priest, 'I don't understand this Father-Son-Holy Ghost thing.

Explain it to me. I don't understand the Holy Ghost, you've got to explain it to me.' I never got a good answer. It was about faith, that's for sure."

Rich was 24 years older than Counsell, old enough to be his father, but their conversation on the way back to the hotel was easy, free-flowing. They connected. Counsell began talking about that day's game and asked Rich what he knew about the opposing pitcher. Rich was impressed by the kid's attention to detail. At the time, Counsell was batting a whopping .352. Had he played a full season, he would've been a leading candidate for Rookie-of-the-Year. Rich patted him on the back as they parted ways and remembers thinking, "What a wonderful kid this guy is. Now I know why my kids are attracted to him." He also found it intriguing that of all the Marlins on the trip—staff, trainers, coaches, players—only two had made it to mass that morning:

Him and the Chicken.

## QUICK HITS & INTERESTING BITS

Craig scored the winning run in the World Series in the 11th inning of 1997, Game 7. You've probably seen the picture.

Craig just crossed the plate. He jumped up in the air in happiness. Coming out of the dugout is this guy in shorts and a T-shirt. He's equally high in the air. They end up being brother-in-laws. That's my son, Michael Rock Hughes. Everybody calls him Rock, except me and his family. Rock married Craig's sister, Jennifer.

*Counsell scored the winning run for the Florida Marlins in the 11th inning of Game 7, 1997 World Series.*

Jennifer was working in Miami. My son Rock was the clubhouse guy with the Marlins. I don't know how they met. The dad is the last one to know.

We love Jennifer. She's great. The two families have meshed together amazingly well. John and Jan are wonderful people. It's been really, really nice. The grandkids get along. It's good.

John is one of those guys who you meet him, immediately he's a friend.

I have no idea when Rock and Jennifer got married. I have eight grandkids. I have nine kids. I have two great-grandkids. I'm not really good with dates.

I'm not surprised in the least that Craig has become a manager. He has a great history in the game, an outstanding person, intelligent, a great feel for the game. He's good with people. There was no reason in the world if he wanted to be, that he wouldn't be a successful manager.

He's done an excellent job as a manager. He's been better than any manager in the National League the last few years.

When I think of Craig, I think of when we were playing at Joe Robbie Stadium. Craig got hit in the face with a pitch. There's blood all over the place. I remember going to the trainer's room and our doctor, Dr. Dan Pinelle was there. He was trying to help Craig as were the trainers. I'm just trying to make sure he's alive. It wasn't a pretty situation. When you get hit in the face, it's not going to be pretty. I knew where his parents were. I said, "Craig, what's your mom's number? What's your dad's number?" I called them and tried to take the pressure off him, give him some relief. I'll never forget that.

I want to go back to that picture of Michael jumping up and Craig jumping up. The Cleveland catcher, Sandy Alomar, was walking away with his catcher's mask in his arms. He had just lost the World Series. He's walking back to his dugout and walking the other way is the home plate umpire. The home plate umpire was Eddie Montague, Jr., whose father got me started in scouting. His father signed both Willie Mays and Sandy Alomar's father.

My first job in baseball was a part-time scout with the San Francisco Giants, and the guy that got me started was Ed Montague, Sr.

—**Gary Hughes, Craig Counsell's father-in-law.**—
A renowned baseball super scout with the **CHICAGO CUBS\***,
Hughes is a grad of Serra High School in San Mateo,
California, also the high school of Tom Brady,
Lynn Swann, and Barry Bonds.

I didn't know anything about Counsell when the Marlins traded for him. I don't know if anybody knew who he was. Bruce Kimm had seen him the year before in AAA, and he recommended

\*P.K. Wrigley and Milton Hershey were bitter business rivals. When Wrigley bought the **CHICAGO CUBS**, Hershey tried to buy the Philadelphia Phillies...and sell chocolate gum. Hershey failed in both efforts.

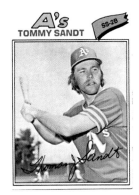

him. That was a good move. He was the guy we needed. We had all of these All-Stars and all of these big-name guys. We needed somebody to do the dirty work, and that was Craig. He did. He'd bunt the guy over. He did a sacrifice fly. He was a big part of our team. He turned us around.

I remember Craig, we first went out for batting practice. Jim Leyland went up to him, he said, "Can you play second base?" Craig was mostly shortstop at the time. Craig said, "Yeah, it won't be pretty, but I'll catch it." I went and hit him ground balls. I didn't know he had said this to Jim. Jim said, "How did he look?" I said, "Well, he isn't very pretty, but he caught everything." That was Craig. That was him.

When I first met Craig, I wasn't surprised at his size. We had John Cangelosi on the team, too. He was 5'6. We had different size guys. Craig looks skinny, but Craig was pretty well put together. His arms aren't little. I was a little surprised by the size of his arms.

As an infield coach, I didn't need to work with Craig Counsell a whole lot. He didn't need a whole lot of work.

Kurt Abbott was our extra guy. He filled in occasionally, but Luis Castillo was our starting second baseman Opening Day. He constantly did something stupid. Luis wound up being a very good player. He wound up being an All-Star. He led the league in hitting. The talent was there. He just was too young to be in the big leagues.

That's okay that Counsell looks so young, even though he's turning fifty. That's not a bad thing. It's bad when you look like you're sixteen, and you're trying to get in the clubhouse.

He's a classy kid, as you know. He was obviously raised the right way. I'm glad he joined us. He won us the World Series.

——**Tommy Sandt** was the infield coach for the Florida Marlins when they acquired Craig Counsell.

I had seen Counsell in the Arizona Fall League in 1995. He was a good fastball hitter and he had good speed. Craig went on to be quite a ball player—he was a manager-type ballplayer. He showed up every day, clear-eyed, and ready to play. He could hit off pitchers and move runners. He just knew how to play and be in the right places. You just turned him loose and let him go.

——**Bruce Kimm** is a former professional baseball catcher, manager and coach

*One happy family after Game 7, 2001 World Series.*

Chapter Six

# A HOT TIME IN OLD ARIZONA

## The Poise that Refreshed

# CLONES ARE PEOPLE TWO

### JOE GARAGIOLA JR.

*Joe Garagiola, Jr. was the first ever General Manager of the Arizona Diamond-backs. He was the reason that Craig Counsell joined the D-backs and became a clutch player in their 2001 World Series win. Garagiola is a Notre Dame grad from Scarsdale, New York.*

I actually followed Craig his whole career; in fact, the first time I met him is when he came out here to play in the Arizona Fall League. John, his dad, had called me because John was the freshman baseball coach at Notre Dame during my extremely brief baseball career. Over the years I've always kidded John that he had me for one season of fall ball and it drove him right into the insurance business and out of coaching. When Craig was with the Rockies, John called and said "Hey, Craig's coming down to the Fall League; if you wouldn't mind just saying "hi" to him and maybe buying him a a meal or something once in a while." I said "Sure!"

That was really how we first met. I had actually tried to trade for him a couple times. I can remember talking to him down on the field in Miami one time and I said, "The problem and the reason I can't get you away from the Marlins is you're not making enough money. If you made more money, they'd get rid of you and I'd have a shot at you!"

He gets traded over to the Dodgers and they release him in Spring Training. Release him! Well, this was the shot we jumped on and got him over here to the Diamondbacks. The rest as they say is history! Craig was without a doubt the most intelligent ball player I was ever around. I say that without qualification. I cannot begin to tell you the number of times we'd be sitting up in the box watching a game and there would be some ball shot off the bat and I'd think "ah shoot." I'd look up and Craig would be standing there in perfect position to field the ball. He knew, he just knew this stuff. I don't know if it was because he was a coach's son or he was studying up on it, I don't know.

The expression "he's like a coach or manager on the field," may be overused but, Craig was like a coach on the field. Of course, he had the great NLCS for us in 2001. This gets forgotten because of all that went on in the 2001 World Series. Books have been written about that. Whether you talk about the way we came back in Game 6 or the three unbelievable Games 3, 4, and 5 in New York. **DEREK JETER***, Mr. November, and Rivera in Game 7 and Gonzo; it just doesn't stop. One of the biggest hits, I might even say 2nd after Gonzo's World Series winning blooper, was Craig's home run in Game 1. We go along and have a great series against the **CARDINALS***; then we have this series against the Braves, which we handled pretty easily. Now we're in the World Series and all of us, when Game 1 started, looked over and thought "Holy crap, that's the **NEW YORK YANKEES*** in the other dugout!"

*<u>**DEREK JETER**</u> was named after former National Hockey League bad boy Derek Sanderson.

*Harry Caray was a legendary St. Louis Cardinals announcer from 1945-1969...In 1949, Harry Caray's first wife, Dorothy, divorced him. In 1979 Harry wrote her: "Dearest Dorothy, Enclosed is my 360th alimony check. How much longer is this _ _ _ _ going to continue?" Dorothy responded: "Dearest Harry, Til death do us part. Love, Dorothy." Harry paid monthly till he passed away in Palm Springs in 1998.

*<u>**BABE RUTH**</u> was the first player ever to hit 30 home runs in one season, the first to hit 40 in one season and the first to hit 50 in one season...and he accomplished those feats in the same season.

Sure enough top of the first they jump right out on us, and you felt this buzz go through the ballpark. You wonder if the clock is about to strike midnight and we're going to turn back into pumpkins. Bottom of the first, up comes Couns and bang, it went over the right field fence. It's all right, now you know that it's a ball game. They're playing, we're playing, let's go. You could just feel that emotion sweep through the ballpark. They're the New York Yankees; that doesn't mean they're just going to be able to throw their gloves out there on the field and we're going to dry up and blow away. We were going to battle them, and that was it.

I'm not making that up when I say I did try to trade for him a few times over the years and just could never get it done. When he was available I jumped right on it that spring. The Dodgers released him in Spring Training and I immediately called his agent Barry Meister, who was a friend. I had dealt with Barry most recently because he was one of Randy Johnson's agents. We worked it out pretty quickly. I got there first, but teams that knew him and knew what he could mean to a team would have been all over him. Couns would have had a job very quickly, which is why I didn't fool around. I wanted him because he was going to be such a good fit for the team we were putting together. We had a lot of players. We were assembling a team of veteran, smart, high character guys, and he was a young guy but he was already a veteran. He'd been in the World Series, scored the winning run in the World Series. In my mind he was a perfect fit

Craig is the definition of a low maintenance guy; in the sense, he knew his job, he showed up every day. You look at him and you think not only was he an accounting major, but he's probably an accountant. He doesn't look like your typical pro baseball player, but let me tell you, he was tough. I remember one time he was stealing second and he slid in head first. He got his thumb underneath the bag and slid over it. He tore all the ligaments in it. It was a bad injury.

We're in the locker room, the doctors were looking at it and they tell him he has all these torn ligaments in his thumb and Craig says, "Ok, do I have to go on the disabled list?" "Well yeah, as a matter of fact you do! You probably have to have surgery!" Craig also had an ongoing problem with his neck. He had this contraption rigged up in the clubhouse. He would sit in it and put his chin on a sling. There were weights and it would stretch his spine. He would do this before games so that he could play. That was Couns; he showed up expecting to play every day. You were going to have to fight him to give him a day off.

People ask me a million times about the 7th game of the 2001 World Series and the 9th inning. I always tell them one of the low moments in that inning was when Craig got hit by a pitch. When he came up, I turned to my guys, we were sitting upstairs, and I said, "Alright, we're alright now, Couns will get this guy in. He'll figure out a way to do it." Then he gets hit by the pitch; I was thinking to myself if this were football I'd decline the penalty. I want him hitting! But it worked out. That was just the confidence that we all had in him. He would have found a way, and I believe that.

Craig is a pure baseball guy. Toward the end of his career I knew he wanted to get home to Milwaukee after he had a great career out here in Arizona. So we worked out the deal and he went back. But I remember we were talking one day and he said, "What do you think I should do?" I'll never forget this; we were at a little Starbucks right across the street from where the Brewers were staying. I said, "Couns, let me tell you something, if you decide you want to work in the front office, one day you will be a general manager and you will be great at it. If you decide you want to stay in the dugout, one day you will be a manager and you will be great at that. That's the kind of ability that you have in this game. So really your decision is what path do you want to take? Do you want to get off the field and out of the uniform? Or do you want to stay down there? Whichever way you go it's going to be a huge hit."

He thought, "I've been in the dugout a long time; I've had a long career, maybe I'd like to try this front office." He went to work for the Brewers as their special assistant to Doug Melvin, the Brewers General Manager. Relatively quickly he realized, and I'm surmising, we never really talked about it, he missed the immediacy of the game-to-game and making decisions, the immediate feedback. It surprised me not at all that he became a manager and equally unsurprising is the success that he has had. He was absolutely born to do that and doing it in his hometown is just terrific. He is one of those people you are just so happy to see his success. That's how I feel, I just love the guy.

In the summer when the Brewers come to Phoenix I always go down to visit with him. Just check in on how everybody's doing. We don't talk baseball, we talk family; make sure everybody's good, nothing heavy duty. I'm lucky to count him as a friend; I'm always pulling for him.

*Craig Counsell and son Brady put a base in place on a new baseball field in Buckeye, Arizona. The field was donated by Counsell and the Arizona Diamondbacks*

# WE SAW IT ON THE RADIO

GREG SCHULTE

*Quad City native Greg Schulte has been the voice of the Arizona Diamond-backs since their inception in 1998. The likable Midwesterner has been a fan favorite ever since.*

When we acquired Craig, I did not know a lot about him other than he scored the game winner for the Marlins in the World Series. Knew he was out of Notre Dame. Looked at him as a utility player. They are the type of players that can be on your team one year and another team the next year. But Counsell just forced his way into the lineup. Was rock solid, as competitive as competitive could be. If you looked at him you'd think, "Who's this little guy? What can he do?" He can do a lot. He was a good defender, he could run counts, he was a battler out there, he never gave up an at bat, and he had some big clutch hits. Bob Brenly, to this day, says with the likes of Luis Gonzalez, Curt Schilling, Randy Johnson, in that 2001 World Series run, the most valuable player on that team might have been Craig Counsell. That's how Bob valued him. Craig was like a **MANAGER ON THE FIELD**\*. Bob just looked at him every day. Counsell was a guy you wanted in the lineup.

Craig was a quiet guy. He paid attention to what he was doing on the field. He concentrated on the job at hand. That was the biggest thing with Craig—he was all work. And I see that in the managerial side of him right now. You look in the dugout and

---

\*Joe Torre was **PLAYER/MANAGER** of the Mets for eighteen days in 1977. Since 1962 there have been four player/managers with Pete Rose (1984-86) the last…In 1935 there were nine player/managers.

he's probably festering with something that's going on—when he's happy you hardly ever get a smile.

No real stories. Craig is just all business. That is the biggest thing I remember about him. If you talk to him he'd give you the time, but he was, like, "Can we make this quick? I want to get back to taking ground balls or I need to work on my hitting: I need to do some soft toss." That's just the way he went about things.

I realized fairly fast that Craig was better than I thought he was going to be because he got off to a pretty good start and forced his way into the lineup. Pretty much every day he played second base or maybe played some short, or maybe even played some third. He handled the bag, he didn't strike out a lot. He worked counts. He was one of those guys that you wanted in the lineup. And he would do something positive every day and that was the biggest thing. He was a very good talent and obviously very smart, knew the game, knew situations. He used those to his advantage and also helped his teammates.

Craig had all the tools. I thought he could be a manager one day. I didn't know if he wanted to do that. We talked about it a couple of different times. I can't even remember what he said. But, if you watched him play the game, he was a thinking man's ball player. He was the kind of man you would want to run a ball club. I envisioned him as the manager of the Diamondbacks some day. I thought he'd be great in that situation. He was good with his teammates. I don't think he was overly talkative to them, but when something needed to be said he would say it. That's the way he is as a manager. He let's them play the game until something needs to be said; either you got to do this or you got to do that, or you're not doing this or you're not doing that. But he's a player's type of manager in the sense that he'll leave you alone if you are doing the job. If you're not doing the job, he'll call you into the office and he will let you know about it.

As I travel, Craig and I will touch base. I'll ask about how the family is. We will talk a little about the team on the field. Basically, it's a relationship that started in Phoenix when he joined the ball club, just a friendship kind of thing. He was so instrumental in what we were able to do as an organization from the time he was there until the time he left and actually came back. It's more of a friendship than anything else. Always have liked Craig.

I had interviews with him when he played. He'd tell you like it was. If he disagreed with something that I asked him he'd let you know about it in no uncertain terms. Nothing rude or anything like that but just say, "No, that's not the way it is, it is like this." Some guys just ballyhoo through the interview and get through it. But Craig, if he didn't agree with something you asked or it was something you said, he'd correct you in that interview.

He just wanted to play the game. He didn't want to be bothered with the interviews and all that. He didn't consider it a waste of time but he would rather be on the field taking ground balls or soft tossing rather than being interviewed and talking about himself.

Craig is a genuinely modest guy. I did not talk to his dad, but I heard a lot about him. Craig was one of my favorite Diamondbacks. He played the game and went about his business. He didn't publicize himself, didn't care if he got any accolades or anything. He was just a total team player. I think the perfect fit for that veteran ball club. Here was a guy who didn't have the career numbers of a Grace, or a Johnson, or a Schilling, or a Gonzalez, or a Finley. You could go on and on; even Reggie Sanders was on that 2001 World Series team, and he played a big part. Craig, until he got to the Diamondbacks, was a role player, and then pretty much became a regular. Without him we don't win the World Series. Without Byung-Hyung Kim we don't win the World Series—because of the job they did. Craig was the MVP of the NLCS Championship Series against Atlanta. We talk about the big hits of the '01 World Series.

There might not have been a bigger hit than the one he got as the second batter of the first game. After the Yankees had scored on Schilling in Game 1 with a big first inning hit by Bernie Williams, Counsell came up against Mussina, second batter, and hit one out. He didn't have that many home runs but that was huge. HUGE!

We got a guy on our team now by the name of Tim Locastro who was with the Dodgers last year. He had been with their organization, they call him up, because he could run the bases, he could steal bases. Well, he was shipped in the off-season to the Yankees; we contacted the Yankees about acquiring him, we picked him up. He gets hit by a pitch all the time. This year he was hit by a pitch 26 different times. His uniform is always completely dirty; he steals bases. His on-base percentage is off the charts. You got to get him in the lineup. He makes things happen. You can't play him every day, but you can play him four or five games a week. He just always makes it happen. And that's a Craig Counsell type. Counsell had better tools than Locastro, but not as athletic as Tim. Counsell is probably a better ball player all the way around. You need those kind of guys. You're going to win with those kinds of guys more than your other guys.

Scouting nowadays is disappearing. I will take the scouting and the IQ's of these scouts over the analytics any day. But that's what the game is right now so you go from there. Everyone always underestimates Craig Counsell. Many consider him the best manager in the Majors.

D-BACKS 3, YANKEES 2

# WE WON!!

## Arizona clinches Series in 9th

Deflucci, right, jumps into a pack of Diamondbacks including Craig Counsell, left, Luis Gonzalez and Curt Schilling after the win Sunday.

## D-lirious fans agree: 'It doesn't get any better'

# LUIS, LUIS, OH, NO, ME GOTTA GO

## LUIS GONZALEZ

*Luis Gonzalez is revered by sports fans in Arizona for three reasons: 1) He drove in the winning run in the 2001 World Series for the Diamondbacks, 2) the 57 home runs he hit that year, and 3) how unfailingly nice he is to everyone. His number 20 was the first retired by the team. He is Special Assistant to Derrick Hall, president of the Diamondbacks.*

Craig is one of my all time favorite teammates. I played with him six years here in Arizona. His passion for the game, people, and his teammates is something else. You knew he had those leadership qualities. When you grow up around baseball like he did it's kind of in your blood. I always loved playing with him.

Everybody always talked about his batting stance because that was very unorthodox, so the first thing you think about when you see that stance is how does a guy like that hit. But he hit, he knew how to get it done. On our team he was the most underrated but one of the most important guys in our club. He knew how to do all the little things to get the job done: move runners, get big hits when we needed it, good at bats, and he knew how to play defense all over the place. Those guys are valuable to a team. I'll be honest, in the 2001 World Series I thought Counsell was going to get the game winning hit. He was so clutch for us in the League Championship Series and he was the MVP of the series before. But he got hit by a pitch and then I came up.

Craig was just one of those players—there are always guys on a team that are sometimes underrated or when a big situation comes up that's the guy you would love at the plate. It's not always the big name guys. If it was a tough situation you always felt good when he was coming to the plate. He would find a way whether it was a base hit or a walk, whatever he had to do to get on base or to move runners or do anything. He knew how to play the game. We both left the Diamondbacks at the same time in 2006.

Craig and I were very close, we would go to dinner and just hang together. You always knew he had good manager traits he was just one of those guys you like being around. He always has positive energy and just knew the game. If you liked talking baseball and the game he was always the guy to talk to. There was no doubt about his managerial possibilities. He was like a director on the field, he always knew the situations. I'm watching him now as a manager and he's still the same and he has that same calmness about him. He never gets frazzled, at least on the outside, nothing seems to get him rattled. He is doing great as a manager, I love it. I've talked to a lot of guys that love playing for him. Craig is still fairly young, he understands what players need. And he understands that the game is evolving differently now. Plus he's got a couple young sons that are in Milwaukee that love it. He's a local, he grew up there and he lives there. Craig grew up watching some of the best of the best play for the Brew Crew when he was a young kid.

Since we left the Diamondbacks we still talk often. We're good friends. When the Brewers come to Phoenix I'm always going down to see him and talk to him for a little while. I always check the box scores to see what the Brewers are doing because I want him to do well.

I think the reason I am still popular around here in Arizona years after I have retired is because of the way I treat people. I've always been brought up that way, you treat people the way you want to be treated and respect. And for me clubhouse guys, parking attendants, people who open your door to come in the clubhouse and things like that, to me are just as important as your teammates. I always knew that I wasn't going to play major league baseball forever. I never tried to change, even when I was at the top of my game. The same people you pass on the way up are the same ones you pass on the way down. I never wanted anyone to say anything bad about me.

Craig is the same way and I think that's why we get along so well. We try to be accommodating to everybody. We were blessed to play a game. Even now I'll tell our guys in the minor leagues that whatever records or impact they make on the field is great but there are going to be better players that come along and break your records. It's the impact you make off the field that is what people are going to remember you by!

Craig Counsell has made a serious impact on and off the field.

*Counsell hit a 3-run home run in the 2001 National League division series with the Cardinals to put Arizona ahead. They went on to win the World Series agains the New York Yankees.*

# IT'S EASIER MANAGING FROM THE PRESS BOX

BOB BRENLY

*Bob Brenly played nine Major League seasons, all with San Francisco, except for 48 games with Toronto in 1989. He was born in Coshocton, Ohio and is a graduate of Ohio University. He was hired to manage the Arizona Diamondbacks for the 2001 season, and won the franchise's only championship his first year. In 2004, he again became a broadcaster with the Cubs until 2012. He now serves as a color commentator for Diamondbacks broadcasts.*

I'm from Coshocton, Ohio. Coshocton is about an hour's drive straight east of Columbus. It's out in the middle of the cornfields and cow farms in the direction of West Virginia.

I'm a big Buckeye fan even though I went to Ohio University. Everybody who's raised in the state has to be a Buckeye fan.

Jerry France was my head coach in baseball at Ohio U. We had better baseball than Ohio State. They wouldn't even schedule us. In my junior year, we played them in Columbus and put an ass whupping on them. The Mid-American Conference (MAC) was strong and used to have really good baseball up and down. A lot of the Big 10 teams used to schedule us just as a patsy early in the season to get in shape for their Big 10 season and they kept getting their butts beat. So they stopped scheduling MAC teams.

Craig Counsell is a very quiet guy. He's close to the vest. You can tell by his body language and by the inquisitive look he had on his face almost all the time that he's processing everything. My first impression was this skinny little kid was going to try to be one of our utility infielders. It looks like you can knock the bat out of his hands and that crazy stance. I had my doubts. I really did. The more you see him play, and the more you see him on the field, and the more you see the way he reacts to situations, you realize he just had tremendous baseball instincts.

In basketball, they call them gym rats. Counsell was a dugout rat. He not only knew what he had to do on every play, but he knew what every other player on the field was supposed to do when the ball was put into play. It sure didn't take long to see that side of him.

Initially, I was skeptical. With each passing day it became clearer and cleared that this was going to be a go-to guy, not just a part of the team, not just a piece at the end of the bench. This was going to be a guy for our 2001 team who was going to play a huge role. As we started to gather before spring training, one thing became really clear to Bob Melvin, Dwayne Murphy, Chris Spier and the rest of the guys on my coaching staff—we had an old team. Our average age was close to thirty-five. A lot of the guys were at the tail end of their careers. We knew we couldn't run Jay Bell out there 145 times. We couldn't run Matt Williams out there 145 times. We were going to need somebody to plug in there from time to time to make sure those guys got regular rest. If they got dinged up a little bit we needed somebody that we could put in that position for maybe a week or two weeks at a time and not miss anything.

As camp started to develop and we got to see more and more of Counsell, it was apparent very early on that this was a guy that we could plug in at second base as long as we needed him to. He could play shortstop as long as we needed him to. He could play third base. I have no doubts we could put him in the outfield if necessary. He was just a great student of the game and didn't make mistakes. Any manager will tell you that it's invaluable to any team if you have a guy you can plug in at multiple positions and multiple spots in the batting order and not worry about what they're going to bring to the team. Counsell was that guy for us.

It's funny looking back at that World Series playoffs now in the age of analytics. I probably misused the hell out of him. With our pitching staff, we were constantly of a feeling that if we can get a lead in the game, we're going to win. With Randy Johnson and Curt Schilling at the top of the rotation, we had some guys in the middle of the bullpen that we were confident in. We had Byung-hyun Kim at the end of the ballgames. We felt that if we could get on the board first, we could find a way to scratch a run early in the ballgame and let Schill and RJ take the mound with the lead, that we had a really good chance to win those ballgames.

I used Counsell to sacrifice bunt four times in one game against Atlanta. Statistically, probably not the proper thing to do, but given our team and where we were at that particular time, my coaches and I were all in agreement that that's what we needed to do. Let's get a run and let our pitching staff make it stand up.

Without a doubt, the biggest hit in the series in '01 was Gonzo's. It was the game winner in Game 7. There's no bigger hit than that. But if you go back to Game 1, the Yankees took a quick lead. It would have been very easy at that point playing against the three-time defending champions to say "Oh sh-t. Here we go again." But Counsell comes up and hits a home run out near the pool at right centerfield and, bang, we're right back in the ballgame. We're here to play. It seems appropriate that it was Craig Counsell who did it. Gonzo hit fifty-seven that year, and some of the other guys we had in the lineup were capable of doing big things when the light was shining the brightest. But Craig Counsell went up there and hit a home run to tie the game and really made us feel like, "Yeah, we can do this. We can play with these guys."

In the first place, obviously Craig's stance looked odd. I used to say he looked like a guy trying to knock a spider off the ceiling with a broom. Nobody hit like that. Milton May, my former coaching partner with the Giants, used to have an unusual stance from the left side, but all the guys who have something unusual like that, their hands were in a good hitting position if you look at them when the ball is released.

During my playing days, I had an ugly-looking stance at the plate, too. But once the ball is released most players get in pretty similar situations, and Counsell was that way. It was just something he did for whatever reason. I don't know how it evolved. I don't know why he felt comfortable doing that, but it didn't bother me a bit. The fans had a lot of fun with it. I'm sure a lot of people made fun of him over the course of his career, but it was something that worked for him. He felt comfortable doing it and he was in a great hitting position once the ball was released.

I thought Craig would be a good manager because he is inquisitive. He wanted to know why we were doing certain things. He suggested other things that maybe we could do differently.

I remember one specific time, we used the hit and run a lot. Counsell was hitting in the eighth spot in the lineup. The number seven hitter reached. We put the hit and run on. He did his job. He got the ball on the ground and moved the guy up to second base. Obviously the pitcher was up next. After a couple of innings had passed, I noticed him standing around behind me, hands on his hips, looking around like something was on his mind. He asked, "Why do we hit and run with the eight-hitter with the pitcher on deck?" He asked it not in a "What the hell is the matter with you?" way. He just wanted to know what my thinking was.

I told him I view the hit and run as an offensive weapon, not necessarily just to stay out of the double play. If I have confidence that the number eight hitter can execute, put the ball in play, find a hole, now we've got first and third, nobody out, with the pitcher at the plate. That makes it a completely different situation for me. He looked up at the ceiling of the dugout for a minute and looked back at me. He said, "Okay, I see that."

It was just one of many situations where he wanted to know, "Why did you do that?" and probably filed it away. At some point he'll either use it or decide he doesn't want to use it, but just wasn't a blind following of orders. He knew that I was in charge. That's what I wanted done, and he was going to do it, but he wanted to know why. That was probably the clearest example of this is a guy who is a thinking player, and he'll probably carry that right into his mind after his playing career is over.

I don't know why players aren't laying down bunts against the shift. Analytics would say that the percentage over the course of 162 games that you're better off swinging away and trying to hit the ball in the air. That may be true, but I think at the same time, do the obvious. Criminy, they're giving you the entire left side of the infield. You're leading off an inning. You're trailing by a run. Bunt the ball. Get on base. Make something happen. Set it up for the guys behind you, especially with guys who may have been struggling, or guys who aren't hitting the ball in the air. They're not hitting it out of the ballpark. They're getting carved up by the opposing pitcher. Take what they give you. Don't try to create something that is tough to create in that situation.

When the Diamondbacks play against the Brewers, Craig and I catch up either in Milwaukee or here in Phoenix. My wife and Michelle stay in close contact. They're on the phone all the time. Indirectly I'm staying in touch with him through the wives.

I have not been surprised by Craig's success as a manager. From my experience being around him as a player and watching the way he approached the game as a player, I had no doubts he was going to be a good manager someday. I think the biggest test that all managers have to face nowadays is how are you going to use your pitching staff. We've seen Tampa Bay and some of the other teams go to the opener. You get the guy who goes through the lineup one time, and then you bring in a starter to eat up three or four innings. Counsell was a manager who was at the forefront of that on the 2018 postseason. I think that's something that organizations all around baseball are going to have to revisit the idea of the starting pitcher going six, seven, or eight innings in a ballgame and then a set-up guy and a closer. I think that model might be outdated.

*Counsell diving for the ball in 2001 with the Arizona Diamondbacks. He played in 141 games at third base, shortstop, and second base.*

# THE HEAT WAS ON COUNSELL WHEN HE REPLACED AN ALL-STAR. BUT IT WAS A DRY HEAT.

## MARK GONZALEZ

*Mark Gonzalez has been the Cubs beat writer since 2005. Prior he was a major reporter covering the Arizona Diamondbacks. Originally from the Bay Area, Gonzalez is a graduate of San Jose State.*

The one story about Craig that always stands out to me was one spring training. They had told Matt Williams is he was going to have to be used as a utility guy. They were going with Craig Counsell as third baseman. I was working on this story on this transition, and I asked Counsell, "Are you prepared for taking over at third base?" He had been a shortstop at **NOTRE DAME\*** and second with the Marlins and some of the time with the Diamondbacks. Craig said, "I watched Matt Williams. That's how I got better." He broke down all of Matt's nuances in playing defense and other tricks.

I thought this was something else, given the fact that here's a guy who was pretty much a journeyman until the 2001 playoffs, and he's admitting to me that he learned from a guy whose job he's taking over who was a multi-Gold Glove winner and perennial **ALL-STAR\***. His candidness in saying how he

*\*Johnny Lattner, the 1953 Heisman Trophy winner from **NOTRE DAME**, didn't even lead the Irish in rushing or receiving that season.*

*\*In the 12th inning of the 1955 **ALL-STAR GAME** in Milwaukee, Yogi Berra complained to Stan Musial that his feet were killing him. Musial told Berra to relax and that he would "get him out of there in a hurry." Musial homered to end the game.*

was going to work to improve by watching the guy he's replacing showed me a lot, especially the way he handled that. Matt Williams was at the end of his career.

Sometimes guys have a lot of pride and don't want to give up their jobs easily. This one was taken away from Matt Williams. Craig admitted that he was looking up to the guy he was replacing who had been established and how he was going to be forced out the door. That winter they were going to trade Matt Williams to the Rockies for three players, and he turned it down because he had ten and five rights—at least ten years in the bigs and five with the last team. That's what it was. Anyway it showed me a lot that Craig was so open about his willingness to learn, the fact that he wasn't as experienced at third, and he was willing to watch Matty and pick his brain told me a lot.

Craig ended up contributing more than I thought. At that point, he was really reaching the peak of his career. It was the culmination of all the things he had worked for, especially coming up with the Rockies and getting traded to the Marlins, and being around a bunch of veterans on that 1997 World Series championship team. When he was with the Dodgers, he didn't play as much as he liked.

That served him in two ways. As a utility guy, he would always be ready. Two, now that he's a manager, he learned that to make sure you communicate with a player and convey the right message, be true and honest, regardless of how tough the news may be to the player. That's served him pretty well with the Brewers, especially with all of the guys they play during a game, the way they shuttle guys back and forth from the minors to the majors and so forth. You never hear guys complaining about him as a manager because he's very direct.

That's one thing he learned from this **DODGER**\* time. He used to tell me that sometimes the manager would say, "We're going to get you in there tomorrow. We're going to get you in there soon," and instead he would sit on the bench. That stuck in his mind.

I'm really impressed by the job he's done as a manager in Milwaukee. I'm somewhat surprised that he's really hit the ground running there. He's helped make them a winner, but it's a sustained success. There have been times when they looked like they were going to fall apart, slip away from contention. Instead they've gotten stronger. You saw that in 2018 in the last month. They were out five games with twenty-six to play, and they, first of all, head to head beat the Cubs four out of six games to get within two, and eventually caught them on the second-to-last game of the series.

The way he runs a game, it's not your typical game, pulling guys early and using your hardest relievers to face your most favorable match-ups. He has done a terrific job of adjusting in each situation and using his best pitchers at the right time, especially guys like Hader.

He's got a pretty good pulse. He's not a guy who's going to go through the clubhouse and spy on guys all the time. He knows his place. It stems from his playing days and knowing the pulse of a clubhouse, knowing the pulse of a player, whether it's the 26th player or the star.

As a manager, I would rate him at a 9 out of 10, without a doubt. He's done the impossible with high baseball acumen. He's done it by maximizing all the talent out of guys. It isn't

---

\***DODGER** Stadium—since the day it opened in 1962—is the only current stadium that has never changed its seating capacity. Because of a conditional use permit from the city of Los Angeles, the capacity is always 56,000....Fenway Park's seating capacity is lower for day games (36,984) than for night games (37,400).

like he's blessed with having a line-up of stars. He finds a way to use the right guys at the right time and use the match-ups to his advantage.

Craig was very professional in interviews. He was pretty classy. You can tell he gets that from his parents. He mentions his dad. I'm not familiar with his dad's background. I believe Joe Garigiola, Jr. played for him at Notre Dame as a freshman. There's some structure there. You can tell he was very well raised just as a player and now as a manager. He's not outlandish by any means by his demeanor. He's the same guy. When you get that consistent vibe, guys know what they're getting from their manager.

The two things that stand out how he was willing to accept anything that came out, especially the third base situation. That was a sticky time for everybody involved. The Diamondbacks were trying to move a big star in Matt. A lot of guys don't realize when their careers are over. Craig, being the pro that he was at the time, it wasn't he was walking on egg shells, but he knew he was replacing a star. Counsell certainly deserved the starts. Matt held on as long as he could. Craig learned how to handle people based on when he was with the Dodgers and not playing as much as he was told he was going to play, conveying that message to his players in terms of how he plays them and how he comes in and says, "Hey, you're in this day," or "No, you're not in this day." That has served him very well.

Great guy! Classy!

Chapter Seven

# HOME, SWEET HOME MILWAUKEE

## Miller Park:
## The Field of Screams
## and Land of Ahs

# IT'S GOOD TO BE THE BOSS

### BUD SELIG

*Bud Selig is a Milwaukee legend respon-
sible for bringing the Brewers in 1970.
He was the Commissioner of Baseball
from 1992-2015 and was inducted into
the Hall of Fame in 2017.*

I have early memories of Craig when he tagged along with his
dad John out at County Stadium. We really ran a family operation in so many ways. I got a kick out of it, that's all I can tell
you. It was a long time ago but Craig was there and it was great.
I like John a lot. Craig used to be a little kid walking the halls.
When we had the '82 team back, I can still see Craig looking at
them. He will remember when it was Cecil, Simba, Molitor or
Yount. That's the team Craig grew up with.

My recollection of the next time seeing Craig was during the
'97 World Series. I was in the Commisioner's Box and he came
over to say hello. I got a big kick out of that. It was hard for me
to believe that there's this young man who I knew so well and
here he is now. I was there when he scored the winning run in
the World Championship. I have to tell you he's a Milwaukee
kid who loves the Brewers and everything baseball.

In 2006 Craig and Mark Loretta came to see me right near the
end of a Players Union negotiation as the Union had asked
them. Of course, we had a great relationship like I did with all
the guys. At the Union negotiations Craig and Mark Loretta
were so mature. Craig was good; he really understood. He was
fair and he was decent. The men at the union said they knew
the relationship and they were right. I have to give credit to
his Mom and Dad for how well he turned out. They oughta

be proud; they did a hell of a job and it shows. You bet I really enjoyed when he came back to Milwaukee and to this day I will say that to you.

I was born and raised here in Milwaukee, and I take great pride in it. It makes me so happy that Craig came back. I mean you have a guy with those great Milwaukee roots, and it's a really wonderful story. All along I heard that Craig would be a managerial quality type of guy.

Craig was always very impressive the way he handled himself, the way he spoke. He was smart; just everything about him was impressive. I'm not surprised and he has done a tremendous job managing. Craig is really popular here. He's already been manager for five years and I think he has a long and very bright future with this organization. The thing I like about Craig is he's a Milwaukee guy and he represents the Brewers, baseball, and Milwaukee as well as anybody could possibly represent it. I'm proud of him and I hope this continues. I'm not the least bit worried because if Craig, God willing, can finish this out; he'll be Manager of the Year soon.

You asked if Vince Lombardi and I had athe same secretary. Yes! Vince Lombardi's secretary Lori Keck became my secretary when Vince went to **WASHINGTON**\*. He left to go to Washington and that was it for her, she just didn't want to live there. We got the Brewers in 1970 and Vince died later that year. I got a telegram from Vince the day we got the team and it's one of my proud possessions. In 1971 Lori applied and she became my secretary-assistant and she was for the next 38 years. Lori's from Sturgeon Bay and lived in Green Bay while working for Vince; then she moved to Milwaukee. She was terrific.

*Bob Long was the only ex-Packer to play for Lombardi with the **REDSKINS**.

# HEAR ME NOW, LISTEN TO ME LATER

### BOB UECKER*

*Bob Uecker has had an incredible life. The Milwaukee native, 85, parlayed a .208 batting average to become Johnny Carson's favorite guest, a TV sitcom star, author, and voice of the Milwaukee Brewers since 1971. Little wonder he is called "Mr. Baseball."*

Players' kids come to the ball park today as 9, 10 or even 12 years old. You can look at some of them and say these kids are pretty good already. They are around an environment that breeds success. They are getting coaching at the best level because their dads are coaches or players. Those kids are around that environment where if you make mistakes or don't do things right, you have a big league coach or your dad telling you how to improve. When you experience that day after day and you are playing in summer league your environment is baseball twenty four hours a day.

I remember Craig as a kid when he came to the ball park with his dad during school breaks. He was no different than the players kids we have out there today out on the field. They are usually chasing fly balls and doing what baseball families do. When you see kids around the ball park you don't really think about whether they are going to make the major leagues. You don't see them play enough. What I remember about Craig as a little kid is that he was little. He was a little thin guy. He

*One reason that <u>UECKER</u> had over 100 appearances on the "Tonight Show" was a standing bet with Carson that he wouldn't laugh at any of Carson's jokes. Carson kept inviting Uecker back trying to win the bet.

was pesky as a hitter. He wasn't a big power guy. Later in the big leagues every once in awhile, he would hit a homer. He would get on base. He was fast. He could run and steal bases. He could aggravate you. He grew from there developing into a pretty good player and World's Champion a couple of times. That's the bottom line. All that rhetoric you hear about somebody as a kid doesn't mean anything. Even as a high school or college kid you can pretty much tell who, may not be a major league player; but will get a chance to play professionally.

When I found out Craig made it to the big league it was no surprise. When you play for a program like **NOTRE DAME\***, you know that guy's got talent.

I've been around a long time and I've seen guys with odd stances from time to time, so Craig's batting stance didn't bother me. Having played and won a World Series we had guys that didn't look right or weren't using the standard batting stance that they taught you in the minor league. Whatever made you comfortable and whatever way you had success with, I didn't care what it looked like if you could do it and it made you a better hitter or a better player that's what you do. I see guys today that have odd stances and I don't think anything of it. That is their strong suits. Those guys that have those big stances like Craig had with holding the bat near the top of the batting cage, that doesn't mean a thing as long as you get to the hitting position in time. And that is what he did.

I was not surprised when Craig hired his former coach from Notre Dame, Pat Murphy, as his bench coach in Milwaukee. There is a bonding there that happens in those programs. This is evidenced by Murphy being a coach for Craig and one of Craig's closest friends. Pat Murphy was a coach for a long time. When

\*Former **NOTRE DAME** quarterback Tony Rice has been on more covers of *Sports Illustrated* than Henry Aaron...when Aaron headed the Atlanta Braves minor league operations, he cut off the pockets on the players' pants so they couldn't carry tobacco products.

you coached and managed in the major leagues, which is what Murphy did, it was no surprise that Craig hired him.

I told our owner long ago that Craig belongs in the dugout. He needs to be our manager. I told Craig that he didn't belong upstairs but it gave him the opportunity to find out what goes on in the front office. Like what the thinking is for players that we are going to draft, players that are available, players that are DFA. I really felt Craig didn't belong upstairs. Upstairs is a good job, don't get me wrong, it's not a bad job; but I told Craig he belonged in the dugout. When they fired Manager Ron Roenicke in 2015 I told our owner, if we hire anybody it has got to be Craig Counsell. I didn't know if he was going to be a success. All I knew was that he had to be the manager. He had managerial capabilities.

Craig can take care of business when it comes to getting tough with people. All I knew was he had all that because I saw what he did as a player with Arizona, Miami and when he finished up with us. Certain guys have managerial capabilities and you don't really find out about it until their waning days as a player comes into being. But you know down the road somewhere this guy could be a coach and a good one. Craig is a good coach. Craig's boys, you couldn't get much better than they get from Craig. Jack and Brady get more from Craig than Craig got from John. John wasn't what Craig is; John was mainly a front office guy. Craig has had a great career and a couple of world championships which is a heck of an M.O. Craig is dead set on seeing his kids play. He watches their high school games. He goes wherever his kids go when he has a chance. He watches them play and he works with them.

Craig, his wife, me and my other half are good friends. Craig trusts me and I trust him. He tells me things that I know I am not going to use on the air. I would never talk about inside stuff. I would never rip players because I know how hard it is to play. I know what it is like to get your brains beat out by the beat writers and other media people.

The big leagues are totally different today. These guys flip **BATS**\* and trot around the bases. That would have never happened in my time, the 50's, 60's. Back in the day, each organization had 15 farm clubs, now they have 3 or 4. Back then you could spend your whole career in the minors.

Knowing how Craig played the game of baseball and watching him walk around the ballpark; I knew he'd make a great manager. Craig absolutely loves Milwaukee and Wisconsin. When I interview Craig in the pregame show him I don't bring up bad or costly things that happened in the game the night before because I don't want to start things on a negative note. I can find tons of things to talk about that accentuate the positive.

Craig as a manager is not really any different than he was a player. He is in the game all the time. If Craig thinks he is right and his players are getting a screw job he is going to fight for them all the way, even if he gets ejected.

We go out to eat together with our families. A lot of managers don't go out with the broadcasters. A lot of managers hate the broadcasters because they think the broadcasters are a pain in neck. They think the broadcasters are picking on the manager or the way the team is playing. It's not like that with Craig.

\*Orlando Cepeda used more **BATS** than any player in history. He felt each bat had exactly one hit in it. When Cepeda hit safely, he would discard the bat. He had 2,364 hits in his career.

# TAKE THIS JOB AND LOVE IT

### DOUG MELVIN

*In his hometown of Chatham, Ontario, Doug Melvin may be better known than another local native, Ferguson Jenkins. After an outstanding prep career, Melvin pitched in the **YANKEES**\* minor league system before becoming an assistant coach in New York from 1979 to 1984. He then became GM of the Texas Rangers where he guided them to their first playoffs in that team's history. In 2002, he became the Brewers' GM, where he hired Craig Counsell as manager in 2015.*

My second year at Brewers we had Richie Sexson, Geoff Jenkins and a lot bad ball players around them. We were in what we call a total rebuild and one of them had to go. Richie Sexson brought the most value back. I made the trade of Richie to Arizona. It was a ten-player trade. Craig Counsell was one of those players we got. I know it was a tough trade for their General Manager Joe Garagiola Jr. because Craig was a very popular player in Arizona. He is still popular down there. Craig still had the ability to play, had great clubhouse presence, and he was a great teammate. That had great value to our organization which was going to be trending with a lot of younger players and a rebuilding program.

Craig might not have wanted to be a part of that trade if it wasn't to Milwaukee where he lived. But we knew from a baseball standpoint what he brought: a class act. He wasn't

*The cement used to build **YANKEE STADIUM** was purchased from Thomas Edison who owned the huge Portland Cement Company.

big, but he did all the other things that are required to bring championships. He goes down as one of the best teammates whenever you talk to the people in the game. Craig and Trevor Hoffman, both those guys, were great teammates.

I didn't know Craig at all until I traded for him. He was here for a year; went back to Arizona, became a free agent, and I brought him back in 2007. He had a rough time his last year in 2011. He was like 1 for 40 there near the end of his career but I kept him on the roster. Today that kind of a player doesn't survive with the way that all the roster moves happen, but Craig brought so much more to the table. I also anticipated that if that was going to be his last year it would give me an opportunity to get to know him a little bit better.

As a general manager I had a difficult time getting real close with players because I knew I was going to have to make moves and changes with them. I treated them with respect, but I wasn't one of the general managers that would go to dinner or go out and have a drink with players. I wanted to keep him around to get to know him a little bit better because I did really feel that he was going to have a future in the game whether it was manager, front office, or whatever. It was 2010 and I gave him a two-year contract at that time and he didn't perform well.

I remember when I said to him, "Do you want to be a manager or a general manager?" Craig said ''I don't know, I just want to be in a position of leadership where I can impact an organization." I told him in both those positions you can have an impact on the success of an organization.

Both jobs are leadership positions. Craig told me to give him a little time to decide which one he wanted to do. In a short amount of time he could decide whether the right place for him was the front office of the down on the field with a uniform back on. I was worried about losing Craig when he was interviewed by the Red Sox to be a hitting coach when he was working for the Brewers front office. He went to the interview when John Farrell was the manager. I was worried we might lose him to the **RED SOX**\* if he decided to go back on the field. But he decided not to take it.

My thoughts were if he wanted to manage maybe it's good to go to the minor leagues to manage. I thought if he wanted to be a coach he might be able to be a coach immediately. I know I had those conversations in my head. I asked, "Do you want to be in the front office?" Because you travel so much managing a team, he felt he would have more time with his kids and see them playing ball and see them growing up if he was in the front office.

When you're managing and coaching, it's tough to see your kids play ball. I had a manager Johnny Oates in Texas that didn't see his son play until he was 19-years-old. Craig wanted to take the front office over managing and coaching the first year. It was family related. I also think that in his mind he thought if he can learn what takes place in the front office with the mechanics of player decision making, dealing with owners, dealing with scouting directors, and farm directors, in the end it would be very helpful to him.

Now that he is managing, it is even more helpful to him that he took that path as opposed to going to the minor leagues. You know, he's a bright guy, a smart guy. He asks questions and challenges you. He loves baseball conversations. That's what you do in the front office. I'm not so sure the front offices do it today like we did. Our people would engage in baseball challenges and conversations all the time. Craig would love those kinds of conversations. When I go into the park now, I will see

*In Babe Ruth's first major league game—as a pitcher for the Boston **RED SOX**—he was removed in the 7th inning for a pinch hitter.

Pat Murphy and Craig sitting there and I'll bring up something to get their minds going. Craig loves that kind of interaction perhaps since he's been around the game as many years as he has.

Craig's a tough competitor; his playing career wasn't always easy. He had been released, traded, and designated for assignment. As General Manager every spring training I would tell players, "Choosing a career in baseball requires that you be prepared, it isn't a negative, it's just preparation. Every one of you in this room will probably be traded, designated for assignment (DFA), released, optioned to the minor leagues or whatever. The people that bounce back up from all those decisions of the game are going to be the ones that are going to survive the longest." Craig was one of those guys, he handled all those situations very well.

I included him in the late 2003 Diamondbacks trade even though I never met him before because we needed an infielder. It was more about his leadership skills. I'm not going to just trade for a local guy. You have to also be a good player; he was a good player. The other factor was, we were in a rebuilding mode and we knew we were going to have younger players who needed a clubhouse presence. Craig might not have thought that. At that time he was 33 years old; he probably wanted to play another five or six years. In 2004 he went back and played two years at Arizona.

Craig had clubhouse presence plus his ability to play. He knew how to play the game; he played the game the right way. He knew when to move a runner over, whether to hold on to the ball, or whether to throw to get a guy out. He had good instincts. He was always prepared; he was a baseball junkie. He came to the park prepared and he practiced well. Also I heard about his influence in the clubhouse. Even though I'm not down there, I hear about it all the time. Any manager that had him wanted him because he's one of those guys. There is always a player on a team that a manager just totally wants. He sees him as a team leader. Craig was a team leader. It's not always your most talented player. Sometimes it's somebody else; Craig was that somebody else.

When I offered and explained to him the job I wanted him to take, I said "Craig I'm in the office here at 9 in the morning." I said "You will get time to go spend with your family, I understand you've been away from it. But come on upstairs and get to know everybody from the scouting to players development to the analytics department, spend a lot time. We're going to have meetings; we'll go over things. We're going to send you on scouting assignments." He went on a scouting assignment for the trade for Jean Segura and had a big impact in our acquisition of Jean Segura for Zack Greinke. He also went out to see a lot of amateur players, he loved that part of it also. Craig had input in a lot of those players. We sent about 4 or 5 people to see Jean Segura who was with the Los Angeles Angels at the time playing in AA. I sent Craig to go see him and he filed a favorable report on Segura. We then traded Zack Greinke at the deadline for Segura.

Craig liked that kind of action going on seeing other teams. He's well respected, always bumping into a lot of people out there. I told him to spend time with family; don't be afraid to leave the office and go watch the boys play ball or the daughter playing sports. Don't be afraid to do that. I respect the fact that he's been away from them all these years in the summertime. He needed to spend some summertime with them.

When we had our games at night I'd have the baseball ops come to the suite every game. We'd sit up there and people would be talking about the game. We'd interact during the whole game about our farm system, other teams. Craig's a great person to interact with in baseball discussions whether its old school whether its new, analytical things, the history of the game. I've always been a believer you can manage sometimes in this business, by storytelling, because there are so many great stories and experiences that we all go through.

In 2014 we had a rough year. Ron Roenicke was our manager. We were in first place 150 days out of the year but we ended up not getting into the playoffs. I asked Craig then if he had an interest in managing. He didn't want to manage then because he didn't like the fact that he was upstairs and that Ron Roenicke might lose his job. I don't think he wanted that perception that he was doing that and he never did. He never was critical of our manager or our coaches, he never did that. That year he said "no" to managing under those conditions.

We kept Ron Roenicke the next year, 2015. We were 23 days into the season and we were 6 and 17 or something like that. I asked Craig, "Craig if we don't get this thing turned around would you be interested now to manage?" He was getting frustrated with losing. I told him that I was not going to be doing this much longer at my age. I am getting ready to transition into a senior role. Once I reached 20 years tenure and age 65 I said maybe it's time to turn it over to somebody. I went to Owner Mark Attanasio on that. But that year when I went to Craig. I said, "Craig, if you want to manage, this is the time. It'd be good for you." Craig was tired of losing at the end of the year and losing at the start of 2015. He thought he could control or have an impact on things. He was ready. After learning what he did after three and a half years in the front office, I think he felt that he belonged with the uniform on.

I'm sure people outside the organization were critical because Craig didn't have any experience coaching or managing. However, he was one of the few guys who did work in a front office. Later on there were some guys, John Farrell worked in the front office in Cleveland and then he ended up being a manager of the Red Sox. A.J. Hinch worked in the front office and he went on and became manager of the **ASTROS**\* and won a World Series. If you look at it, that part may be more important than managing a AAA team.

The processes that you go through and your interaction in the front office as a manager is important to have. You're not going to be a successful organization if your manager and your GM aren't getting along. Craig went through our minor league system. He knew our players better than the other managers had in the past. When I hired Ron Roenicke, Ken Macha and Ned Yost they knew nothing about our system.

Craig had time under his belt knowing our minor league players, knowing our prospects, knowing our minor league managers and coaches. The front office gave Craig perspective of the interaction you have with ownership.

Ownership interaction is very important. Mark Attanasio is a very active owner; he is very hands-on and very fair. He will challenge you with tough questions and a lot of "Whys?". That helped Craig and he was ready. In baseball, managers and coaches don't even make close to the money some of the college football coaches and NBA coaches make. Craig took a cut in pay from a player's salary to a manager's salary. It wasn't about money for Craig, but he did want to be treated fairly. Craig has a union stance; he has very strong opinions with a union standpoint for the players. The players union protected him for his 16-year career and so he's very respectful of that.

When I hired Craig as manager I didn't have any major worries other than his coaching staff. He needed to select his own coaches by the end of the year; people that he felt comfortable with, and I understood that. If you're going to manage,

\*Larry Dierker threw a no-hitter for the **ASTROS** in 1976 and was given a thousand-dollar bonus check by the team. He gave the money back because the team was in receivership saying "A no-hitter is a good enough reward for me."

you can't have people telling you that you have to hire certain people. It's always tough, and I wasn't sure who his coaches would be. You want to make sure he hires the right people to coach for him because they are going to have a major impact on his career.

Craig brought in Pat Murphy as a bench coach. Pat was Craig's college coach. He brought in Carlos Subero from our minor league system. He kept Eddie Sedar, and they hired a new pitching coach that Craig didn't know from the **CUBS**\*, Derek Johnson. Craig also kept Lee Tunnell. I've always felt that both parties have to agree on the individual coaches. A general manager might have had an issue with a particular coach or a player, and you just have to put that behind you. Both have to be pretty well in agreement, but you also have to have the flexibility to let a manager feel comfortable with whom he is hiring.

Craig has done a really good job managing. After I transitioned out of the GM position there was a philosophical difference with the front office and I think Craig was on board with that. There is more analytics in the game today and he is smart enough to know how to utilize that. He's got a good enough baseball background to know what numbers are just a bunch a noise and what numbers are good to utilize in helping a player's performance. Craig has a really good memory and I'm sure when he got the manager's job he probably had about 30 former players call him about a coaching job. I asked him one time which manager he respected the most that he played for; that is always a tough question when you've played for different guys. He told me it was Jim Leyland. Leyland was the guy he respected the most and it was because he could jump your butt one day and the next day he'd come up to you and pat you on the back.

*On July 1, 1943, the first night game was held at **WRIGLEY FIELD**. It was an exhibition game for the All-American Girls Professional Baseball League (AAGPBL). Portable lights were used.

Craig's the guy who would not be afraid to do that. He probably had some unhappiness during his career; there are certain years he didn't play as much or whatever. At the end of his career, he just struggled and I told him, "Get some hits, get some hits; I don't-want to have to release you." To release a fan favorite, a guy that's a favorite of the players; I didn't want to do that. I was rooting for him to get some hits.

I worked with the Yankees as a coaching assistant back in 1979-85. I then went to Baltimore and became assistant general manager to Roland Hemond and his farm director. My first GM job was in Texas and the situation here in Milwaukee was very similar to Texas. When I went to Texas as a GM they had never been to the playoffs and they had been in existence for 25 years. Then when I came here, the Brewers had not been to the playoffs since '82. They had 11 straight losing seasons so it was 25 or so years that they hadn't been in the playoffs. The fans here were very hungry to get back to winning baseball after having had a real dry spell. Everybody wanted the Younts, Molitors, and Ted Simmons like the '82 team. We had a lot of younger players who said, "Hey guys we weren't even born in '82 and don't know anything about the '82 team." If you give a good blue collar effort the fans understand that. The fans understood that we were not a large market club and we had to find different ways to win.

We have great fans here; we get almost 30,000 every night. Living in Milwaukee you get to know the people and they get to know you. I've been out of the GM chair for four years now. They are Brewer hungry here. It's a statewide team, and if you drive up to Green Bay, La Crosse, or Madison you'll see Brewer apparel. Milwaukee itself is so hungry for the Brewers I think it is something that will always be here. Right now there is this new generation of interest that was missing from 1986-2002.

The manager has to be concerned about the criticism on social media. I felt that Craig could handle it because he played as many years as he did. If you're not personally having success;

if you're making player moves, you're going to have to read about it; your family is going to have to read about it, and you have to have really thick skin to be able to handle that. He's here all off-season and can hear it on his radio. If I was going to give Craig some critiquing on his interviews I would tell him to keep his head up more, look into the camera, and look at the people that are asking the questions. Brewers' fans realize how good a manager they have, but there is criticism from the fan base no matter who is managing. Craig will handle it okay. I'm not in the position of General Manager anymore, but I've seen it before with all the other managers I've had: there are certain things you can critique and talk to them about. When I see him I ask him, "Hey, Craig how you doing?" Sometimes we will have several games in a row, but I will just tell him to keep your chin up, it's a long season.

Craig is a great family person. I know how much he admires and loves his family, from his mother and his dad, to Michelle and the kids. He knows how to separate that when he gets away from the game. I have a place out in Park City, Utah and they go out there once in awhile. I know sometimes you need to get away from it and Michelle understands it. It's good to get away and spend time with the family. That is a tough thing to do; a lot of times you are with your family and you're still thinking about baseball.

Craig goes out with baseball people like the Mark Kotsays and the Trevor Hoffmans. They are all good friends of his and he probably has a lot of other baseball friends and family. Also, Craig can take criticism. He may challenge you on it at some point, but he can handle it. He respects the game and the history of the game and he respects how hard the game is to play. That's why he is a good manager.

1 never promise things in baseball. I always said it's a bad habit to promise somebody something. I do believe Craig read the fact that I knew he was going to have some important job with the organization whether it be a manager, coach, or

assistant GM grooming him for my position. He could have done my position too as a general manager, if he wanted to go that route when I transitioned. He would have figured it out, surrounded himself with good people. When he got up there in the front office with me, he saw it's pretty complex when you're a general manager. You got 6 minor league teams, a major league team, international scouting, amateur scouting, pro scouting, analytics, medical staff, and dealing with ownership. The manager's job is not easy because you're exposed every night on TV with your decision-making. But Craig is able to manage all of that.

One of the best decisions I ever made in all my years in baseball was trading for Craig Counsell and later naming him the Brewers manager!

*The riding lawnmower pitcher Trevor Hoffman bid on at an auction. All the players signed it with a silver Sharpie. Trevor gave it to Craig as gift.*

# INSIDE TRAITOR

Harrison Bader

*Harrison Bader was drafted by the Cardinals early in the 2015 MLB draft from the University of Florida. Two years earlier he played in Milwaukee or the Lakeshore Chinooks in the Northwoods Collegiate League. In the penultimate game of the 2017 regular season, the Brewers were playing the Cardinals. The Brewers needed to win to catch the Rockies or a wild card spot. The Brewers were leading 6-0 when Bader, a rookie outfielder with the Cardinals, drove in the winning run with a hit in the bottom of the eighth inning. Cardinals 7, Brewers 6.*

When the 2013 college season was done I played summer ball as everybody does. I was placed in the Northwoods League by my coaching staff at Florida. I played for the Lakeshore Chinooks in Milwaukee. Teams house players in homes of team supporters. Just by chance I was hosted in Craig Counsell's house. I guess just pretty serendipitously. I didn't choose it, it was just given to me, but it was great. I had heard of Craig before because I was a Yankees fan growing up. So I was aware of what he did in that World Series in 2001. When I got to their house they gave me a car to drive, a Lamborghini, just kidding. It was a 2004 GMC Tahoe, one of the old school ones. It was great—like one the best cars I've driven.

When I was there, Craig's boys were really young and a lot shorter. Whenever we go to Milwaukee I see them at the stadium. Craig came to one of my games, but he didn't really talk about baseball much. He was pretty reserved. He was super laid back. I think his growing up, going through the baseball process and the different levels make me understand why he didn't really talk about baseball. Success in the Major Leagues really does come from within. You have to understand who you are, no one can do it for you. So he can provide wisdom and everything but I understand why he didn't talk much because it's all about your own journey. Which I appreciated and I understood.

I never really looked to Craig for baseball talk, I was just very appreciative that he opened his house to me and allowed me to live comfortably. Michelle was very sweet and super nice. She was helpful with anything I needed or wanted. She was like a second mother when I was in Summer Ball. Unfortunately I hurt my heel that summer so I only played there for about a month.

But the time I was there they were always super friendly. The kids were always out playing. They had two big dogs that were always there. It was great and they were awesome! My mother actually still keeps in touch with Michelle. The kids were big baseball fans and played baseball all the time. I went to some of their games when I was there. They asked me to play catch with them, which, of course, I did.

The Northwoods League was a good league. Talent-wise it was definitely below the Cape Cod League. I played in the Cape League the following season. Lakeshore was good—the only issue was the travel, the travel was tough. Besides that it was a great league with talented players everywhere. Paul DeJong and Pete Alonso were there. A lot of guys if they don't make the Cape their first summer, get sent to the Northwoods League which is still good.

I never bragged about staying with a former Major League ball player. I could tell that Craig and his family wanted to keep their private lives separate. So I never broadcasted it. I was just there to do my to best play some ball. Like I said before it just serendipitously worked out to where I was staying with an ex-big leaguer. Since I got to the big leagues I've talked to Craig briefly just saying hello. But again he keeps it super professional and I get it. It's a frame of mind too. I'm here to compete and win a ball game. I understand the dynamic of how that works.

# THE FOURTH ESTATE DOESN'T TAKE THE FIFTH

TODD ROSIAK

*Todd Rosiak is a big-time survivor as a Wisconsin* **SPORTSWRITER**\*. *He graduated from UW-Milwaukee and has been with the* Milwaukee Journal Sentinel *for 27 years.*

My first exposure to Craig Counsell was in 2011. I had just been moved from covering Marquette University's basketball team over to covering the Milwaukee Brewers at the Milwaukee Journal Sentinel. I'd been around awhile; my first real experience on a pro beat was in 2001 when I moved to Green Bay to cover the Packers for the Journal Sentinel's weekly "Packer Plus" magazine. I was shifted to Marquette—which featured an up-and-coming junior guard named **DWAYNE WADE**\*—in the Fall of 2002 and remained on the beat while also helping cover the Packers during the college basketball offseason until the Spring of 2011.

Marquette advanced to the Sweet 16 that season before being trounced by North Carolina, and that prevented me from heading to spring training—a huge detriment that I wouldn't be aware of until later. It's where relationships are formed between players and reporters, with the media typically

\*There are many times more **SPORTSWRITERS** than there are religious reporters.

\*Tom Crean coached **DWAYNE WADE** at Marquette. Football coaches Jim Harbaugh and John Harbaugh are his brother-in-laws. Crean is married to Joani Harbaugh.

allowed 1 ½ hours of access to the clubhouse every morning, and those relationships are vital to covering the team on a daily basis once the grind of the regular season begins.

Having been deprived of those ultra-valuable six weeks, I had no choice but to jump right into the 2011 season in **CINCIN-NATI***, where the Brewers were opening the regular season. There was a workout day on March 30 and then a walk-off loss to the Reds the following afternoon. It took me a long time to feel comfortable navigating a baseball clubhouse—years, really—and I don't think I ever even interviewed or spoke to Counsell for the first couple months.

I knew who he was, of course. Not only was I an avid baseball fan coming up in the business, but I was also a Milwaukee native who was well aware of his World Series exploits and the fact he was from the suburb of Whitefish Bay. I also found his batting stance incredibly weird. But he had toned it down quite a bit from his earlier days in this, his last year in the major leagues. He had one of the most desired lockers in the Brewers' clubhouse at Miller Park—way in the back, closest to the showers—but I don't remember him being at it much.

I do remember him seeming mostly uninterested in small talk. Which is why I almost fell over when one day, as I was walking down the corridor that led from the clubhouse to the dugout, Counsell asked me how I thought Marquette would be next season. I'd seen him coming toward me but expected at best a nod but more likely nothing, which is what reporters get many times from players when they walk past—almost as if you're a ghost.

I don't remember much of what I said, probably something to the effect of they'll be pretty good because they had a lot of talent

*In 1998 the **CINCINNATI** Reds started an outfield trio of Chris Stynes, Dimitri Young, and Mike Frank. You might know them better as Young, Frank, and Stynes. (The author couldn't resist. He'll show himself to the principal's office now.)

coming back. I do remember asking him how he knew I covered Marquette. He said he went to games at the Bradley Center, their home arena in downtown Milwaukee, and had seen me there and also read my stories. Then we parted ways, with me feeling like I finally had something of a connection with a player.

Counsell played sparingly that year—187 plate appearances over 107 games—on a team that finished with the most victories in franchise history to that point (96) and advanced to the NLCS. He had just one homer and nine RBI, so talking to him about his effect on games didn't happen all that often. The first time I ever interviewed him about something he'd done in a game was on July 10, the final day of games before the All-Star break.

The Brewers had beaten the Reds, 4-3, at Miller Park on a Counsell walk-off sacrifice fly. He hadn't managed a hit in exactly a month (0 for his last 28 at that point) and in the scrum at his locker afterward I clumsily opened by stating, "Well, you didn't get a hit but you still won the game." He was nice enough to provide a quote suitable for my game story, and that was that.

Fast-forward another few weeks, and the calendar had flipped to August. Counsell was still without a hit—0 for 45 at that point, which was believed to be a major-league record. Ryan Braun was in the midst of an MVP season, Prince Fielder was crushing homers and the pitching staff featured Yovani Gallardo and Zack Greinke, but my bosses wanted a story on the hometown kid who just couldn't get a hit.

As the guy who was going with the team to Houston at the start of a road trip (my beat partner, the venerable Tom Haudricourt, had the second half of the trip) the story fell into my lap. I immediately knew this was going to be a tough story to write, because what veteran player would ever want to talk about something like that? Tom suggested I call Counsell's father, John, for some insight into Craig and his struggles, and he passed along his phone number. John had been a longtime

Brewers employee, and Tom said he'd be amenable. So, I traveled to Houston on the off day before the series opener and called John Counsell, not knowing what to expect.

John Counsell couldn't have been kinder. He gave me all that I needed and more to write a suitable story. But I didn't have to file it for several more days, so on the afternoon of the opener I warily approached the then-40-year-old Counsell at his locker (for comparison's sake, I'm only a year younger). I started by telling him that I was pretty sure I knew what his answer to my question was going to be, but I had to ask it anyway since I had my marching orders. "I'm writing a story about your slump. Can I ask you some questions about it?" He gave me a look like I was crazy and said, "I'm not talking to you about that." I told him I understood. I also told him, in the interest of full disclosure, that I'd already interviewed his Dad. He said, "If he wants to talk to you, that's fine. But I'm not talking about it."

Later that night, a funny thing happened. In the ninth inning of an 8-1 Brewers victory over the **ASTROS**\*, Counsell singled to right field off Enerio Del Rosario. Slump over. Counsell's teammates went crazy in the dugout in the aftermath. Following the game, I collected what I needed for my game coverage for the newspaper and then made another run at Counsell. He was all smiles then, and with the pressure lifted, he spoke at length about how tough the previous two months had been for him. I was greatly appreciative, and always respected him for that. I also wrote what I thought was a pretty good story. Then, wouldn't you know, Eugenio Vélez of the Los Angeles Dodgers surpassed Counsell in late September with an 0-for-46 streak at the plate that actually dated to the 2010 season.

---

\*When the Houston **ASTRODOME** opened in 1965, it was hailed as "The Eighth Wonder of the World." Bud Adams, the owner of the AFL's Houston Oilers (now the Tennessee Titans) agreed but said the rent was the "ninth wonder of the world."

Counsell retired following the Brewers' loss to the St. Louis Cardinals in the NLCS, and he eventually wound up in the front office as special assistant to general manager Doug Melvin. He learned all the workings of the front office in that role and was around the ballpark quite often. It wasn't unusual to bump into him, and we'd share pleasantries from time to time.

I'll admit I was as surprised as anyone when he took the reins to the team after Ron Roenicke was fired as manager early in the 2015 season following a 7-18 start. The Brewers had won two straight against the Chicago Cubs at Wrigley Field, and three of four overall, and seemed to finally be getting back on track when Melvin removed Roenicke. I remember I had just walked in the house after covering what was Roenicke's final game, getting a phone call that the move was being made, and hurriedly making plans with Tom for what would be a terribly busy following day.

Counsell was announced as interim manager late that Monday morning and was impressive in his introductory news conference. I was assigned the "scene-setter" feature story about his life and career to that point that would go onto the front page of the *Journal Sentinel*, and after writing that I remember shaking Counsell's hand and congratulating him in the clubhouse as the team prepared for its game that night against the Los Angeles Dodgers. Having already built a relationship with him since 2011, I felt confident he'd give me a fair shake as the new head man. As it turned out, I was right.

His managerial debut was a success, with unknown shortstop Hector Gomez hitting the only major-league homer of his career off the great Clayton Kershaw in the eighth inning of a comeback, 4-3 victory. Since then Counsell has become the fourth-winningest manager in franchise history, taking the Brewers to within a game of their second World Series in 2018, as well as a tailor-made spokesman with his local roots, understanding of the state's sports scene, distinguished background as a player and unflappable demeanor.

Counsell has also become adept at handling the media. He clearly enjoys the daily give and take and will provide insightful answers to good questions. But he also doesn't suffer fools and will call out reporters for not being prepared. While he never hesitates to throw a barb at a member of the small group that covers the Brewers on a daily basis, it's always done in fun. I've even seen him chastise media members he doesn't know, or people who don't cover the team regularly, if one happens to crowd out a beat reporter in a scrum during the regular season or take a seat regularly assigned to a beat reporter in his office during his morning briefings in spring training.

It's all much appreciated.

# WHEN MILWAUKEE CALLS
# YA GOTTA ACCEPT THE CHARGES

BILL SCHROEDER

*Bill Schroeder had a solid eight season MLB career mainly with the Brewers after they selected him in the 1979 draft. Primarily a catcher, he successfully moved on to a second career announcing Brewer games for 25 seasons.*

I worked with Craig's father a lot when I was playing, and he was a community relations director. I'd seen Craig tag along here and there. It was a wonderful family, John and Jan Counsell. In my early days with the Brewers, they were real important to us. They were my family. They brought us along. Craig was just a little squirt at that time. He was always at the ballpark, always had his ears open and his eyes wide open and listened, sucking up all the information he could.

You knew at that time that that guy had something special. He wasn't one of these young kids who were just expecting things to fall into his lap. That's kind of the way his baseball career was, too. He wasn't the most talented guy on the field, but he was probably one of the smarter guys on the field at that age, what he likes to call "a good baseball IQ." He got the most out of his abilities.

That's how he manages his team. His team was not always the most talented group out there, especially in the way he managed in the last few years in September. It's just incredible work that he's done. He's just a smart guy, well respected. His wife, Michelle, and his family, it's just a great little family he's got there. Quintessential Milwaukee let's put it that way. That's what he is.

He's smart. In this age of analytics and all the spreadsheets, he has a good way of blending all of that with personal relationships with his players. He's great with us, me in the TV business. He's great with the media. He's not condescending at all with the media. As you imagine, I sit around in those little media conferences in the dugout a lot before games. Some of the questions are just mindboggling; that somebody could actually ask such stupid questions. But he gives every question due concentration and doesn't belittle anybody. he has never done that. He's always understood that that's a big part of it, to deal with the media.

I was not at all surprised when Craig was named manager. Did you hear the story about the players when he retired and worked in the front office with Doug Melvin and learning different aspects of the organization. He'd be on the field in uniform every now and again. The players put together an outfit for him that was half suit and tie and half baseball uniform. It was really funny. This was in spring training, and he wore it one day because he wasn't quite sure what his role was going to be, but he knew it was going to be something.

He had opportunities to coach in other organizations. He wanted to stick around. He wanted to be a Brewer. The success of the Brewers means everything to him. He takes it very seriously because he grew up around here, and he understands how important it is to the people in this community to have a winner. The organization has put together a number of winners lately. It's good to see, and Craig's been a big part of it.

When he was young, in the clubhouse, Craig would do errands for everybody. He would be on the field. Robin Yount took him under his wing and Molitor. If you want to be with baseball people, there're no two better guys to hang out with. I remember Craig hanging out. He's a sponge, and he continues to be. He doesn't pretend like he knows everything. He never was that. He always finds a way to learn something from a lot of different people in interesting circumstances. You never know who you're going to learn something from. He's really good at that. He did a good job at identifying situations and listening to everybody, and sometimes things make sense to him.

As far as Brewers managers, Craig understands the modern day player better than any of them. He's the manager who hasn't been out of the game that long. The other managers have been, and the game has changed so much. There are a lot of good game managers out there. Craig Counsell is certainly at the top of that list. If he doesn't win Manager of the Year, there should be an investigation, doing as well as he does. He should have won it in back-to-back years in 2018-19…doing such a good job at the end of each season while everyone else was throwing dirt on the team in mid-August for two years in a row and doing it without Yelich in 2019.

He understands players and the psychology of being a manager and getting the most out of his players, making that player feel important. No manager in the National League on the teams that we played used all of his players as well as Craig did. It's an old stale cliché by saying you put players in a position to succeed—he did a fabulous job of that, working his lineup. He very rarely had the same lineup in back-to-back dates. It's all about match-ups and getting guys in familiar spots. Everybody talked about how short the starters went, but it worked. It worked in September. You'd get a guy, going through the lineup a couple of times, and take him out. He'd get into the bullpen where he had fourteen guys. He used the roster that he had at his disposal. He and David Stearns did a great job of that all season long. It really highlights itself, how great the team was in those two Septembers in the last couple of years.

It's like a novel that's written every year, the way you win this division. These teams beat up on each other so much.

It's amazing how good a manager becomes when he's got good players. I've been doing this 25 years at Milwaukee games. I see different teams come in. I sit up there, and I think to myself,

"What's this? What's the manager doing? That doesn't make any sense." I never feel that way when Counsell's managing the game. There's always a reason, whether you like the reason or not. He's very good at giving those reasons at the end of the game at the press conference. He gives the reasons why he does things. They make sense. You might not agree with him all of the time, but he has a reason, and they make sense. That's why he makes the decisions that he makes. The biggest thing is he's learned how to use his bullpen incredibly well.

I don't spend much time with Craig on the road or in the off-season. We don't really run in the same circles a whole lot. I don't really hang out a lot with players and coaches. The team is giving events all the time. He's very giving in the offseason. He's speaking to groups all the time. He doesn't disappear in the offseason. Most of the players are somewhere else. None of the players anymore live in Milwaukee. Those were the days when Molitor, Yount, Charlie Moore, and everybody lived here year-round. The whole team was pretty much here.

Players today have no problem renting a really nice house in the summer and living where they want in the winter. Back in the old days, you had one house. The big league minimum my first year was 40 grand. How many houses can you buy for that? Now it's $575,000. Where would you want to live in the wintertime when you're getting ready for baseball? You want to be in the warm weather. That's where most guys hang out.

It's the economics of the game. Guys can rent these penthouse suites downtown or a nice lake place and go back to Arizona or Texas or **FLORIDA\*** in the winter. The economics of baseball are such that they don't have to live in a cold-weather town.

---

\*The **FLORIDA** Marlins are the only MLB team that travels north for spring training...80 miles to Jupiter where they share a facility with the St. Louis baseball Cardinals.

Milwaukee is a fabulous city. The more you dive into it, the better it becomes. It's a great place to raise a family. After my playing days, I stuck around here. I've been doing Brewers television for 25 years. It's been good to me. Paul Schramka said, "Be good to the town when you play, and they'll be good to you when you're done." No truer words have ever been spoken. I never forgot that. I tell people that.

*Counsell turning a double play vs. the Cincinnati Reds, 2009.*

# THE SON ALSO RISES

### JON SPOELSTRA

*Spoelstra lives in Portland, Oregon and has been president or general manager of NBA's Nets, Nuggets, and Trailblazers. He is the father of Miami Heat Head Coach Erik Spoelstra and a Notre Dame classmate of John Counsell, father of Craig Counsell. He has a unique perspective of how the parents of a big-time coach or manager must navigate a tricky road with their son's job.*

I gave my son two pieces of advice when he became head coach. These probably would work for Craig too. He cannot listen at anytime to sports talk radio and he can't read things online. He can't be involved with Twitter because there are all these people that shouldn't have opinions; they do have an opinion on Twitter and that will just make you feel bad. Do what you are doing but you can't listen to sports talk, you can't listen to Twitter and you really can't listen to the fans. I don't know about Craig, but my son doesn't have a Twitter account and I really don't think he reads the sports page about the Heat. I didn't want him to read the sports page because his opinion of how he is doing must be formed by himself and not by outsiders.

In any walk of life you know how you are doing. The difference in sports is that there are a lot of people who have an opinion about how you are doing. If you start to shape your job by those peoples' opinions, who really aren't experts, you will soon be sitting with those people watching a sporting event. My son told me a couple of days before it happened that he might get the head coach job for the Miami Heat. I asked him if he was ready and he said yes. He had been thinking about being a head coach for quite awhile; maybe not the Miami Heat but someplace. Just like any young guy he was ready. The fact that he had never played pro ball didn't hurt him because he had been a video coordinator.

When he got the job with the Heat as a video coordinator I told him that he would be watching more video that anybody in the United States, maybe in the world. When he got that job he was one of the first video coordinators in the business. Football had video coordinators; they did a lot of video. In basketball, Pat Riley had done it in New York with the Knicks. When Riley came to **MIAMI**\*, Erik had been there for a couple of months and because of his contract Riley couldn't bring his video coordinators from New York. I told Erik, you are going to see some things that most basketball people wouldn't see. When you see something interesting put it on a VHS tape and give it to Riley. He said, "No, I've got my job to do with offensive sets and defensive sets." I said, "If you see something interesting, do a little write up, a paragraph or so, why it is interesting and then give it to him."

A month later Erik called me up and said, "I did it. Remember that conversation about the video, I gave it to Riley two days ago. I put it on his chair at 2 a.m. with a little note." A few days a week Erik used to sleep at the Arena because of the volume of work. Erik said, "He hasn't responded to me at all." I said, "So what, he is the president and coach, he doesn't have to respond to you about anything. But when you find something that is interesting, again, put it on his chair."

About a month later Erik found something again. He called me back and said, "Riley didn't say anything." Normally Erik would give the edited tapes to Stan Van Gundy, the lead assistant. I told Erik that Riley might not even know who you are

---

\*The **MIAMI** Heat retired uniform No. 23 in honor of Michael Jordan. Go figure....The coach of the Miami Heat, Erik Spoelstra, is the grandson of famed Detroit sportswriter Watson Spoelstra. Watson Spoelstra is the man who started Baseball Chapel, a Sunday service that has spread to all other major sports.

because you are down in the basement in the video room. He did it about three or four times that year. The next year he is in the video room and it's the first part of the season and who shows up in the basement in the video room when Erik is editing, but Pat Riley himself. Eric didn't even know that Riley knew where the video room was. And Riley is chatting with him; saying he just wanted to know what the place looked like. Then he said, "By the way, how come you are not sending me those tapes anymore?"

That is what really led to Erik becoming the lead scout about a year later. They would have to scout a team twice within two weeks before they would play that team. The previous scout would do a report that was two to three pages. Erik would do sixty pages. I knew basketball-wise he was ready. His knowledge of basketball far exceeded mine and I thought my knowledge of basketball was pretty good. When we would have conversations while we were sitting at a game, his conversation was at a level that I didn't understand.

What you don't know when somebody becomes head coach is what kind of coach they are going to be. It takes a lot more than just knowledge of the game to become a great head coach. This may apply to Craig too. The first year I knew that Erik was going to be a great head coach. He had a team that in the previous year had won fifteen games. At that rate you are looking for somebody who is going to win twenty-five games. Erik won forty-three games with a ragtag group of players. I knew then that this kid's got it. If he has the right talent he could really do something. Ninety-nine percent of basketball knowledge Erik knows he learned from **PAT RILEY***. He had been there as a video coordinator, then a lead scout and then an assistant coach

*It is true that NBA Coach **PAT RILEY** never played college football, but was drafted by the Dallas Cowboys. His brother, Lee, played seven years in the NFL. It is not true that Pat Riley combs his hair with a pork chop.

under Riley for eleven years. Erik absorbed everything. If you are going to step down like Riley did, and you are still the general manager and president, you want a guy that believes in the same things you believe in. You don't want to reach out and get some head coach that coached Houston the previous year or Indiana or whatever. You want your guy. He picked Erik because I think he was a natural extension.

As a parent, I was proud of what Erik had achieved. Thank goodness for television because I was able to watch every game on television. I wouldn't normally watch every game of the Miami Heat. The stakes were a lot higher when I was watching those games than when I was the General Manager of the Portland Trailblazers. The wins and losses were more important to me when Erik was coaching than when I was the General Manager of the Trailblazers or President of the New Jersey Nets because it was my son. I want him to succeed. When I watch the games I feel like 99 percent of the time he makes the right moves. I kid him that I am going to give him an I-phone to put in his pocket and at half-time I will ring him up and give him some suggestions! There is very rarely a time that I would give him a suggestion to change something. Even the substitutions, I agree with him on that. When he makes a mistake, I cringe a little bit but I don't bring it up to him. I'm not coaching him. I coached him earlier in his life. I gave him some suggestions along the way, like don't listen to sports talk shows.

Once in awhile when I have a conversation with my son I will bring up a stat. They have stats for everything now a day. I will say, "I read that you are number two in efficiency on out of bounds plays." He would ask me where I got that information and we will talk about it. But if he makes a mistake that I think is a mistake during a game, I probably don't question whether it was a mistake or not because his knowledge is so far superior to mine. If we were all sitting at an NBA game like just three guys watching the game, you would be shocked at his knowledge of the game versus ours.

I prefer to watch the games on TV. I only go to about five or six games a year in Miami, not including playoffs. I'm just like a regular cheering fan and I feel bad when they go into a funk.

I read the Miami papers but I don't listen to sports talk. They used to have a feature In the Miami papers where fans could write in on the game story. They discontinued it because an experienced writer, who has covered the Miami Heat since its inception, would write a great game story explaining what happened. Then guys would comment about how the Heat blew the game or about how Spoelstra was an idiot. They would use profanity and rough language. It was the Sun Sentinel allowing guys to take over the paper. Guys who shouldn't have an opinion were giving their opinion in very profane ways. I stopped reading because I didn't respect their opinion and it hurt. You could tell from the comments that some of those people might have been drinking. But also their apparent knowledge of the game wasn't that great. I followed that same advice I gave Erik. You can't listen to sports talk and you can't read Twitter or things online about Erik. It could be the same for Craig. On the other hand, don't get me wrong: every team has some very knowledgeable fans whose criticisms are well-founded.

Early on, there was talk about Erik not getting along with LeBron James. I expected that. I didn't think it was going to be easy, but I didn't expect it to be as vitriolic as it was. But Erik came out with nine wins and eight defeats early in that first LeBron season. Once the rumor mill starts it picks up steam. But that's where Pat Riley is sure in his place with the Heat. He is not a general manager looking over his shoulder. Micky Arison, the Heat owner, who owns Carnival Cruise Lines, is not prone to knee-jerk reactions. They withstood that and the next two years they won championships.

The support of the owner is vital. The key to this business is the owner. Are they level-headed? Is this team a toy? Do they understand the game? Take a look at the owner of the Phoenix Suns. He is a very successful businessperson but as the owner of the Phoenix Suns, he makes knee jerk reaction decisions. Solid and self-assured is what you want in an owner. When a blip comes up like that nine and eight start with LeBron, they don't panic. If it had been up to half of the owners in the NBA, they probably would have fired Erik. Micky and Pat didn't panic and they won two back-to-back championship. They have a coach that has been there eleven years and they have a solid franchise. They don't have the musical chairs of always rebuilding. That is vital. From what I've heard from my sources is that the Brewers owner is terrific!...and their GM, too.

I was there both times Erik won the NBA title. It was unreal and difficult to explain. I have a picture at home with my son and me holding the trophy after the game. Sometimes I think that picture was Photoshopped.

*Jon and son, Erik Spoelstra*

Once a year, the Heat comes to Portland, but my wife Lisa is way too nervous to go to the game. I've been to over 1,000 NBA games. I can watch a game and enjoy what is going on. There is no huge upside or downside. With Lisa, it's all downside. She gets extraordinarily nervous. She prefers not to go to the game at all, and she meets up with Erik afterwards. The last few years Erik has come to Portland a day early so we can meet up for dinner. We are proud as can be. I bet Craig's folks would understand...but I know the pressure and worry Jan and John have about Craig can make for sleepless nights. What a mentor Craig has had with my old classmate John.

**CRAIG COUNSELL** | **INF** | **#30**

# A REAL PRO IN EVERY WAY

## DOUG GLANVILLE

*One of few Ivy Leaguers to make the Major Leagues, Doug Glanville became an ESPN reporter upon his retirement. During his nine years in the big leagues he hit .277.*

We tend to think that it is the superstar who gets to ride off into the sunset on his own terms. The one who called his own shots for a career, the one who was so talented that he is retiring because he is bored and broke every record known to the game. Everyone else goes out kicking and screaming. But Craig Counsell showed us that is not the case at all.

Don't get me wrong, you have to be some kind of superstar to play 16 seasons in the big leagues. So when Craig Counsell retired from baseball, I too went online to look up the number. Sixteen? Kids were born and then halfway through high school, and Counsell was still playing in the big leagues. And he pulled this off by just being a force of nature.

Counsell was truly the underdog. Not the self-proclaiming obnoxious player who is holding a championship trophy over his head and saying, "No one believed in us. Blah. Blah." But truly a player whose ability to believe in himself trumped every label that usually gives others more opportunity than him.

I first heard about Counsell in the minor leagues. I don't know why the conversation about him stood out above all others, but so many players talked about how he was a "stone-cold hitter" and that he was buried in the minors unfairly. It was the first time I learned that the major leagues didn't always reward the ones who looked the best and the brightest or the ones with the best numbers. Since this was before the Internet, information like that took a long time to get around, so it said a lot about Counsell that Cubs minor league players were so concerned about someone from an entirely different organization.

Then I finally played against him and his image did not fit the aura. He could run, he could pick it, but it was not sexy. It wasn't an "all eyes on me" kind of moment. His batting stances reminded you of someone trying out for Cirque du Soleil, not trying to turn around a 95-plus **MPH**\* fastball.

But he got it done. He was always in the mix, doing something to put his team in a winning position. He dove to stop a ball from driving in two runs, holding the opposition to just one. He got the bunt down, he backed up a base, or he got the big hit. He did everything you needed to win that would not put you on the home page of a website. And trust me, coaches knew it and wanted him on their team.

I remember when the Cubs decided one season to create a chart that rewarded minor league players for executing winning baseball. You had to move runners over, hit the cutoff man, hit behind the runner. Small ball. It did not show up in your batting average, but it put your team in positions to win. Even after I won a few rounds, evaluators from afar would go back to spitting out my batting average as the end-all, be-all stat, but coaches knew that to win, you had to be selfless and want to win. They needed a Counsell on their team.

Counsell did this every day at every level, before it was fashionable. He had a knack for knowing what needed to be done. Sort of like a field general without a need for directions from leadership. He was programmed to play to win, as a team.

---

\*The speed limit on the University of Mississippi campus is 18 **MPH** in honor of Archie Manning's uniform number.

But his execution style did not grab you at first. You were almost nervous for him because you thought this guy was a breath away from being out of the big leagues. You kept saying, "Eventually someone will figure him out and neutralize what he can do." He somehow reminded you that everyone's days are numbered. But then he just kept adding days and became an inspiration.

It is a testament to Counsell that he had so much going against him on a superficial level to still become such a fixture in the game. He wasn't silky smooth or endowed with a bodybuilder's stature. People had to look deeper to see what he brought to the table, and he was so good at it that he made you look deeper. And those who did were rewarded for it.

A ridiculously long 16 years—and two World Series titles—later, he was the one who decided when to pack it up, not the other way around. Counsell just quietly slipped baseball the pink slip so that he could move into the corner office on his own terms.

That isn't what happens to guys who look like Craig Counsell—the underdog who has to prove himself every minute, playing through injuries that require surgery just so he could show up and get a look. But now, who is the one evaluating talent? It's Counsell, managing the Brewers after being special assistant to Brewers then-General Manager Doug Melvin.

Many players had more than him—in talent and marketability—yet he was the one who came out a champion and a respected player from all across the game. He worked hard for players' rights, he taught an entire school of players how to play the game with your heart and your mind. When you look back, he is the one who outlasted just about everyone. And in the end, that is what counts.

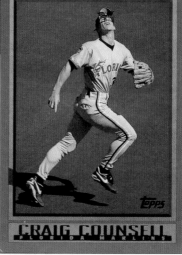

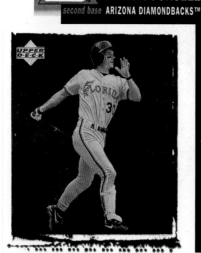

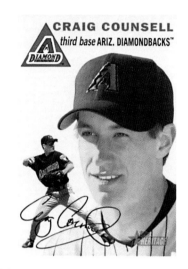

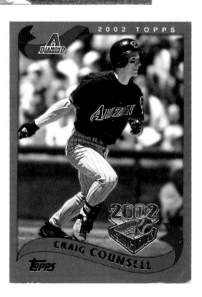

# OTHER BOOKS BY RICH WOLFE

*I Remember Harry Caray*
*Ron Santo, A Perfect 10*
*For Cubs Fans Only*
*For Cubs Fans Only—Volume II*
*Da Coach (Mike Ditka)*
*Take This Job and Love It! (Jim Harbaugh)*
*Tim Russert, We Heartily Knew Ye*
*Oh, What a Knight (Bobby Knight)*
*There's No Expiration Date on Dreams (Tom Brady)*
*He Graduated Life with Honors and No Regrets (Pat Tillman)*
*Take This Job and Love It (Jon Gruden)*
*Been There, Shoulda Done That (John Daly)*
*Jeremy Lin, The Asian Sensation*
*And the Last Shall Be First (Kurt Warner)*
*He Left His Heart in San Diego (Tony Gwynn)*
*I Saw It On the Radio (Vin Scully)*
*The Real McCoy (Al McCoy, Phoenix Suns announcer)*
*I Love It, I Love It, I Love It (with Jim Zabel, Iowa announcer)*
*Personal Foul (With Tim Donaghy, former NBA referee)*
*The Least Likely to Succeed (Food Network Founder)*
*Remembering Jack Buck*
*Remembering Harry Kalas*
*Remembering Dale Earnhardt*
*Sports Fans Who Made Headlines*
*Fandemonium*
*For Notre Dame Fans Only—The New Saturday Bible*
*For Cardinals Fans Only—Volume I*
*For Cardinals Fans Only—Volume 2*
*For Yankee Fans Only*
*For Yankee Fans Only—Volume II*
*For Red Sox Fans Only*
*For Browns Fans Only*
*For Mets Fans Only*
*For Bronco Fans Only*
*For Michigan Fans Only*
*For Milwaukee Braves Fans Only*
*For Nebraska Fans Only*
*For Buckeye Fans Only*
*For Georgia Bulldog Fans Only*

*For South Carolina Fans Only*
*For Clemson Fans Only*
*For Oklahoma Fans Only*
*For Mizzou Fans Only*
*For Kansas City Chiefs Fans Only*
*For K-State Fans Only*
*For KU Fans Only (Kansas)*
*For Phillies Fans Only*
*For Packers Fans Only*
*For Hawkeye Fans Only*


*All books are the same size, format and price.*
*Questions or to order? Contact the author directly at 602-738-5889.*

**Note: No actual Chicago Cub fans were harmed in the making of this book.**